100 GAA GREATS

FROM CHRISTY RING TO JOE CANNING

JOHN SCALLY

MAINSTREAM
PUBLISHING

EDINBURGH AND LO

D0280881

First published in Great Britain in 2010 by
MAINSTREAM PUBLISHING COMPANY
(EDINBURGH) LTD
7 Albany Street
Edinburgh EH1 3UG

ISBN 9781845965648

The author has made every effort to clear copyright permissions,
but where this has not been possible and amendments are required,
the publisher will be pleased to make any necessary arrangements at
the earliest opportunity

A catalogue record for this book is available
from the British Library

Typeset in Florencesans and Palatino

Printed in Great Britain by
CPI Mackays, Chatham ME5 8TD

To Dermot Earley:
A hero on the pitch,
An absolute inspiration off it.

ACKNOWLEDGEMENTS

I am very honoured that the legendary Eddie Keher agreed to write the foreword for this book.

This book has been over 20 years in the making and draws heavily on interviews with many of the greats of both football and hurling whom I have had the good fortune to meet, including some who have passed on to their eternal reward, such as Jack Lynch, Seán Purcell, Enda Colleran, John Wilson and Eddie Boyle. There are too many to name individually, but I am really appreciative for all their insights. As always, I am very grateful to my good friends Seán Freyne and Peter Woods for their assistance.

My gratitude to Mick Bermingham, John Boyle, James Brennan, Iggy Clarke, John Murray, Seán Duggan, Ann Colleran, Pat Lindsay, Dermot Flanagan, Babs Keating, Máirín McAleenan, Karl McDonough, Willie McGee, Paddy Prendergast, Paddy Quirke, Jimmy Smyth and Henry Wills for help with photos.

Thanks to the wonderfully hospitable Kathryn Brennan of Castle Bookshop in Castlebar for her ongoing love affair with books.

Thanks to my good friend John Tiernan for his supply of amusing GAA stories.

My thanks to the great and generous Liam Horan for his practical assistance.

Thanks to Bill Campbell, Graeme Blaikie, Alex Hepworth and all at Mainstream for their help.

CONTENTS

FOREWORD

The annals of the GAA have a special place for the great players who, by their genius on the field over a period of years, have claimed a permanent place in the memory of all who love the game. Every county has furnished its stars. This book honours 100 of them.

From the world of hurling come giants of the ash of the past like Lory Meagher, Mick Mackey, Jack Lynch, Jimmy Doyle, Nicky Rackard and, of course, the great Christy Ring; and more recent stars like D.J. Carey, Nicky English, Brian Lohan and Joe Canning.

My father was from Roscommon, and that is why I am particularly glad to see my old friend Jimmy Murray featured here. I have fond memories of visiting him in his famous pub in Knockcroghery. Many other great footballers, including Mick O'Connell, Seán Purcell, John Joe O'Reilly, Peter Canavan and Maurice Fitzgerald, also feature.

As the GAA is a national movement, I am particularly pleased that players from counties that seldom get the limelight also figure, such as Carlow's Paddy Quirke, Leitrim's Packy McGarty and Sligo's Micheál Kearins.

The role of women in the GAA has not always got the attention it deserves, which is why I am delighted that some are included in this book. In the 1960s, I came up against a great Tipperary side that featured Len Gaynor, so I am thrilled to see Len's daughter Ciara in these pages, in the company of the great Angela Downey.

In recent years, managers have become hugely important in the GAA, so it is appropriate to see the top ones honoured here, like Mick O'Dwyer, Kevin Heffernan, Seán Boylan, Liam Griffin and Brian Cody.

I hope you enjoy this trip down memory lane.

Eddie Keher
July 2010

THE THROW-IN

My mother always told me I would not amount to anything because I procrastinate. I said, 'Just wait.' I have been waiting for many years to write this book, but it presented many selection headaches.

What makes a great player? Is it natural talent or the ability to inspire others? Alternatively, is greatness essentially a question of spirit or attitude, a never-say-die mentality, an innate drive to overcome all the odds and to give every ounce of energy for the glory of the team? To what extent is greatness a matter of style? Does a great player shape a match in the same way as a great artist uses paint on a canvas? Is physical presence a factor to be considered? How long does a player have to maintain the highest standards on the playing fields to be considered 'great'? Can the quietly effective player attain the same status as a gifted 'star'? Who decides? And who decides who decides?

Greatness, like beauty, is an extremely subjective concept. It could also be argued that to ask about the characteristics that make a great player is to ask the wrong question. The proper question, since the different positions in a football or hurling team require such specialised skills, is what are the traits that make a player great in a particular position?

The problems of attempting the task of selecting 100 GAA greats are magnified when one attempts the hazardous task of selecting the greatest players over different eras. It was much more difficult to decide whom to exclude than whom to include. I could have easily filled this book with just Kerry footballers and Kilkenny hurlers. How do you decide between the great Kerry full-forward line of Mike Sheehy, Eoin Liston and John Egan? So dominant have Brian Cody's Kilkenny been in recent years that not only any member of that team but even some of his subs could be considered for inclusion! However, as the GAA is a national movement, I wanted all 32 counties to be included. As a native of Roscommon, I support a team who have not won a senior

THE THROW-IN

All-Ireland since 1944. Some would call this a famine. We prefer to say we simply missed a lot of dinners. It has made me keen, though, to feature players from counties that were starved of success.

As we saw in the recent 125th anniversary of the GAA, the high-profile players of past and present get acres of space in the national media, but remarkable players often lose out because they have never won an All-Ireland medal. The tragedy is that they are often forgotten. So many heroic players' stories are woven almost anonymously into the tapestry of GAA history, even though they deserve individual recognition. This book makes some attempt to redress that balance.

While it features many of the greatest names in the rich history of the GAA, I did not want to simply 'round up the usual suspects': the chosen few beloved by pundits who suffer from irritable vowel syndrome. As someone whose own football and hurling career was a total failure, I have deliberately picked a few less obvious choices and a few who regularly lit up games with the box-office appeal of two bald men fighting over a comb.

One test of greatness is the amount of nostalgia a player creates. The memory of a 'great' lingers for life in the minds of those fans who grew up with them, leaving a warm afterglow to light up numerous conversations years later. These obsessive followers are de facto stakeholders in their performances, the intimacy of the relationship reflected in the thousands who have never even met the stars of the past and present thinking of them as friends.

A community reveals itself not in the men and women it produces but in the people it chooses to honour. In making my final selection, I was searching for a common bond that would unite the chosen few, and I found it.

The ancient Greeks didn't write obituaries. They just asked one question: did he have passion? All of the players featured in this book played with passion – whether on sunny days in Croke Park before a full house or on cold January Sundays in challenge matches in front of two men and a dog. They are a group of men and women who graced and honoured their clubs, counties and provinces not just with a series of great performances but because they share a sacred trust, a common code: one that spoke of sacrifice and led each of them to forfeit every fibre of their being, every everything, to the interests of their team. Their stories embody the living history of the GAA.

A number of options presented themselves in the writing of this book. One was to take a statistical approach and present the facts and figures of the chosen players' careers. Another was to recycle lengthy accounts of their most famous matches. I decided in the main to forego such approaches and go beneath the surface to present a more personal style of portrait, showing their characters, the controversies they faced, and sometimes created, their triumphs and setbacks – through their own eyes or the eyes of those who played against them. I hope these portraits will in some way capture the unique magic and humour of the GAA.

John Scally
July 2010

1

LORD OF THE RINGS
CHRISTY RING

The *Pall Mall Gazette*'s tribute to W.G. Grace, the greatest cricketer of them all, was, 'He has drained the language of eulogy and it is no use applying superlatives to him any more.' If any GAA player deserved such an encomium, it was Christy Ring. He won eight All-Ireland medals in his career with Cork, playing in four decades from 1939 to 1962. Above all, hurling fans loved his all-action style – like a mighty atom – and relentless pursuit of every chance of taking off on an incisive run.

One of the many stories told about Ring is that, one day, leading his team out of the tunnel, halfway out he turned them back to the dressing-room. Then he took off his Cork jersey, held it up and asked his players to look at the colour and to think what it meant to them. After that, the team went out with fire in their bellies and played out of their skins.

Ring was not a man to call a spade an agricultural implement. Famously, after the 1968 Munster final when Babs Keating gave a magnificent performance, scoring 1–3 for Tipperary, Ring congratulated him by saying, 'Great performance, Babs, but imagine what you would have done if you had concentrated for the whole game.'

In Ring's days as a selector, Cork's ace forward Seánie O'Leary got a belt of a hurley across the nose and was withdrawing from the field when Ring shouted at him, 'Get back out there. You don't play hurling with your nose.'

Former Tánaiste Dick Spring had an 'almost encounter' with Ring.

'My father attempted to introduce me to Christy Ring after Cork lost a Munster final to Tipperary, but he was so disappointed at losing the game that he stormed off and wouldn't talk to anyone.'

Asked about the greatest player he has ever seen, Dublin's Mick Bermingham answers with speed.

'It has to be Christy Ring. I first got to know him when he was working in Dublin and he used go training in Islandbridge. I was 15, and he was in the autumn of his career. My uncle played against him in the Railway Cup final in 1947, so that gave me the courage to go up and speak to him. We pucked a few balls together.

'I got to know him better when I played with him later in the Cardinal Cushing Games in America. He was very intense. There were no short cuts with him. It was a great education to watch him. He had great anticipation and was a master of judging the flight of the sliotar. I learned a lot about how to play corner-forward from him. If he got a score, he'd dance a little jig to annoy his opponent and straight away won the psychological battle.'

Few hurlers are better equipped to evaluate Ring's career than Tipperary's greatest hurling legend John Doyle.

'Christy Ring was by far the best hurler I ever saw. He had unbelievable skill and could do anything with a ball. He thought and dreamed only about hurling. Once, after we beat Cork in a Munster final in Thurles, I saw him in Hayes' Hotel telling another Cork player what they needed to do to beat us the following year. How could you a keep a man like that down?

'He was also a very tough hurler. I think back to a great tussle between Christy and another Tipperary player in a game in Cork. Though I was not involved in the scuffle, I happened to be lying on the ground close to it and I got a fierce belt of a hurl as they both drew on the ball together. As a result, I needed four stitches on my chin and ended up with a scar for life.

'He was a true perfectionist. He was always trying to perfect and practise his skills. The interesting thing was that, unlike most players, the older he got the better he performed.

'I saw a side to Christy that few hurling fans got to see. He was a very kind, helpful person. Back in the 1960s, I ran for the Senate, and I went down to Cork to do some canvassing. I went into Johnny Quirke's pub, and sitting in the corner, drinking a mineral, was Christy. When I explained what I was doing, he immediately volunteered to go canvassing with me, and we went around all his friends, who not only promised to vote for me but actually did. It was a mark of the man that he was so generous with his time.'

One of Ring's biggest fans was the RTÉ Gaelic games correspondent, the late Mick Dunne. He recalled a conversation he had with Ring for me.

'Everybody knows how brilliant a hurler Ring was, but what is less

CHRISTY RING

well known is that Christy was a brilliant analyst of the game. After he dissected the course of a Munster final for me with extraordinary insight, I jokingly said to him, "You are the nearest thing that hurling has to a Pope." His reply, though spoken half in jest, was very revealing: "The only difference is, when it comes to hurling, I really am infallible!"

'Although Ring was the David Beckham of his day in terms of name recognition, he was very humble in many ways, but, equally, he was very aware of where he stood in the game. There was no false modesty about him. That trait was probably most evident when an irate county board official asked him, as he jumped over the stile instead of displaying his pass as he went into a match, "Where's your pass?"

'Christy replied, "I don't have it."

"'But, Christy, you ought to have. You won no less than eight All-Ireland medals."

'"And if I hadn't been carrying passengers like you, I'd have won at least eight more!"'

When Ring died in 1979, up to 60,000 people lined the streets of Cork for his funeral. In his graveside oration, Jack Lynch said of his great friend, 'As long as young men will match their hurling skills against each other on Ireland's green fields, as long as young boys swing their camáns for the sheer thrill of the feel and the tingle in their fingers of the impact of ash on leather, as long as hurling is played, the story of Christy Ring will be told. And that will be for ever.'

Not surprisingly, Ring was an automatic choice on the Team of the Century. That team was:

1 TONY REDDAN (TIPPERARY)
2 BOBBY RACKARD (WEXFORD)
3 NICK O'DONNELL (WEXFORD)
4 JOHN DOYLE (TIPPERARY)
5 JIMMY FINN (TIPPERARY)
6 JOHN KEANE (WATERFORD)
7 PADDY PHELAN (KILKENNY)
8 LORY MEAGHER (KILKENNY)
9 JACK LYNCH (CORK)
10 CHRISTY RING (CORK)
11 MICK MACKEY (LIMERICK)
12 JIMMY LANGTON (KILKENNY)
13 JIMMY DOYLE (TIPPERARY)
14 NICKY RACKARD (WEXFORD)
15 EDDIE KEHER (KILKENNY)

2

THE ISLAND MAN
MICK O'CONNELL

Great players pride themselves on their ability to rise to the challenge. The bigger the challenge the more they like it. This approach was typified by Mick O'Connell. Once when O'Connell had been knocked to the ground, an opponent said to him, 'Get up, you lazy f***er.' O'Connell replied, 'You should catch a few balls while I'm down here, because you'll catch no more when I get up.'

O'Connell is the most iconic name in Gaelic football: the game's first superstar. He was the catch-and-kick footballer par excellence and played the game as though his motto was 'Catch it like you love it, and kick it like you hate it.' He is the yardstick by which all subsequent midfielders with aspirations to greatness have been judged, and, not surprisingly, he was chosen in that position on both the Team of the Century and the Team of the Millennium.

At the beginning of every year, Kerry footballers put two dates in their diary: the Munster final and the All-Ireland final. Mick O'Connell knew this phenomenon better than most. He won four All-Ireland medals (in 1959, '62, '69 and '70), six National Leagues and was chosen as footballer of the year in 1962. In the 1962 All-Ireland final, O'Connell was the driving force when Kerry beat the men in primrose and blue from Roscommon by 1–12 to 1–6.

More than any other footballer, there was an aura to O'Connell, a mystique heightened when he was reputed to have left the dressing-room immediately after captaining Kerry to win the All-Ireland in 1959 and headed straight home for Kerry. Asked why he had to forego the celebrations, he is said to have replied, 'I had to go home to milk the cows.' In Kerry's 1972 All-Ireland semi-final against Roscommon, his perfectionist streak was vividly illustrated in the long time he spent sitting down in the middle of the pitch tying his laces.

The fact that he lived on the island of Valentia, and rowed himself on his boat to the Kerry coastline for training and games, added to his aura as a man apart. Although the game's most public figure because of his wonders on the field, he remained an intensely private man off it. Experience has taught him that, for someone in his position, reserve is an indispensable virtue. Those who have penetrated his inner circle testify that he has the gentle nature typical of country people.

The late Micheál O'Hehir was often asked to compare the respective merits of Paddy Kennedy, Kerry's star midfielder in the 1940s, and O'Connell in terms of their place in the hierarchy of Kerry greats. He answered with typical diplomacy.

'When Paddy retired, it was a huge blow for Kerry, and I suppose many of us felt we would never see his like again, but, lucky enough, within a couple of years we discovered another great star in Mick O'Connell. I don't really think you can or should compare players from different eras, and it's not fair to either Paddy or Mick to compare one against the other. Both were superb players over a long number of years, and both had tremendous dedication.'

Many of O'Connell's peers recall being almost in awe watching him play. Mayo star of the 1960s and '70s Willie McGee observes, 'I remember the one player who stuck out like a sore thumb was Mick O'Connell, especially as Kerry beat us in the All-Ireland semi-final and two league finals and he played so well against us on all three occasions. He was always very fit and loved playing against Mayo, because we never set out to hurt him or take him out of the game. Mayo tried to play football with him, and, as a result, we always came out second best. He was the best footballer I ever saw.

'He was a great fielder of a ball, as were Noel Tierney and P.J. Loftus. I think that I never saw anybody give as good an exhibition of fielding as Willie Joe Padden gave for Mayo against Dublin in the replay of the 1985 All-Ireland semi-final. The difference was that none of them could touch Mick O'Connell for distributing the ball.'

Ace Kildare midfielder Pat Mangan's view of O'Connell is unreservedly positive.

'Mick was a tremendous player. He played football as I liked to play it. He concentrated on the ball, and it was never a man-to-man situation when you were playing on him. He went for a ball, and he caught it in the clouds, and I think one of the great thrills is seeing a high ball floating in the sky and someone grabbing it.

He also kicked superbly and was a tremendous man to lay off the ball. His accuracy was tremendous. He had a very sharp brain, and in my opinion he was one of the all-time greats.'

Offaly's Willie Nolan was another big fan.

'Mick O'Connell was the best natural footballer I ever saw – because of his sheer ability, class and fitness – although he played on some average enough Kerry teams. In 1972, he had great tussles with Offaly's Willie Bryan. In the second half of the replay, Willie pulled ahead, and in the last 20 minutes he was something special, but I'd love to have seen them clash when they were both at their peak.'

While no one has ever questioned his extraordinary skills, there are those who questioned O'Connell's ability when he was tightly marked. Regardless of how much natural ability a forward has, there is not much he can do without the ball. As Con Houlihan once said of a struggling Kerry forward, 'He was like a gunfighter roaming the streets without his gun.' Maurice Hayes, in an indictment of the modern game rather than a criticism of a legend, said, 'Mick O'Connell would not last five minutes today with the blanket defence.'

As a man, O'Connell could be very generous to teammates. During a training session in Killarney in the early 1970s, he soared majestically to pluck the ball from the clouds. John O'Keeffe did the same, only to leap that little fraction higher and catch the ball tightly in his grasp. O'Connell turned to his opponent and said, 'John, I can retire now.' The torch was being passed to the next generation.

Gaelic football needs every nostalgic prop it can muster, and when many of the stars of today have been forgotten, the powerful grip Mick O'Connell exerted on the popular imagination will endure.

O'Connell was chosen on the Team of the Century. That team was:

1   DAN O'KEEFFE (KERRY)
2   ENDA COLLERAN (GALWAY)
3   PADDY O'BRIEN (MEATH)
4   SEÁN FLANAGAN (MAYO)
5   SEÁN MURPHY (KERRY)
6   JOHN JOE O'REILLY (CAVAN)
7   STEPHEN WHITE (LOUTH)
8   MICK O'CONNELL (KERRY)
9   JACK O'SHEA (KERRY)

MICK O'CONNELL

10 SEÁN O'NEILL (DOWN)
11 SEÁN PURCELL (GALWAY)
12 PAT SPILLANE (KERRY)
13 MIKE SHEEHY (KERRY)
14 TOM LANGAN (MAYO)
15 KEVIN HEFFERNAN (DUBLIN)

3

BARRY-MURPHY'S LAW
JIMMY BARRY-MURPHY

Many Gaelic players have been known to suffer from 'Orson Welles syndrome'. Like the famous star of the screen, their crowning moment of glory comes at the very start of their career. Nothing that follows can match it. Jimmy Barry-Murphy is the exception to the rule. He exploded onto the scene when, at the age of nineteen, he scored two fine goals in Cork's All-Ireland football final triumph over Galway in 1973. In his commentary, Micheál O'Hehir said, 'He may be 19, but today he's joined the ranks of the football immortals.'

Galway defender Johnny Hughes still recalls the day vividly.

'We scored 2–13 and lost the All-Ireland by seven points. I have no cribs about losing in 1973, because we were comprehensively beaten. We couldn't match their firepower. Jimmy Barry-Murphy and Jimmy Barrett caused us untold trouble. Jimmy Barry-Murphy, even then, was a most difficult opponent. He was both very confident and very skilful and could take you to the cleaners, and he had two great feet – but, above all, he had a great head. Had he stuck to football, he would have gone on to become one of the all-time greats.'

Like other players featured between the covers of this book though, JBM's collection of football medals is much smaller than it should be – because his career coincided with the golden era of Kerry football. I asked him how difficult it was to keep going when Cork were losing the Munster final every year.

'God, there were times when it was hard. It does get demoralising. However, I would have to say that we never went into any of those Munster finals not thinking we were going to win. We never had an inferiority complex, even though they beat us well a few times. We always enjoyed those matches, even though Mick O'Dwyer always hyped us up by saying Cork was the most difficult opposition he expected to meet all year. We always got on well with the Kerry lads. I played with most of them on the Munster team, and I always felt they gave the Cork lads plenty of respect.

JIMMY BARRY-MURPHY

'I suppose what kept us going was the enjoyment we got from playing. We were all passionately in love with the game. We had a lot of craic and fun. Although we had a lot of disappointments in the Munster championship, we at least had the consolation of getting to a league final in 1979, which we lost to Roscommon, and of beating Kerry in the league final the following year, which was a big thrill for us – to at last win another national title.'

Who were the characters on that Cork team?

'Dinny Allen was the only Cork player to be chosen on the Centenary Team of players who have never won an All-Ireland. Five years later, he put that omission to right when he captained the Cork team to win the All-Ireland in 1989. A lot of hurlers on the ditch alleged that Allen hadn't contributed much to winning Sam. As a result, Dinny christened himself the "non-playing captain"!'

Donegal great Martin Carney saw the more relaxed side of the legendary JBM.

'I played for Ulster in 1975 and remember it as Seán O'Neill's last game for Ulster. Jimmy Barry-Murphy had played the day before in a senior club hurling final for the Barrs against Johnstown, and I remember meeting him that night and, let's put it this way, he was enjoying himself. And yet the next day he produced a devastating performance. Jimmy scored 4–1 in that game from five kicks of the ball.'

Despite having won All-Stars in 1973 and '74 in football, Barry-Murphy's talents were most often seen in hurling on the national stage, because Kerry ruled supreme in Munster. The ultimate sign of a great player in any sport is that they have the power to make the pulse skip a beat whenever they are in full flight. Once they get the ball, a buzz of expectancy goes around the ground. Before D.J. Carey came onto the scene, the one hurler who consistently had this effect was Jimmy Barry-Murphy. In his many magic moments, he lit up the stage like a flash of forked lightning, shining brilliantly. He was thrilling and, from the opposition's point of view, frightening. He is probably the greatest dual star of all time, having won five All-Ireland hurling medals and five hurling All-Stars. With characteristic modesty, he downplays his role in Cork's three-in-a-row winning side of 1976 to '78.

'There are those who will say that we were in the right place at the right time, because other teams like Kilkenny were not as strong as they usually were. But look at the players we had at the time, such as

Martin O'Doherty, John Horgan, Gerald McCarthy, Charlie McCarthy, Ray Cummins and Seánie O'Leary. The fact that we won those All-Irelands had much more to do with their brilliance than anything I ever did.'

He also had the honour of winning an All-Ireland medal in Centenary year on the hallowed sod of Semple Stadium against Offaly. The side's preparation for the game was rather unorthodox, as Barry-Murphy's teammate Tomás Mulcahy recalls.

'Before the 1984 Centenary All-Ireland final, our trainer, Canon Michael O'Brien, wanted the team to be shielded from all the fuss in Thurles. Finding such a sanctuary was difficult, but, as a resourceful man, Canon O'Brien rang up the local convent and asked if the team could rest up there. When we got there, we were fed by the nuns and had a light puck around in the grounds.

'To ensure the team's focus was not compromised, Canon O'Brien gave strict instructions to the nuns that, once the team bus arrived, the gates were to be closed and under no circumstances was anybody to be admitted. The problem was that, a short while later, the chairman of the Cork County Board drove up in his car to the gates of the convent. When he requested entry, he was greeted by two formidable nuns who left no room for ambiguity in the way they told him he had no prayer of being admitted. I think Jimmy Barry-Murphy was the nuns' favourite, and their prayers for him worked in that final.'

Irish soccer legend Niall Quinn has his own reason to recall JBM.

'I always have a hurley in my car. I paid a small fortune for a hurley signed by Jimmy Barry-Murphy at a charity function in London, only to discover later that Jimmy hadn't signed it at all! That evening, I was trying to get a taxi afterwards, but no one would stop for me with the hurley in my hand.'

JBM's sublime overhead flick against Galway in the 1983 All-Ireland semi-final was voted as the greatest hurling goal of all time in 2009. His goal-scoring powers were immortalised in a piece of graffiti in Cork: 'Jesus saves – but Jimmy Barry-Murphy scores on the rebound.'

4

A TRUE DUB

MICK BERMINGHAM

Mick Bermingham's career with Dublin spanned four decades. He first played senior inter-county hurling with Dublin as a 16 year old in 1959, and his last game for Dublin in 1982 was at intermediate level. He enjoyed great success with Leinster, winning six Railway Cup medals, including a four-in-a-row between 1971 and '74. In 1971, Mick was selected at right corner-forward in the inaugural All-Stars. In 1984, he was chosen at left corner-forward on the Centenary Team of greatest players never to have won an All-Ireland final. Additional achievements include ten senior club championship medals. The highlight of his career came when he captained Kilmacud Crokes to win the Dublin title. Mick considers this side unlucky not to have won a Leinster club title. He was also a prolific scorer for Kilmacud Crokes in the All-Ireland Sevens competition. He had an impressive family lineage.

'I had hurling on both sides of the family. My mother's brother, Paddy Forde, played full-back in the 1947 Connacht Railway Cup side that beat Munster. My father's first cousin, "young" Mick Gill, was on the 1938 Dublin side that won the All-Ireland.'

However, Bermingham was denied the same opportunity to perform on the highest stage.

'In 1961, I broke a few fingers in a club match and I missed out on the chance to play for Dublin in the All-Ireland. It was agonising to watch the Leinster final, let alone the All-Ireland final. Dublin could have won. We lost to Tipperary on a scoreline of 1–12 to 0–16. We had a lean year in 1962 and qualified for the Leinster final in both '63 and '64, only to lose to an emerging Kilkenny side who went on to have 15 years of great success. The consolation came for me in the Railway Cups, which had a massive profile back then.'

One of his best moments came in 1964 when Dublin scored a shock win over Kilkenny in the Walsh Cup final in Nowlan Park by 5–4 to 2–12. Bermingham was the winners' hero, scoring 4–3 of his side's total despite receiving an injury that forced him to retire for a spell. He had the ball in the Kilkenny net twice in the opening two minutes: the first coming from a free and the second in the melee that caused his injury. The corner-forward's return created an immediate impact, and he went on to score two further goals and three points. His last point proved to be the winner. The match had a comical postscript.

'I didn't know it at the time, but I had dislocated my shoulder. Des Ferguson was in charge of the team and asked me if I could go back. I was patched up again and took my place. The circulation went out of my arms, and my shoulder was paralysed after the match. There was great jubilation in the dressing-room. It was like winning the Leinster final because we had beaten Kilkenny. I was having great, great difficulty changing my clothes. When I came back from having a shower, our dressing-room was empty. As I finished dressing, I found out that some so-and-so had tied my shoelaces together!'

However, Bermingham's best match was for Leinster.

'When we beat Munster in the Railway Cup final for my first medal, I couldn't believe how excited the great Kilkenny and Wexford players were: legends of the game and multiple All-Ireland medal winners, but they were like children because they hadn't won the Railway Cup before. I had an exceptional day. I was on John Doyle, a giant of the game. And who was I? Only a nipper from Dublin. Coming out of the dressing-room, another of the hurling immortals, Jimmy Langton of Kilkenny, came up to me and congratulated me on how well I played. It meant a lot.'

While Bermingham was working abroad, Dublin lost the 1967 All-Ireland under-21 final to Tipperary. They were beaten only by a point scored in the last minute by John Flanagan. Dublin at least had some talent coming on the scene.

'I resumed my career with Dublin when I came back in 1970. We won the Leinster intermediate championship, beating Kilkenny, which was a great boost. The year 1971 was a particularly good one for me in the scoring stakes. Dublin had won the minor All-Ireland in 1965, and seven or eight of them had come through. Things started to move with the senior team. Kilkenny beat us in the Leinster semi-final two years. They were at their peak then. In 1974, we got to the league semi-final, but Cork beat us by a point. They went on to hammer the reigning All-Ireland champions, Limerick, in the final, and that Cork team went on to win three All-Irelands. So, although we never got there, we were thereabouts.'

One of the impediments to Bermingham's hurling career was his job in the bar business, which led to him regularly working antisocial hours. There was one memorable moment, though, when his occupation came back to haunt him on the hurling field.

'I played in the 1963 Leinster final against Kilkenny. It was a lovely sunny day, and I was the free-taker. At the time, a friend of mine was working on a luxury liner, so he asked the captain if he could listen to the match on whatever frequency it was available. In fact, he talked my skills up so much that the captain decided to listen in with him. Micheál O'Hehir had been praising me in his commentary, so my friend was feeling totally vindicated. Then we got a free into the Canal End goal and Micheál said something like, "The diminutive Mick Bermingham is about to take a free for Dublin, and this will surely be a point." When I was lifting the ball, it tilted away from me, and I put it wide. The captain turned to my friend and said, "He wasn't much of a hero there."

'I ran back into the corner after the free, where I was marking the young Fan Larkin. Then I heard a Dublin voice ringing out clearly among the 40,000 crowd, saying, "Ah sure, Bermingham, you can't score a point, and, what's worse, you can't f***in' even pull a pint!"'

Bermingham's dream team is as follows:

1 OLLIE WALSH (KILKENNY)
2 FAN LARKIN (KILKENNY)
3 NICK O'DONNELL (WEXFORD)
4 TOM NEVILLE (WEXFORD)
5 MICK ROCHE (TIPPERARY)
6 PAT HENDERSON (KILKENNY)
7 MARTIN COOGAN (KILKENNY)
8 JOHN CONNOLLY (GALWAY)
9 FRANK CUMMINS (KILKENNY)
10 JIMMY DOYLE (TIPPERARY)
11 DES FOLEY (DUBLIN)
12 EDDIE KEHER (KILKENNY)
13 CHRISTY RING (CORK)
14 TONY DORAN (WEXFORD)
15 ÉAMONN CREGAN (LIMERICK)

5

THE NICE GUY WHO
DID NOT FINISH LAST
SEÁN BOYLAN

After Meath sensationally trounced reigning All-Ireland champions Kerry in the 2001 All-Ireland semi-final, Kerry manager Páidí Ó Sé said, 'Meath football is honest-to-goodness football. It's from the heart; it's passionate. To succeed, you need the two ingredients, and you have both in abundance.' Ó Sé could just as easily have been talking about the Meath manager, Seán Boylan, a man who always wears his heart on his sleeve.

Graeme Souness famously said, 'I have come to the conclusion that nice men do not make good managers.' Seán Boylan is the exception that proves this rule. He is an absolute gentleman, yet he has an inner steel to him. In 1987, he sensationally resigned as Meath manager because he felt that the team needed to make a bigger effort in training. The players asked Joe Cassells to ring him and persuade him to return. The call was made, and a change of heart ensued. At the first training session afterwards, Boylan said, 'I believe I owe you ten pence for the phone call.' To riotous laughter from the Meath squad, Cassells replied, 'Nah, it's okay. I reversed the charges.'

Seán Boylan is generally considered the second greatest manager in Gaelic football behind Mick O'Dwyer. He was appointed Meath manager in 1982, but it would be '86 before he would lead the team to their first Leinster title. Colm O'Rourke said at the time, 'Leave Seán around long enough and we'll make a decent manager out of him.'

The tide finally turned when Meath beat Dublin in the 1986 Leinster final. Defeat followed in the All-Ireland semi-final against the great Kerry team, thanks in no small part to a freak goal from Ger Power. Despite the defeat, the foundations were laid. Meath went on to win back-to-back All-Irelands in 1987 and '88 and five out of six Leinster titles from 1986 to '91 in the greatest run in the county's history, losing All-Ireland finals in 1990 and 1991 to Cork and Down respectively.

Dublin reigned supreme in Leinster from 1992 to '95. Boylan confronted another apparent crisis in 1995 when Meath lost the Leinster final to their great Dublin rivals by ten points. Boylan had to face another election. Again, Seán reacted to major defeat by rebuilding the Meath team – and was rewarded with another All-Ireland title in 1996. Three years later, he took Meath to his fourth All-Ireland title. In 2001, his Meath side were hotly fancied to add another Sam Maguire victory to their collection, but, in an amazing match, Galway ran out as easy winners in the All-Ireland final. The football world was shocked and frantically searched for an explanation for this tale of the unexpected – but not so the Meath manager.

'It was very simple. Galway were a better team on the day. It was very tight for a lot of the game. Then a few things happened very quickly that changed the game. Firstly, Ollie Murphy broke his arm. Secondly, Nigel Nestor was sent off. People talk about Trevor Giles missing the penalty, but that wasn't the reason why we lost the match. Galway won because they produced outstanding football. Nobody wants to lose an All-Ireland, but if I had to choose to lose to another manager, it would be to John O'Mahony. A lot of the credit for that All-Ireland has to go to John.

'It wasn't easy for him in 2001. He had to face a lot of problems early on in the season, but he dealt with the problems in the dressing-room in his own way. He worked at it behind the scenes. What is said in the dressing-room is like what is said in the confessional. It's not for outside consumption.'

In conversation, Seán Boylan laughs a lot. He laughs heartily when I suggest that he appears to have a strong spiritual dimension.

'I suppose you could say I'm a very spiritual person, but I'm not always very spiritual! When I was young, I thought seriously about becoming a priest. I was attracted to the contemplative life. To this day, I still like to visit a monastery regularly. I find it very peaceful.'

It is clear that his father was the formative influence on his life.

'He was a wonderful man. He was an army officer and had a great authority to him. He commanded respect wherever he went or whomever he met, but he always believed that you should help people if you could. I worked with him for years as a herbalist, and he was able to help a lot of people in that way. That's the path I have taken in life, and it's very rewarding when you can help people or bring them relief from pain.

'There's the other side though, when people come to you and you can't offer them a solution for their particular problem. That's very sad, and unfortunately I come across people who have to carry huge crosses in life far too often. All of us get very caught up with football and with the importance of winning All-Irelands, but when you meet people who have to face huge problems every day of their lives, it really puts football in perspective.'

Boylan has witnessed the funny side of the game.

'When Dublin played Meath in the 1996 Leinster final, Meath's Tommy Dowd was in a clash of heads with Dublin's Keith Barr. Some time later, Keith's brother Johnny was also in the wars with Tommy. After the match, Tommy was going up for an interview when he banged his head against a bar in one of the barriers: an injury that subsequently necessitated four stitches. As Tommy held his head in agony, a passing Dublin fan said to him, "I see you made the hat-trick."

'"What do you mean?" Tommy asked.

'"Johnny Barr, Keith Barr and iron bar!"

'Little things can break the tension for a team. In the strain of an All-Ireland final in 1996, against Mayo, Colm Coyle reduced his teammates to laughter when he asked President Mary Robinson – as she was being introduced to the Meath team before the match – with the familiarity of intimacy, "How are things at home?" For the rest of the lads, the pressure evaporated immediately, and, happily, we went on to beat Mayo and win the All-Ireland.'

6

THE GIANT FROM THE WEE COUNTY
EDDIE BOYLE

At the top of the list of Louth immortals is the late Eddie Boyle, an outstanding full-back for Louth and Leinster. He played for Leinster between 1935 and '48 and won five Railway Cup medals during that period. He won Louth senior championship medals with Cooley Kickhams in 1935 and '39 and a Dublin senior championship medal with Seán McDermotts in 1947.

In 1932, he made his debut in a Louth jersey with the county minor side. In 1934, he was a member of the Louth junior team who reached the All-Ireland final, but after the semi-final he was promoted to the senior team and was therefore ineligible for junior grade when Louth won the final. However, he was awarded a junior medal. In 1990, he became Louth's first All-Star when he received the All-Time All-Star award.

Born in picturesque Greenore in the Cooley Peninsula, spiritually, he never left it – as was evident from the name of his Dublin home, Greenore. The archetypal gentle giant, nothing seemed to faze him on or off the pitch until the sad death of his wife in 1997. Given his height, strength, fetch, mobility, anticipation, positional sense, and his long, accurate kick from hand or ground, he was the complete full-back, though, as a youngster, he once scored 30 points in a game at centre-forward. He also once played full-forward for Louth in a challenge game against Monaghan.

The highlight of his inter-county career came in 1943 when he won his first Leinster senior championship medal. Boyle was the spine of the team, along with Jim Thornton at midfield and the classy Peter Corr in the forwards. In the Leinster semi-final, Louth had trailed Offaly by four points, but with his bucket-like hands repelling virtually everything Offaly could throw at him, Boyle and his fellow backs kept them to a solitary point in the second half – while the Louth forwards notched up 1–7 to win comfortably. In the Leinster final, Laois could only manage two points in the second half, while such was the service to the forwards that the final margin in Louth's favour was fifteen points.

Although Louth were to lose the All-Ireland semi-final to Roscommon in 1943, Boyle had the small consolation of keeping the late, great Jack McQuillan scoreless for the 60 minutes. His second Leinster medal came in 1948, when Cavan beat them in the All-Ireland semi-final.

Surprisingly, though, neither victory ranks as his most memorable match.

'I will always remember a National Football League match against Cavan in the Athletic Grounds in Dundalk. The Grounds were packed, as Cavan were All-Ireland champions and it was their first game after they won the title in New York. Cavan were hot favourites to win, as we were having a bad time, but it was a sizzler of a match and we played some inspired football. And we won by two points. The town was talking about the match for days afterwards.'

Boyle commanded great respect among his peers. When he retired, his Louth colleagues presented him with a magnificent gold watch. On its back were the words, 'To a great player, from all Louth footballers.' Louth goalkeeper Seán Thornton once said that when playing behind Eddie Boyle he often felt like bringing a chair to relax in!

The great Mayo forward Eamonn Mongey said of Boyle, 'It was immaterial how the ball came to him: high or low, left or right, carried or kicked. Eddie invariably collected it. Sometimes he came bursting through with it; sometimes he came through sidestepping like a bullfighter to avoid the forward rushes, but he came away to clear it. And when Eddie Boyle cleared the ball, it stayed cleared for quite a while!'

While Eddie Boyle was chosen on the Centenary Team of greatest players who never won an All-Ireland, Meath's Paddy O'Brien was chosen on the Team of the Century in the full-back position. Coincidentally, both had played club football with Seán McDermotts. Asked once how he compared to Boyle, O'Brien said, 'Eddie was undoubtedly the greatest, and you could put me somewhere in the bottom of the league table.'

The late Paddy Kennedy of Kerry was a close friend of Eddie. Boyle also retained a particularly close friendship with Peter McDermott and said of McDermott's team, 'I really liked playing against Meath; there was always great football between us.' This friendship had made the former Louth great more sympathetic to the plight of referees and the difficulties they have to contend with.

How big a disappointment was it for Boyle not to have won an All-Ireland medal?

'I was always playing to get into an All-Ireland final, and if I had succeeded in getting to it, I would certainly have been playing for a medal. But I always enjoyed the game so much. That was what was important. Yet, while saying that, I don't mean that I wasn't always all out to win.'

As his firm contention was that forwards could be prevented from scoring without infringing any of the rules, he was a strong believer in sportsmanship.

'At the very longest, it's only a very short period, really, that you'll be playing the game, so it should always be played properly for everyone's enjoyment.'

According to Aristotle, the unexamined life is not worth living. Eddie Boyle was a very reflective man and gave a lot of thought to the secret of his success as a player.

'I loved being in the action. When the ball was up at the other goal, I was longing for it to be at my end, even if it meant danger. There is one thing you need in any position, and that's anticipation. My intention was always to close down all traffic to the goal. You cannot afford to allow anything to develop in the play, otherwise anything can happen and you are in trouble. I was always blessed with good anticipation, but in playing full-back I was never relaxed. I was always on my toes, even when the ball was way up the field.

'My biggest asset was my ability to read the game. I never knew how I knew where the ball was going, but I did. I'd be going out to the ball like a bullet. If you waited, the other fella had as good a chance as you of getting it. That's why I never looked for my man at any time; the ball was always all I was interested in. When the ball came in, my man was looking for me, but I was already clearing the ball.'

When I asked him to pick his dream team, he selected the following:

100 GAA GREATS

1 DAN O'KEEFFE (KERRY)
2 ENDA COLLERAN (GALWAY)
3 PADDY O'BRIEN (MEATH)
4 SEÁN FLANAGAN (MAYO)
5 SEÁN MURPHY (KERRY)
6 JOHN JOE O'REILLY (CAVAN)
7 STEPHEN WHITE (LOUTH)
8 MICK O'CONNELL (KERRY)
9 PADRAIG CARNEY (MAYO)
10 SEÁN O'NEILL (DOWN)
11 SEÁN PURCELL (GALWAY)
12 PADDY DOHERTY (DOWN)
13 MAURICE FITZGERALD (KERRY)
14 TOM LANGAN (MAYO)
15 KEVIN HEFFERNAN (DUBLIN)

7

BROGAN BRILLIANCE
ALAN BROGAN

As hot favourites, Dublin were swamped by a tsunami of green and gold in the 2009 All-Ireland quarter-final, losing to Kerry – who should have been beaten by Sligo and who had been struggling all year – by a demoralising 17 points. The Dublin forward line went absent without leave, apart from the two brothers Bernard and Alan Brogan. It was a relatively new experience for Bernard, but Alan had been lighting up the Dublin attack for years, with All-Stars and five Leinster medals to show for it. Alan's father, also Bernard, had been a star midfielder for the great Dublin team of the 1970s and will always be remembered for scoring the decisive goal in the 'greatest game of all time', when the Dubs beat Kerry in the 1977 All-Ireland semi-final.

For all his accomplishments in Croke Park, Alan has not been carried away with his success, and in his career he has learned the hard way that there is a fine line between victory and defeat.

'Dublin fans will never forget years like 2002 when we were a "nearly team" and were unlucky to lose against Armagh. There is a very thin gap between laughter and loss. Who will ever forget Ray Cosgrove's free coming off the post at the end of the game that would have given us the equaliser? We lost the game by a point, and Armagh went on to win the All-Ireland.'

What was the lowest point of Brogan's career?

'I would say losing the 2006 All-Ireland semi-final to Mayo was a low point. We were winning and, with 65 minutes gone, seemed unbeatable, but, depending on who you ask, we threw it away or Mayo rose from the dead and snatched victory from us heroically. We met a few weeks after the Mayo defeat. We tried to come up with reasons, but it's hard to put your finger on it. When you look back, you have to look forward as well. If we're in that situation again, we have to do something different and make sure it doesn't happen, whether it's holding on to the ball or making sure we get that extra score when we're under pressure – if someone gets a goal, to make sure we get the next score.

'When we came back in November, it meant that we could look each other in the eye again. We weren't like, "Remember, you did this" or "I did that." We cleared the air. We got rid of the bad feelings after we were beaten. That was a good way to have it.

'It was important. There would have been bad feeling, not towards each other but that we lost the match. Fellas would have been thinking, "Where did it go wrong?" But the meeting cleared the air. Losing to Tyrone in '08 and Kerry in '09 were also crushing disappointments.'

Why have Dublin lost so many games they seemed certain to win?

'There's no point in hiding from the fact that we have lost a few leads over the last number of years. It's hard explaining why it happens. We've nearly started every championship game well, bar a couple, but we have been clawed back a few times when we had big leads.

'Maybe teams raise their games for us. We've been burnt a few times. The important thing is, if it happens again, that we make sure to respond. We know it's there and people are talking about it. We know in our hearts and souls we've let very good chances slip away. It's up to us to make sure, if situations arise again, we hold onto the lead and close the games out.

'In the last few years, people have said that Dublin teams found it difficult to put two big-name performances together. Looking back, we have put our fans through a roller coaster of emotions, often raising hopes that we were on the road to an All-Ireland after a good performance only to put in a bad one in the next match to bring everyone crashing back down to earth. Probably, the key for us is that we make the most of the periods in the game when we are dominant, which we didn't always do in the past. Possession needs to be converted into scores.'

Many Dubs fans were very critical of Dublin's managers, like Tommy Lyons, and blamed them for many of Dublin's defeats in previous years. Was that criticism justified?

'I tried to stay away from all that. Maybe the players didn't take the responsibility we should have taken for losing games I think we should've won – games that we had the squad to win, anyway. Maybe the players got off lightly. Maybe we didn't get as much flak as we deserved.'

ALAN BROGAN

Given his roots in the GAA, Alan surprised many people when he once said in an interview that his hero was David Beckham. Why does he admire Becks?

'It has nothing to do with his tan or his trendy haircuts or clothes! If you have that flair, that ability to do something exciting or outrageous, it's important to do it. Winning is the bottom line, but you need that entertainment factor. That's something I always admired about Beckham. He wasn't afraid to try something.'

Does he enjoy the fame that goes with the sport in the way that Beckham seems to?

'Unlike players like David Beckham, I have no interest in the celebrity side of the game. I'm not interested in being recognised in public. I'm not interested in proving anything. I don't have to convince myself of what I am. I know what I am. I work hard. I am not interested in image or pretence. I want my team to be the best that they can be. Some people seem to think it's ambition. I don't think it is. I am not into making rash promises.'

What are Brogan's hopes for the future?

'To win an All-Ireland. We feel we have a maturity now. We just need to find that extra bit to take us that final step.'

8

ONE-IN-A-ROW JOE
JOE BROLLY

In the 1990s, Derry football produced one of the greatest characters in the history of the game, Joe Brolly. He did things his way, such as blowing kisses to fans after he had scored a goal. This caused one fan to remark, 'At the best of times, Joe Brolly is objectionable, but when he blows kisses he's highly objectionable.'

Although Brolly was an Irish basketball international as a schoolboy, Gaelic football was part of his genetic inheritance.

'I always wanted to play for Derry because of the great team of the '70s that won back-to-back Ulster titles. We were totally dyed-in-the-wool Gaels.'

As a prominent member of Sinn Féin, Joe's father, Francie, was interned in the 1970s. That experience was to be a formative one in shaping Joe's career choice as a defence lawyer.

'Criminal defence is very important in a civilised society. When I was a boy, we would regularly have the house searched by the army. I remember, as a very small child, being dragged out of bed and the bed being searched.'

With a typical laugh, he makes a joke out of his career as a legal eagle: 'I often quote Billy Connolly's line, "I'm fabulously wealthy."'

In 1993, Brolly was at the heart of Derry's most famous day when they won their only All-Ireland. However, he jokes that because the county failed to win another All-Ireland, he has become known as 'One-in-a-row Joe'. Brolly believes that there were a number of reasons for the triumph.

'It was very clear from an early stage the team was going somewhere. We had a lot of very strong characters on the team. An important catalyst for our success was Lavey winning the All-Ireland club title in 1991. Our captain was Henry Downey from Lavey, and he was driving us on. He would tell us we were not training enough. So when Lavey won the All-Ireland club title, we all bought into the belief that the Downey way was the right way. We were training five nights a week.

'Our manager, Eamonn Coleman, was crucial. He was jolly and a great character. He always played cards with the lads down the back of the bus. He was a teetotaller himself and didn't understand drink. Eamonn was a small man, so it was a sight to see him berating a giant like Brian McGilligan about drinking. The best man to hold his drink in the squad was Johnny McGurk. Eamonn would say to him, "Wee man, wee men can't drink." The boys would be laughing, because Johnny could drink any member of the squad under the table! Eamonn wasn't a great tactician, but he was a real leader, 'cause the boys loved him very dearly – because he was a man's man. He once told me I needed to do weight training, saying, "Brolly, you're like a girl."

'Then Mickey Moran came in. He is a quiet man who is a terrific coach and a football fanatic. He worked very well with Eamonn. The broad-brushstroke man who had the philosophy behind everything was Eamonn, while Mickey was the nuts-and-bolts man. I know in hindsight that Eamonn was not a good trainer, but when Mickey came in, all of a sudden everything was right.

'I've never seen either the 1993 semi-final or All-Ireland final, but anyone who has tells me they never had the slightest worry that we would win either, although it was very close against Dublin in the semi-final. And even though Cork got a whirlwind start, scoring 1–2 in the first five minutes in the final, we beat them without any problems.

'To this day, people speak about time – they talk about winning the All-Ireland to fix other things by. I especially recall people queuing for the Credit Union, because nobody worked for two weeks. We had a banquet in the Guildhall. It was organised by people who wouldn't know if a football was pumped or stuffed. It was like the end of the world. The spiritual side was very important. To Kerry, winning an All-Ireland is just routine, but to Derry it was cathartic. At last, we could take our place among the football counties with self-respect.'

Although he was a classy forward, Brolly is most remembered for his flamboyant style. His exuberance did not endear him to his opponents.

'I remember once lobbing the Meath keeper in Celtic Park. He was a big, tall fella, and I just popped it over his head. Colm Coyle came charging over to me and drove his boot into me. I needed about 13 stitches. Brian Mullins was managing us at the time and said, "You deserve that, you wee boillix!"'

Over the last ten years, Brolly has become one of the best-known faces on Irish television as a straight-talking pundit on *The Sunday Game*. During the Connacht semi-final in 2004 between Mayo and Galway, as Colm O'Rourke was engaged in a typically incisive analysis, Brolly butted in to describe ponytailed Kieran McDonald: 'He looks like a Swedish maid.' As Michael Lyster tried to get serious again, Brolly decided to interject a comment about Mayo's Conor Mortimer: 'He would be better off spending more time practising his shooting and less in the hairdresser's.'

To his credit, Brolly was also hard on himself. After a poor performance against Galway, he said, 'My only consolation was that I held Tomás Mannion [the corner-back] scoreless.'

After Armagh beat Down in the 2008 Ulster semi-final, the Armagh manager, Peter McDonnell, explained, using the saying in its broadest sense, 'We were riding the donkey close to the tail.' At times like these, an analyst is indispensable to help decipher the hidden treasures of such a comment. Brolly stepped up to the plate and said, 'Riding the donkey close to the tail? I presume that's something you do in south Armagh. It's a very odd part of the world.'

9

HIS KINGDOM COME
PADDY BAWN BROSNAN

The many legends of Paddy Bawn Brosnan, on and off the field, hold a special place in the annals of the GAA. He was one of the all-time great Kerry footballers. His commitment to football was evident at an early age. Attending the local Christian Brothers' school, he was asked to conjugate the Latin verb *venio*. Paddy Bawn simply shrugged his shoulders and said, 'Ah sure, Brother, I'm only here for the football.'

He played senior football for Kerry, winning thirteen Munster medals, three Railway Cups, and All-Irelands in 1940, '41 and '46. He captained the team in the 1944 All-Ireland, only to lose to Jimmy Murray's Roscommon. One player who has never forgotten his encounter with 'the Bawn' that day is Roscommon's Brendan Lynch.

'You have to remember it was a very different time because of the war years. Some people listened to the news on the battery-set radio, which was the only programme we were allowed to listen to because of the Emergency, but they kept it on to hear Seán O'Ceallachain reading the sports news. Most people heard that either Roscommon had won or Kerry had lost on the radio. The belief then was that you hadn't really won an All-Ireland until you beat Kerry in a final, so we were all keen to do that. I was marking the famous Paddy Bawn Brosnan. He was a fisherman and fond of the women, fond of the porter and fond of the rough and tumble!'

For his part, the Bawn believed that the pivotal incident in that final was when Lynch had a head collision with Kerry's great midfielder Paddy Kennedy, who had to be stretchered off. Kennedy asked Lynch, 'Jaysus, what did you do to me?' Brosnan was a massive admirer of Kennedy, one of the greatest midfielders of all time, and endorsed the sentiment they wrote on his tombstone when Kennedy died:

God rest you, Paddy Kennedy,
Your reward you've surely won,
When duty called, you gave your all
Both off the field and on.

Early in his career, Paddy Bawn had played in the forwards, but later he switched to the defence. As a defender, his most famous encounters were with the late Mayo great Tom Langan. One player had the inside story on their most memorable exchange. Seán Freyne captained the Mayo minors in 1953 but missed out on the final because he had entered the seminary in Maynooth and was precluded from playing because of the rules of the Catholic Church at the time. He finally got the opportunity to play for Mayo seniors in 1956 against Galway. Before the match, Tom Langan told him that he would send him in the perfect ball. Uncharacteristically, he failed to do so. Ten years later, Seán was walking into Croke Park and met Langan for the first time in ten years.

'I got a very revealing insight into Langan's perfectionism. Tom's immediate response was to say to me, "Jaysus, that was an awful ball I sent you."

'Langan had a rare off-day in the 1951 All-Ireland final. Kerry were leading with moments to go, and Paddy Bawn Brosnan, described by Langan as a "strong fella who was very butty", had dominated him. Brosnan took a kick out, and a high ball was sent in and Langan flicked it into the net. Paddy Bawn's verdict was, "He stood inside me while I was taking a kick out. It was probably illegal, but it was very effective." The goal secured Mayo the replay they needed, and they went on to reclaim the title.'

One of the stars of that Mayo team, Paddy Prendergast went to work as a Garda in Kerry, where he formed a close friendship with one of the icons of Kerry football.

'Kerry had such wonderful players. I always felt that Paddy Kennedy was the prince of footballers. He was majestic, but Paddy Bawn Brosnan was something else: a great player and an exceptional man. He was a lovely human being and at that stage had a pub in Dingle. He had a great feeling for Mayo, and I spent a lot of time with him. One time Seán Flanagan came down to visit me, I brought him to see the Bawn. We went into a quiet nook of the pub and chatted for hours. What I most remember about it, though, was that, over the course of the evening, 30 people must have peered into the nook just to get a glimpse of Paddy Bawn, such was his legendary status. It was like going to Lourdes.'

Paddy Bawn was celebrated for his keen intelligence and his quick wit. This latter trait was evident from an early age, if a story heard in Kerry is to be believed. When he was a young man, Brosnan entered the confessional box and said, 'Bless me, Father, for I have sinned. I have been with a loose woman.'

The priest asked, 'Is that you, Paddy Bawn?'

'Yes, Father. It is.'

'And who was the woman you were with?'

'Sure, and I can't be telling you, Father. I don't want to ruin her reputation.'

'Well, Paddy Bawn, I'm sure to find out sooner or later, so you may as well tell me now. Was it Mary O'Malley?'

'I cannot say.'

'Was it Monica Kelly?'

'I'll never tell.'

'Was it Lizzie Ward?'

'I'm sorry, but I'll not name her.'

'Was it Patsy Kearney?'

'My lips are sealed.'

'Was it Fiona Hession, then?'

'Please, Father. I cannot tell you.'

The priest sighed in frustration. 'You're a steadfast lad, Paddy Bawn, and I admire that. But you've sinned, and you must atone. Be off with you now.'

Paddy Bawn walked back to his pew. Paddy Kennedy slid over and whispered, 'What you get?'

'Five good leads,' said the Bawn.

10

PETER THE GREAT
PETER CANAVAN

In 1996, after the All-Ireland semi-final, two irate Tyrone fans were loud in their condemnation of the Meath team, particularly of their alleged ill-treatment of Tyrone's star player, Peter Canavan. A Meath fan made an interesting and revealing slip of the tongue in response, 'You can't make an omelette without breaking legs.' Having almost won the All-Ireland final against Dublin for the county on his own, scoring 11 of his team's 12 points when they lost by a single point, it was a backhanded compliment to Canavan that he was singled out for 'special attention' by the Meath men.

A great player's career is like a rose on a bush: it blooms brilliantly only to fade away. Yet Peter Canavan's fame is destined to endure for many years. He captained the county to All-Ireland under-21 glory in both 1991 and '92, and in 2003, despite struggling with injury, captained them to their first senior All-Ireland. He won a second All-Ireland in 2005.

As a boy, Canavan shopped local for his hero.

'In 1984, I followed Tyrone's Ulster championship when they defeated Derry and Down before facing Armagh in the Ulster final. That decider was to provide me with a tailor-made hero. This, to me, was Frank McGuigan's final. When I went home, I decided that I was going to try my best to emulate Frank McGuigan. He became my constant inspiration as I practised alone or with others.'

Joe Brolly sees Canavan as pivotal to Tyrone's triumphs in the noughties.

'The advent of Peter Canavan was critical to Tyrone's success. Any team he had been involved in were champions: Errigal Ciarán were Ulster champions, and he had won minor and under-21 All-Irelands with Tyrone. Suddenly, he found himself in his mid 20s, wondering what was going on. In his first four years as a Tyrone senior, they didn't win a single match in the Ulster championship. In 2003, they had great young players like Eoin Mulligan and Co. arriving on the scene, but Canavan was still there to give the leadership on and off the pitch they needed.

'Armagh had won the All-Ireland the previous year, playing a defensive brand of football, but there was something to admire about it, something heroic about it. Even Armagh couldn't cope that year with Tyrone's play. In Tyrone, the individual was anonymous. Peter Canavan was able to play in that final, kicking on only one leg. People started to ask, is that football at all? But they won their All-Ireland.'

In the classic 1994 film *The Shawshank Redemption*, the hero escapes through a tunnel of human effluent after 17 years in prison for a crime he didn't commit. Morgan Freeman, narrating, describes his escape: '. . . crawling through a river of sh*t and coming out clean on the other side'. For fans of Tyrone football, that win was such a moment of epiphany. As he lifted the Sam Maguire Cup, Canavan said, 'They said we were like the British Army, that we lose our power when we cross the border, but we've proved we have power today.'

Canavan is very aware of the spiritual importance of the victory.

'To take back the Sam Maguire trophy to Tyrone for the first time meant so much to so many, and we were very aware of that. The memory of the celebrations will live with me for ever. However, what I really appreciate now is going around Tyrone and seeing young children wearing their county jerseys or displaying the flag of their county team with pride. You really can't put a price on that.'

Hopes of consecutive All-Irelands received a devastating setback with an event that Canavan and his teammates could never have foreseen.

'Cormac McAnallen's death did keep things in perspective. It showed us that, when football is a matter of life and death, our priorities are warped. It was a watershed for people.'

Few people had the opportunity in their careers to see Canavan up close and personal more regularly than Armagh's Enda McNulty.

'Against Tyrone in 2003, we decided we were going to show the whole country that we could win by playing nice football. We tried to play less tough football and more champagne football. We needed to marry the skills with the physical dimension. We could also have been more intelligent on the day on the pitch – I'm not talking about management. For example, I was marking Peter Canavan and he wasn't fit to walk – and I marked him man to man. I should have come out in front of him and covered off Eoin Mulligan as well. So I am taking the blame for my own performance. The player I always knew I had to be unbelievably focused on, when I was marking him, was Peter Canavan. You knew you had to be incredibly switched on for every single ball, because if you even blinked, he would stick the ball in the net.'

Although he played with a very serious manner, Canavan also has a light side. In 2003, he was speaking at a reception to launch his book. All the Tyrone team were there apart from the delayed Eoin Mulligan. Canavan explained to the crowd that Mulligan was late because his mother had bought him a new mirror and he was still admiring his reflection.

Canavan has shown a new side to himself since becoming a pundit with TV3. Commenting on the Munster semi-final replay in 2009, he remarked on the small dressing-rooms in Páirc Uí Chaoimh.

'Senan [Connell] was telling me about a National League match that Dublin played here. It was that dark that one of the Dublin players, when he was changing, actually put his leg into someone else's shirt.'

11

NO ORDINARY JOE
JOE CANNING

The rich history of the GAA is studded with personalities who have retained for ever a niche in the memory of those who have had the good fortune to see them in action. Joe Canning is unusual in that he had already gained a place in the hurling immortals as a teenager, given his exploits with his club Portumna and with Galway's underage teams – winning two minor All-Irelands and captaining the team as they sought a three-in-a-row, only to lose to Tipperary. Canning is a sports writer's dream: boy-next-door manner, quick-witted, intelligent and, above all, immensely talented.

Such adulation brings its own problems. It can push young players into fostering delusions about their own importance, encouraging them to imagine they are better than they are – only to become embittered when their careers fail to deliver what they appeared to promise. Far more damaging than anything opponents can do to them is the burden of unrealistic expectations. Although still a minor, in 2006 Canning was given the opportunity to join the senior squad. He declined then, though he did win an All-Ireland under-21 medal that year.

In 2008, he made his senior debut for Galway. The prophets of doom had said that Canning was fatally handicapped by inexperience. Such reasoning is as devoid of logic as the injunction 'Don't go near the water until you can swim.' Success is impossible without opportunity, and opportunity in hurling is created with the right blend of skill and character. Canning showed what he was made of when he starred in Galway's narrow loss to Tipperary in the league final. However, he really announced his arrival on hurling's centre stage, in bold print, with a stunning performance against Cork in the championship. Although Galway lost, Canning scored two goals and twelve points of Galway's total of 2–15. He was rewarded with an All-Star and the young hurler of the year award.

In 2009, he once more lit up the championship, notably in his first-half performance against Kilkenny when he strode through the defence like a colossus. Again, disappointment came when Galway were surprisingly defeated by Waterford in the All-Ireland quarter-final, but still Canning finished the top scorer in the championship with 3–45. He scored 4–7 in the All-Ireland under-21 semi-final defeat to Clare. Consolation came for Joe in the form of his third All-Ireland club medal with Portumna and his second All-Star award.

The GAA will succeed and progress as long as it has the support of people; the club is the cell of growth and renewal. Hurling is woven into Irish history. The roar of the crowds, the whirr of the flying sliotar and the unmistakable and unique sound of the ash against ash have enthralled sports fans for decades. Canning combines the old values with new realities: a master of a game that has its roots in an ancient Celtic civilisation but also a star of YouTube, where he can be seen scoring line balls. When he takes a sideline cut, it is as though an invisible hand guides the ball over the black spot on the crossbar. When he takes off on a solo run, the hurley becomes part of his hand. As his goal in the 2010 league final showed, close to goal, his senses are heightened like those of a wolf in the wilderness, the crowd's cheers and jeers dissolving like supermarket background music.

Canning's exploits have elevated him to the status of hero, but his innate self-possession has saved him from being overwhelmed by the celebrity that has engulfed him. His self-deprecation is most evident in his own jocose description of himself as 'slow and one-sided'. Despite his tender years, he has already produced performances as consistently sublime as anything that has been seen before. When Canning plays well, the hurling fans tingle and tears of pure joy come to their eyes. The tingles last well into the night when they lie in bed, with no chance of sleep, and replay the finest moments, often in slow motion, like an overzealous commentator with his finger on the replay button. Canning plays the game with the vitality and inspiration that give hurling fans the knowledge that theirs is the chosen game.

As one of the greatest forwards in the history of the game, few people are as well equipped as Nicky English to evaluate Canning.

'I had heard all the hype about Joe Canning, and I wasn't sure, the first time I saw him playing for Galway minors, it was all justified. Then I saw him scoring line balls for fun in the Fitzgibbon Cup, and I began to reassess him. For me, the turning point was the 2008 league final. He had excelled for Portumna in the club championship and had just come onto the Galway panel, and I couldn't believe the way he was able to run through the Tipperary defence. It changed the way I viewed him. I thought to myself, "This guy can become anything."

'I was lucky enough to see him play against Cork that summer. It was incredible to watch him almost pushing his own players out of his way because he was so confident he was going to get the scores. In the second half especially, he was a one-man show, and it was just incredible to see three of the finest players we have seen in recent times – John Gardiner, Ronan Curran and Seán Óg Ó hAilpín – in a panic because they had absolutely no idea how to handle him. After that game, I felt, "This is a guy who has the potential to become one of the all-time greats."'

12

LEGEND OF THE ASH
D.J. CAREY

Big hurling matches are often settled by explosions of effectiveness, and nobody exploded more lethally or plundered more consistently than D.J. Carey. Was he the greatest of all time? Was he as good as Christy Ring? The answers have never been clear-cut, but the mere fact that these questions have been asked so often is testament to Carey's genius. His collection of honours includes nine All-Stars, five All-Ireland medals and four National League medals. When he announced his retirement in 1998, it was a major news story that year, but Carey came back and played on until 2005.

As a player, he deserved all the plaudits heaped upon him – with a string of performances as captivating as the sport can offer. Opposing him in top form was like trying to defy a succession of breaking waves. Whenever danger lurked, he responded like a wounded lion. He was at his best when the stakes were highest, with the adrenalin flood that sharpens the senses and boosts the appetite for living.

D.J. was what he had to be, an excellent craftsman with a superb fighting spirit and the stamina of body and mind to cope with the long haul. His athletic body generated astonishing power, which was complemented by an even more profound strength of spirit. D.J. believed in the importance of thinking like a winner.

'Winning games is not just about who can swing the hurley the best. A lot of the time it is about who has the right attitude and who wants to win the most.'

The American football coach Bill Parcells said of his sport, 'This is not a game for well-adjusted people.' He might just as easily have been speaking about hurling. The clash of the ash is not a game for emotional neuters. It is a sport for those addicted to ferocious, helter-skeltering emotional rides, whether they manifest it or not.

Hurling is the ultimate virtual reality, because it can take you anywhere you want to go. The heart of all sport is the quality of experience it provides. Contrary to everyday life, sport offers us a state of being that is so rewarding one does it for no reason other than to be a part of it. Such feelings are among the most intense, most memorable experiences one can get in this life. That is why for Carey the main rewards of the game were spiritual.

'A lot of people think we do what we do for the medals and the glory. It's not about that. It's about fun and pride in one's parish and county.'

Ger Loughnane has radically revised his views on the mental toughness of the master executioner of hurling.

'There was a lot of talk before the 2000 All-Ireland when D.J. Carey wasn't on the Team of the Millennium. I was of the opinion that he didn't deserve it because he hadn't proved himself in an All-Ireland final. The test of a really good player is to produce the goods against a top-class player on the really big occasions.

'In '97, before we played Kilkenny in the All-Ireland semi-final, I was asked in an interview what I thought of D.J. He had been absolutely brilliant in the All-Ireland quarter-final in a thrilling game against Galway in Thurles. He practically beat the westerners all on his own. I said, "D.J. will prove himself to be an outstanding player when he plays really well against one of the best players in the country in a big match. Next Sunday, he will be playing in a really big match against Brian Lohan, and if he plays really well against him, he will prove himself to be a really great player, but I won't regard him as a great player until he does it against somebody like Brian on the big day."

'Nicky Brennan was Kilkenny manager then, and he taped the interview and played it on the bus on the way to the match. According to the version I heard, and how true this is I don't know, he said, "Listen to what that cu*t Loughnane said about one of our best players." Eddie O'Connor is supposed to have piped up, "He's f***ing right!"

'In 2000, we went to play Kilkenny down in Gowran on D.J.'s home pitch. He put on an exhibition. I never realised he had the skill, the pace and the wit to the degree he showed that night. All that night, he was like somebody on a different plane. He left Brian Lohan totally and utterly stranded. I met Brian Cody coming off the field, and he said, "He's something else." I answered, "He's a wizard."

'In 2000, I was delighted that he played a great game in the All-Ireland. What people underestimate about him is his courage. Down the years, he has collected many injuries. Yet his nerve remained as good as ever. His one instinct was to go for goal no matter what kind of punishment he was going to be subjected to. Under every category of defining a great player, he is without doubt the finest player of his generation, if not ever.'

Brian Cody's description is equally fulsome.

'He brought everything to hurling. He's a great tackler, he's a great player, he's a great winner of a ball. His skills – he just had them all. And he's been the most exciting player in hurling for a long time.'

13

THE FOOTBALLER FROM WESTMEATH
MICK CARLEY

If not fortune then fame is the deserved reward of those players who have the good luck to play for a team who enjoy great success. However, for great players who line out for the so-called 'weaker counties', celebrity status is much more difficult to achieve. A case in point is Westmeath's Mick Carley.

He first came to prominence in 1955 when he helped St Mary's CBS win the Leinster Colleges Senior B championship. He later enjoyed the rare distinction of playing with both the minor and senior Westmeath team on the same day in the Leinster championship. That occasion was in 1958 against Louth in Páirc Tailteann, Navan – in both games playing at full-back. His inter-county career, which spanned 20 years, had begun the previous year.

Carley quickly established a reputation as a top-class player, which led to his selection in 1961, '62 and '63 on the Leinster Railway Cup team. At that time, Railway Cup football and hurling were prestigious events, and to be selected to play was the highest accolade of recognition for a player of exceptional talent. By then, Carley had blossomed as a centre-fielder, and it was in this position that he scaled his greatest heights. Leinster won the competition in 1961 and '62 and were beaten in the final in '63. In 1961, he was selected on the Rest of Ireland team in the annual fixture with the Combined Universities. This remains one of Mick's most cherished memories, because of the privilege of lining out with and against the cream of footballing talent in the country. In 1966, he was chosen to tour America for the Cardinal Cushing Games. There were two crushing disappointments in his career.

'The first that stands out was not beating Kerry in 1969 in the league final in Croke Park: a game we could have won. The second was the day Laois beat us in the championship in Tullamore. At half-time, we were leading by ten points, and when Noel Delaney scored his second goal in as many minutes – and in the dying seconds of the game – I could feel the hair literally standing on my head. I just could not believe it.'

Although he never won medals with Westmeath, one of the rewards of Carley's career was to meet so many characters.

'My favourite character in Gaelic games is Tipperary's John Doyle. We were room-mates in the Cardinal Cushing Games in America. He was some operator. Meath's Patsy [Red] Collier was another. I went with Red to the Cushing Games. He was great craic. We were walking in Washington one day, and we passed what we thought was just a public house. Red looked in and called us back and said, "Jaysus, come back here, lads. Ye never saw anything like this." We went back to see what he was so excited about. There was a woman up on the bar doing a striptease!

'Colm O'Rourke displays a very compact character on television. He was also a very clever and able forward for Meath. I liked his strength and accuracy as a forward, and I enjoy his observations on television.'

Offaly great Willie Nolan was a big admirer of Mick Carley.

'He was a great player. I won two Railway Cups with him. It was a great competition then, because it didn't matter whether you were from a weak county or a strong one. All that mattered was talent, and a good player always stood out because the cream always rose to the top. Mick was more than a match for the star players from Down or Kerry.'

Club football provided Mick Carley with the most memorable incidents of his career.

'I was marking Seán Heavin, who I played with for Westmeath in a club match. I was playing centre-forward and I was at the end of my career, so my legs were going. At one stage, the ball came in to us and was about ten foot in the air. Seán was younger and much quicker than me, so there was no way I was going to beat him. Just as he was about to jump and claim the ball, I let a roar: "Let it go, Seán!" He stopped and let down his hands, and the ball fell into my arms. The whole field opened up for me, and I just ran through and tapped it over the bar.

'I once was playing a club match in Offaly against Walsh Island, a club most people will know about because of Matt Connor. After the game was over, I togged in and was about to go home when a fella called me over and told me I should stay for a junior match between Clonbullogue and Bracknagh. I didn't really want to, but he was adamant that I should stay. I agreed to stay for five minutes. There was nothing special for the first couple of minutes, and suddenly a fracas developed and all hell broke loose. Everyone was swinging and punching. I found out later that they were all intermarried and there was a lot of history there.

'It took about five minutes for the referee to sort things out and get order back. He sent one of the lads off, but your man didn't do the usual thing and go back to the dressing-room and take a shower. Instead, he stood on the sideline waiting for things to boil over again so he could get back into the thick of the fighting. He didn't have long to wait! Another melee broke out, and they went at it again, only twice as hard. The referee finally restored order. But almost as soon as he threw the ball back in, another scrap broke out. I swear that there was no more than five minutes' football in the first half. In fact, things were so bad that at half-time the priests from the two parishes went in to try and calm things down. Things went fine for the first 20 minutes of the second half, and then another scrap broke out. I thought the fights in the first half were bad, but this one was really, really bad and the match had to be abandoned.

'Obviously, the man who told me to stay knew what to expect. My only regret is that nobody made a video of the game. I would love to watch the match again. It would have made a great comedy.'

Carley's dream team is:

1   ANDY PHILLIPS (WICKLOW)
2   JOHN BOSCO MCDERMOTT (GALWAY)
3   PADDY O'BRIEN (MEATH)
4   JOHNNY EGAN (OFFALY)
5   MICK O'DWYER (KERRY)
6   PADDY HOLDEN (DUBLIN)
7   MARTIN NEWELL (GALWAY)
8   SEÁNIE WALSH (KERRY)
9   MICK O'CONNELL (KERRY)
10 TONY MCTAGUE (OFFALY)
11 PADDY DOHERTY (DOWN)
12 PAT SPILLANE (KERRY)
13 SEÁN O'NEILL (DOWN)
14 SEÁN PURCELL (GALWAY)
15 KEVIN HEFFERNAN (DUBLIN)

14

THE MAGNIFICENT SEVEN
IGGY CLARKE

Iggy Clarke was part of the beginning of a new era in Galway hurling when he captained the county to their first All-Ireland under-21 title against Dublin in 1972. Three years later, a National League medal came to Clarke.

'The watershed, and one of my hurling highlights, was beating Tipperary in that final, for in those days the blue-and-gold jersey of Tipp had for us a hue of invincibility attached to it.'

There would be disappointment, though, later that year, when Galway lost the All-Ireland final to Kilkenny.

'We beat Cork by two points in the '75 semi-final. After that, euphoria in Galway was unbelievable. The county was on a roller coaster. But the expectations weren't based on reality. We were still unready to face a team of the calibre of Kilkenny and learned that in the final.'

In 1979, Clarke had been ordained to the priesthood when Galway played Kilkenny again in the final, only to make a present of two soft goals to the men in amber and black.

'We wasted a lot in the first half. I don't think the rain suited us. Kilkenny were spurred on by the defeat at the hands of Cork the previous year and didn't want a second successive defeat. There is a photograph [of me] as I'm walking off the field disconsolate and downhearted and Eddie Keher saying to me, "You'll be there again next year." But I was not even looking at him. I was just thinking to myself that we could have and should have won that game.'

Unfortunately, injury prevented Clarke from lining out in Galway's historic All-Ireland triumph over Limerick in 1980. However, his presence was publicly acknowledged following Joe Connolly's tour-de-force acceptance speech.

'In the All-Ireland semi-final against Offaly, I was flying it. A high ball came in, falling between the half-back and full-back line, which I retreated to gather. I gained possession from Mark Corrigan and dodged his tackle. Out of the corner of my eye, I saw Pádraig Horan coming to tackle me, and I avoided him, but I failed to see Johnny Flaherty, whose tackle from behind drove up my shoulder blade and broke the clavicle. As I went down, I could feel the heat of the rush of blood. I knew I was in trouble. I waited for the free that never came. Seán Silke was behind me saying, "Iggy, let go of the ball." I opened my hand, and he cleared it down the field. I was removed on a stretcher and faintly heard the applause of the crowd in my ears, but in my mind I clearly saw my prospects of playing in the All-Ireland disappearing fast.

'The pain was unreal. I was placed against the X-ray machine in the Mater Hospital, and I was afraid I was going to faint. A nurse tried to take off my jersey, but it was agony, so I told her, "For God's sake, cut it off." I suppose I kept half-hoping for a while that I might be back for the final, but it was not realistic.

'During the second half [of the final], I came out from the dugout and went up to the Hogan Stand. I had to mind my shoulder and didn't want to be crushed by people at the presentation. I had an inner feeling, you might say a premonition, that the lads were going to win, even though the game wasn't over. On the way, people kept asking me if we were going to win and if I was praying. After his wonderful speech, Joe Connolly handed me the cup, which enabled me to feel part of the whole victory. It was such a beautiful moment to hold it up in front of the crowd. We all felt that we were part of a turning point, a special moment in hurling history when Galway would take its rightful place at hurling's top table.'

There was further disappointment for Clarke in 1981.

'We were coasting in the All-Ireland final at half-time, despite John Connolly's disallowed goal. We looked like winning until Johnny Flaherty's goal, and even then I thought we were good enough to come back. It was a bitter pill to lose, but the defeat didn't hurt me as much as '79. That year, we hadn't won an All-Ireland, and I was very aware of the so-called curse on Galway hurlers, which said we would never win an All-Ireland. As a priest, I wanted to disprove that rubbish, and we had achieved that in 1980. I often wonder about priests' curses. I wish somebody had used them for positive things. I often think of the peasant who refused to hold a priest's dancing horse. The priest said to him, "I'll put a curse on you that will stick you to the ground." The peasant replied, perfectly reasonably, "If you can do that, why don't you do it to the horse?"'

Having won four All-Star awards, Clarke retired at the tender age of 32 in Centenary year: 'At that stage, I didn't have the passion for it any longer.'

In 1997, Clarke left the priesthood. He is now married to Marie. He works as a deputy principal in a school in Galway and also on a part-time basis as a professional counsellor. However, it was his experiences in the priesthood that provided him with his most amusing memory from his career.

'The morning of the All-Ireland final in 1981, I was saying Mass for the team in the hotel. The gospel that day was about the parable of the mustard seed: the smallest grows into the biggest seed. In my sermon, I gave a very eloquent philosophical presentation on how the story of the mustard seed equated with our journey as a team. In '75, we were a tiny seed, but in '81, it would really go into fruition. That night, at the meal, we were all down because we felt we had left another All-Ireland behind us. Joe Connolly turned to me and said, "Jaysus, whatever happened to that f***ing mustard seed?"'

Clarke selected a dream team he would have liked to have played on, restricting his choices to players from his own era:

1 NOEL SKEHAN (KILKENNY)
2 FAN LARKIN (KILKENNY)
3 PAT HARTIGAN (LIMERICK)
4 JOHN HORGAN (CORK)
5 JOE MCDONAGH (GALWAY)
6 SEÁN SILKE (GALWAY)
7 IGGY CLARKE (GALWAY)
8 JOHN CONNOLLY (GALWAY)
9 FRANK CUMMINS (KILKENNY)
10 JIMMY BARRY-MURPHY (CORK)
11 PAT DELANEY (KILKENNY)
12 MARTIN QUIGLEY (WEXFORD)
13 NOEL LANE (GALWAY)
14 RAY CUMMINS (CORK)
15 EDDIE KEHER (KILKENNY)

15

COOL FOR CATS
BRIAN CODY

When Cork hurlers went on strike in 2009 to replace Gerald McCarthy, they got their desired result. McCarthy's successor, Denis Walsh, had his first match in charge in a league clash against Kilkenny. Cork were annihilated. After the match, rumours emerged that the Cork hurlers were about to go on strike again – this time to have Brian Cody sacked. It was a story told in jest, but it reveals Cody's place at the very top of the hurling hierarchy. Proof of that assessment comes every time he walks into a room of hurling people. As soon as he enters, everyone turns a questioning eye on him. His opinions are avidly sought, his every remark hailed and his judgement accepted without question.

A member of the great Kilkenny team of the 1970s, Cody won four All-Irelands as a player and captained the county to All-Ireland success in 1982. He won two All-Star awards. He also won an All-Ireland club medal with his beloved James Stephens in 1976.

For many years, Ger Loughnane has witnessed Cody's performances on and off the pitch.

'Brian was a year behind me in St Pat's teacher training college and lived in the room opposite me. We got on really well, and when we played together in college he could do things with the ball that'd make you look completely stupid. His level of skill was a delight. He wouldn't say much, but when he spoke everybody listened. After he retired from playing, I thought he'd be managing Kilkenny minors or under-21s, because I remember that when he came on the field at Pat's he had a very strong presence. I really admire him as a man and as a manager, but when he was appointed manager of the Kilkenny team, I said, "Everybody's in trouble now."'

Tommy Lyons famously said, 'The most important skill for any manager these days is to have a good excuse.' Since he was appointed Kilkenny senior manager in 1998, Cody has not needed excuses. He won his first All-Ireland in 2000, back-to-back titles in '02 and '03 and completed a memorable four-in-a-row in '09 in an epic tussle with

Tipperary. The basis of his success is that he is not only a proven judge of players but has the extra, invaluable ability to recognise exactly where, how and in which on-field circumstances they can best serve his teams. Moreover, he brings analytical assessment, passion and a talent for motivating players individually to transcend their former limitations. A side's self-belief soars when the manager's methods work, and no manager's methods in hurling history have worked as well as Cody's.

Of course, he has occasionally disappointed himself and others. In fairness, the perfect talent has never existed. As rabbits and hedgehogs quickly learn not to become transfixed by the headlights of oncoming cars, Cody learned speedily from his rare failures, notably the defeat to Galway in 2001. Yet, with Cody seeming to get his bearing from signs known only to him, the level of success was unprecedented. After the loss to Galway, Cody introduced a more robust style of play to Kilkenny hurling. Nobody was going to push them around any more.

Aside from Cody's great achievements as a manager, Nicky English believes that Cody's legacy will be profound.

'I don't believe in the cult of a manager. The way I see it, a bad manager will stop you from winning an All-Ireland but a decent manager will win the All-Ireland for you, if he has the players – and that's the key. It is players who win the All-Ireland not managers. The one exception I would make is that I rate Brian Cody very highly. He has achieved so much over such a long period, but above all he has changed the tradition of Kilkenny hurling. He has brought in a new system and a way of playing which has become part of the hurling culture now in Kilkenny.'

Although best known as a twice world cross-country champion and for his silver medal in the marathon at the 1984 Olympics, John Treacy, head of the Irish Sports Council, is a keen hurling fan and a big admirer of Cody.

'I think of Brian as the Alex Ferguson of Irish sport. He is an incredible manager. He sets the bar very high and demands and gets the highest standards off his players. If you don't reach them, you have no future as a Kilkenny hurler no matter how much skill you have. He knows everything about every promising player in every corner of the county. He is always looking for ways to improve the team. He leaves nothing to chance, and everything about his preparations is always well thought through.'

BRIAN CODY

The hallmarks of Cody's catalogue of triumphs have always been his unassuming professionalism and his unparalleled eye for a player. His genius lies in his ability to look at an unproven hurler and evaluate and imagine his likely development. Then, when the player moves to the first-team stage, Cody displays an almost mystical, intuitive understanding of the player's psychology.

With coaches, as with players, the cream rises to the top – and good coaches tend to have success follow them. With the obvious exception of his memorable lynching of Marty Morrissey after the 2009 All-Ireland final, Cody's answers at press conferences may not be entertaining in the style of Babs Keating, but players would follow him over the trenches. He is, without doubt, hurling's greatest-ever manager. Many attempts have been made to explain his genius. But one way to think of his managerial career would be that he came and planted a seed in a barren ground – when Offaly, Clare and Wexford had challenged the natural hurling order in the 1990s – and he watched the seed grow. He loved it and nurtured it till the branches started growing outwards and upwards, and All-Ireland success came back to Kilkenny in 2000. Then the tree was struck by lightning when Noel Lane's Galway knocked them out of the championship in 2001. He started all over again, loving and nurturing it and changing its style of care in a fundamental way, and the branches grew and grew to the ends of the hurling world, leaving everything else in their shade.

16

CAPTAIN MARVEL
ENDA COLLERAN

Initially, the chief football analyst on *The Sunday Game* was the late
Enda Colleran, who was a key part of the Galway three-in-a-row All-
Ireland-winning side of 1964 to '66, captaining the side in the latter
two years. He was selected at right full-back on both the Team of the
Century and the Team of the Millennium. He used the knowledge
he acquired to telling effect as an analyst and blazed the trail for the
rest to follow. Colleran's first taste of All-Ireland success, in 1964, was
shrouded in sadness.

'After half-time, John Donnellan and I were walking out together.
John was right half-back, and I was right full. He turned to me, and he
said, "I think there's a row in the stand." In one portion of the stand,
there were an awful lot of people moving around, and I said to him,
"There must be." We didn't take any more notice at all. We played the
second half, and we won. We were in such good form, but I noticed
our officials were very subdued when they came in.

'We went into the dressing-room after all the presentations. John
said, "I want to go out to show the cup to the old man." Up to that point
they couldn't get an opportunity to take him aside and tell him. At
that stage, they had to tell him, and then everybody changed. Actually,
it wasn't a row at half-time, but John's father [Mick Donnellan] had
passed away in the stand. John's father had captained Galway and
was a fantastic footballer.

'It's amazing, really; you think that an All-Ireland is the most
important thing, but everything changed. The atmosphere was totally
subdued, as you would expect. The next evening, the Sam Maguire
Cup was brought home in a funeral cortège, rather than with a blaze
of glory, as is the norm. In fact, Mick Higgins, who played on the same
team as him [Mick Donnellan], was actually watching the game at
home, and he collapsed and died as well. According to rumour, when
Mick Donnellan went to heaven when he died, and when he reached
the gates, St Peter said to him, "Who won the All-Ireland?" And he

said, "Well, when I was leaving, Galway were winning well, but Mick Higgins will be up soon and he'll have the final score."'

Enda had no hesitation when I asked him his outstanding personal memory from the three-in-a-row triumph.

'It was the All-Ireland semi-final against Down in 1965: my best ever game. The ironic thing was that I had a terrible start to the match. I was marking Brian Johnson, and he scored two points off me in the first few minutes. I felt that, if I didn't get my act together, he would end up as man of the match – and decided to change my tactics. Down were storming our goal for most of the second half, and I found that, no matter where I went, the ball seemed to land into my hands. I seemed to be in the right place all the time and made all the right decisions. Often, I took terrible decisions and went forward and left my man, and still the ball came to me. I was so thankful that a thing like that happened to me in an All-Ireland semi-final rather than in a challenge game with no one to witness it.

'At one stage, Seán O'Neill had the ball around the midfield, and Paddy Doherty, completely unmarked, came at speed to the full-forward position. I had two options: one was to stay on my own man, and the other was that Seán O'Neill would pass the ball to Paddy Doherty. I took the chance and ran for Paddy Doherty, and Seán O'Neill passed the ball to him, and I actually remember coming behind Paddy, trying not to make any noise so that he wouldn't hear me coming towards him, and, at the last second, I nipped in front of him and got possession. I felt he had a certain goal, only for that. It's amazing, with 60,000 people present, that I still thought my approach had to be as quiet as possible.'

A more tense occasion came the following year, when Galway were to face favourites Meath in the All-Ireland final. Colleran was due to mark sprint champion Ollie Shanley, who had given a top-class performance in the semi-final.

'Everybody was saying to me, "You've an awful job in the final to mark him; you'll never mark him." Martin Newell and I went out to the Aran Islands for a few days, just before we started training for the All-Ireland final, and we were sleeping in the one room; he was on one side and I on the other. He woke up at one stage of the night, and I was standing over him. I was sleepwalking! Martin told me the next day that I said, "By Jaysus, if I can keep up with Shanley, I'll mark him." It just shows you the pressure I was under.'

What was the secret of Galway's success?

'We also had great belief, which meant that we would always believe we would win a game when it was tight at the end. Other teams choked in that position.

'We also had that vital ingredient you need if you are to win anything: that bit of luck. I think back especially to the Connacht championship in 1965. Both Sligo and Mayo should have beaten us. It was there for them if they had kept their heads. We were in terrible trouble against Sligo, after they got two early goals, but we just sneaked victory by three points. Against Mayo, we were losing by a point in the dying minutes when they got a 50. Three Mayo players were fighting over who should take it when one of them rushed up and kicked it straight to one of our half-backs. He cleared it up the field, and we got the equalising point. And then we got the winning point almost immediately. Mayo were all over us that day and without doubt should have won. It's amazing how a tiny incident can make all the difference in deciding who gets their hands on the Sam Maguire Cup.'

The dream team Enda selected for me was:

1 JOHNNY GERAGHTY (GALWAY)
2 DONIE O'SULLIVAN (KERRY)
3 NOEL TIERNEY (GALWAY)
4 PADDY MCCORMACK (OFFALY)
5 JOHN DONNELLAN (GALWAY)
6 KEVIN MORAN (DUBLIN)
7 MARTIN NEWELL (GALWAY)
8 MICK O'CONNELL (KERRY)
9 MATTIE MCDONAGH (GALWAY)
10 MATT CONNOR (OFFALY)
11 SEÁN PURCELL (GALWAY)
12 PAT SPILLANE (KERRY)
13 MIKE SHEEHY (KERRY)
14 SEÁN O'NEILL (DOWN)
15 LIAM SAMMON (GALWAY)

17

A FOOTBALLING ARTIST
MATT CONNOR

Some pleasures, like marrying a woman for love and later discovering that she has lots of money, creep up as surprises. Others are more obvious, like the sight of the consummate footballing artist Matt Connor at his immaculate best in the early 1980s, driven almost by a lust for scores. Former Roscommon great Tony McManus speaks for most players who lined out against him.

'Matt Connor was the best player I ever played with or against. At times, I was in awe of his skill and class.'

Matt will be for ever imprinted into GAA immortality because of his scoring feats. He was Ireland's top marksman for five consecutive years from 1979 to '83 and scored a remarkable eighty-two goals and six hundred and six points in one hundred and sixty-one matches for Offaly. His silken skills on the ball, his free-taking ability, his power and his speed of movement and thought made him stand out from everybody else. He scored a stunning 2–9 (2–3 from play) in the All-Ireland semi-final in 1980 against Kerry, when the final score was 4–15 to 4–10 in Kerry's favour.

A football career is measured in moments rather than in days. One vignette that typifies Matt's career came for his club, Walsh Island – whom he steered to six consecutive county titles between 1978 and '83 – in Newbridge, in a Leinster club match. His side were under pressure and needed a score. Matt collected the ball 25 yards out from his own goal and went the length of the field on a solo run. In his green-and-white-hooped jersey, he swerved, feinted, sold a dummy and slowed up or accelerated to lose his man. He left everybody that came to tackle him behind, stretched on the ground, without any of them even touching him. As the ball went over the bar, some of the players he had beaten were still on the ground, some were picking themselves up and one or two were on one knee. All were pictures of dejection, beaten by superior skills.

Dublin's status as kingpins of Leinster was ended abruptly by Offaly in the 1980 Leinster final. Offaly's manager, Eugene McGee, was to mastermind one of the biggest upsets in football history when Offaly beat a Kerry team seeking a five-in-a-row in the 1982 All-Ireland final. The undisputed star of that team was Matt Connor, who scored seven points that day, and his points, when Offaly were under pressure, enabled the team to claw their way back.

Connor is a very private man living a public life. Given his exalted place in football's elite, he is in much too strong a position to go rushing wide-eyed and eager towards the beacons of welcome. Even those journalists closest to him have never quite penetrated the reserve that masks his rich wellspring of humanity. His is a protective spirit raising a wall against the outside world. Though the pitch of his conversation is undramatic, almost downbeat, the depth and authenticity of his experience fills my mind with images of a score of summer afternoons in Tullamore and elsewhere and of poorly attended league fixtures, when the sound of thunder cracked the air and rain spilled down onto the stand roof, rattling like applause on metal slats. Anyone interviewing him is unlikely to be offered a stream of cosy reminiscences, but there are one or two. As we spoke, his talk came initially as a trickle, then, as he cast away his inhibitions, swelled into a flood.

'The build-up in 1982 suited us very well, because all the pressure was on Kerry. They were probably the best football team ever. They had a lethal forward line, an extremely good back line and a great midfield. They really had no weakness. We had to work hard on the day and never give up. One very important thing was that our manager, Eugene McGee, put my brother Richie in at centre-forward. That was a key decision on that day because, the year before, Tim Kennelly had absolutely cleaned up at centre-back. He was going to make sure that the main reason we were beaten in 1981 wasn't going to happen again. He put Richie as a kind of stopper and a playmaker at centre-forward, and that worked a treat. Another thing was that Eoin Liston was the key man in the Kerry forward line, and we had to stop him and stop the supply of the ball to him. Liam [O'Connor, Matt's cousin] did quite a good job in that sense on the day, and the players out the field did a lot of hard work and hard grafting to stop the ball going into the Kerry full-forward line.'

MATT CONNOR

A sadness so deep that no tears would come fell over football fans everywhere – devoted to the flickering images of a rich history – two years later, with the news that, at the age of 25, Matt Connor's career had come to a premature end.

'I was going home from Tullamore on Christmas Day to my Christmas dinner. My car went out of control, and I was thrown out of the car and landed on my back. I damaged my spine, and I suffered paraplegia from that accident. That finished my football career. When I had the accident, I suppose football wasn't the main priority at that stage. It was just a complete change of life that I was not able to walk again.'

Seldom has one man brought so much pleasure to so many. Former Donegal star Seamus Bonner is one of Matt's many admirers.

'Offaly's Matt Connor was the best player I ever saw. He had it all: brilliant from frees and brilliant from play and could do it with either foot. I know him well through working in the Gardai together. It was such a shame that his career ended so early.'

18

THE GOOCH
COLM COOPER

Success in football comes in cycles. When he was president of the GAA, Jack Boothman – at a time when Kerry football was in the doldrums in the 1990s – went to the funeral of the legendary Paddy Bawn Brosnan. Because of the pressures of time, he was unable to make it to the church and went to meet the funeral at the graveyard. As he waited for the cortège to arrive, he chatted with a few gravediggers. One of them gave him a guided tour of the graveyard and pointed to the graves of all the famous footballers. It seemed that every second grave belonged to a former Kerry great. The gravedigger turned to Boothman and said, 'It's a very impressive collection, isn't it?'

Jack replied, "Tis indeed, but the way things are going at the moment, you'll have to dig them all up again if Kerry are ever going to win anything!'

With the arrival of Colm 'Gooch' Cooper on the Kerry team in 2002, there was no longer any need to dig up old heroes. A multiple All-Star winner, he was chosen as Texaco Footballer of the Year in 2004.

Most people focus on the team and the bigger picture rather than on the individual, but fans of all ages have heroes. From the start, Cooper was to be one of them because of his supreme skills and his attitude – it is about doing everything as well as you can and no acceptance of second best, whether it be on or off the field. It is about the commitment to excellence.

Incredibly, though, before Kerry's 2009 All-Ireland quarter-final with favourites Dublin, Cooper was being written off in some quarters. His early season form had not been vintage, and he made front-page news by getting dropped for the qualifier against Antrim, having been caught drinking after a narrow victory over Sligo. Cooper responded in the best way possible: with a goal in the opening minute and a five-star performance in Kerry's demolition of the Dubs by seventeen points. A new joke was born: What's the difference between Dublin and a school uniform? The school uniform will be seen in September.

COLM COOPER

Cooper kicked six points in Kerry's thirty-sixth All-Ireland final victory, when they beat old rivals Cork, and finished the year as top scorer in the championship.

The highlight of his career so far is no surprise.

'The first time that something great happens is special, because there can never be another first time. So winning my first All-Ireland title in 2004 against Mayo is probably the greatest, especially because we lost my first All-Ireland final in 2002 to Armagh. It was very emotional when the full-time whistle went.'

Cooper also played for Ireland against Australia.

'From my point of view, it was a tremendous honour to be invited to play for my country, and I was delighted with the chance to be part of the experiment to give an international outlet to Gaelic football. Of course, it did come as a shock, when you were on the ball, that an Aussie player could come up and knock you to the ground by any means necessary and keep you pinned down. I do think we could learn from them. There is a very high emphasis on the basic skills, but, as Kerry showed in 2004 in their defeat of Armagh, there is still a major place for "catch and kick" in Gaelic football.'

Cooper has had the privilege of playing with legends of the game like Darragh Ó Sé.

'Nothing celebrates the game like a player of his skill – just like the way players like Brian Mullins and Jack O'Shea lit up Gaelic games in the 1970s and '80s. In a different way, Maurice Fitzgerald had lit up the game with his skill and artistry. As a kid, I marvelled at Darragh, because he was fantastic. When Darragh retired in 2010, we lost one of the all-time great midfielders. We will never see his like again.'

Despite winning All-Irelands in 2004, '06 and '07, disappointment was to follow in the All-Ireland final against Tyrone in '08.

'Before Tyrone played Dublin in the All-Ireland quarter-final in 2008, people were ready to write their obituary, but they produced the performance of the year and came out and totally demolished the much-hyped Dubs. They played with composure, class, total commitment, teamwork, flair and skill. They put up a great score in the most atrocious conditions. In short, they played football the way it should be played. Any team could learn from them on that performance, and they would prove that they were a great side when they beat us in the final that year.'

Cooper was an ardent supporter of the GAA's decision to allow other sports into Croke Park.

'The GAA showed real leadership in revoking Rule 42 and opening up Croke Park to rugby and soccer. Nobody will ever forget the atmosphere and the sense of history in 2007 when Ireland beat England in Croke Park. It was a defining moment for many people, and it meant so much to everybody in the country. For an amateur organisation, it is a staggering achievement to have created an incredible stadium like Croke Park, especially in the middle of Dublin. They have shown incredible leadership. The GAA has adapted to the changing times. They are keenly aware of the need to bring modern marketing methods into Gaelic games. I think a critical step came in the 1990s, with the decision to introduce live coverage of a large number of games on the TV. Young people get their heroes from television. If you go down to Kilkenny, you will see almost every young boy with a hurley, because they want to be like their heroes. It is the same with football in Kerry.'

19

WHERE WE SPORTED AND PLAYED
BRIAN CORCORAN

In 1999, after a young Cork side defeated the hot favourites Kilkenny in the All-Ireland hurling final, Jimmy Barry-Murphy stated that Brian Corcoran was the greatest Cork hurler of his generation. Barry-Murphy is not a man given to wild statements or hyperbole, so it was not a remark to be taken lightly. The hurling pundits nodded sagely in agreement.

Corcoran exploded onto the Gaelic games scene in 1992. A series of masterful performances in the Cork colours saw him crowned as hurler of the year. In 1999, he reclaimed that honour. Not long after that, the cumulative wear and tear of unending training sessions and games took their toll, and Corcoran retired prematurely from inter-county football and hurling. The arrival of a young family also played a major factor in his decision to quit at the top of his game.

'To be honest, hurling had become a chore. I'd be on my way home from work, and all I wanted to do was play with the baby, and instead I was being dragged away to do something that I didn't want to do. By the time I came home from training, she was asleep. It got to the stage where I was getting up in the morning and saying, "Oh no, I've got training tonight."'

Initially, he did not miss the game. For a time, it seemed as though Cork could get on without him too, and as though Cork hurlers were more interested in off-the-pitch activities than in contests on the pitch, when they famously went on strike to get better facilities and conditions from the county board.

In 2004, the time was right for Corcoran's second coming, not least because the expectation of a success-starved county awaiting retrieval of its oldest sporting prize demanded another All-Ireland. Setanta Ó hAilpín had departed to Australia, and, after a relatively unconvincing league campaign, Cork were ready for the return of the legend.

The Cork County Board seems to favour austere personalities. They had appointed Dónal O'Grady as their hurling manager. His demeanour was captured in Keith Duggan's comment in *The Irish Times* in September 2003: 'When Dónal O'Grady smiles, you can hear the cello in *Jaws.*'

O'Grady commanded such respect as a manager that Corcoran felt compelled to respond to his invitation to rejoin the hurling panel.

'It was a big gamble to come out of retirement. I could have fallen flat on my face, and Cork could have struggled. Some people told me that I had twice been hurler of the year and I had nothing to prove. But you make decisions and you live by them. To be honest, I was half-afraid of going back. I wasn't sure if the lads would welcome me back, with me being out so long.

'Then I returned to the inter-county scene after a break for a couple of years, and it showed me just how professional Gaelic games have become. When we came into training, our gear was up on a hook for us. All we needed to bring in were our boots and hurleys. After the training was over, we just left the gear behind us and someone washed it for us. In terms of fitness, the drills that had been in vogue three years previously were considered obsolete. The biggest change I found, though, was that when the manager came into training he brought his laptop and could pull out clips from any of the Cork games. That, in a nutshell, sums up the modern game.'

A Hollywood scriptwriter could not have written such a fairy tale for Corcoran's championship story in 2004. It began and ended with him on his knees. On his return, in his opening match of the Munster championship against Limerick, he scored a wonder point while still on his knees. In the dying seconds of the All-Ireland final, he sprinted on to the ball, rode a tackle, turned on his left, shot and scored the insurance score. He fell onto his knees just as the final whistle went and roared in triumph. It was nice to be back. Yet there had been a few anxious moments on the way.

'Waterford were the form team in the Munster championship and had an excellent league campaign, apart from the final, when they flopped against Galway. They beat us in the final, but I hadn't come back to the game to win a Munster medal. I came back to win an All-Ireland, and after that game we put things right and achieved our goal.'

Corcoran found himself unexpectedly embroiled in controversy before the All-Ireland quarter-final. The Antrim manager, Dinny Cahill, adopted an unusual strategy before the match when he publicly

BRIAN CORCORAN

rubbished Cork's chances. Corcoran was singled out for special criticism.

'Cork have to have a problem when they recall Brian Corcoran. They have to have problems. They have a dreadful inside forward line all season, couldn't get the scores. They had to recall a man who finished playing. Well, he will be finished after Sunday; there's no doubt about that. If you look at their games, they had a dreadful centre-forward but got away with it. We have a class centre-back. We know how to stop that man from hurling. We are going to win the All-Ireland this year. We can win the All-Ireland. After getting over this game, anything can happen.'

Corcoran responded in the best way possible and scored the two goals that obliterated Antrim's chances and helped Cork beat Kilkenny by 0–17 to 0–9 in the All-Ireland final.

In 2005, he was at the centre of one of the defining moments of the championship: his wonder goal against Waterford in the All-Ireland quarter-final. He remembers that magic moment with characteristic modesty.

'A hit-and-hope high ball was brilliantly rescued by Joe Deane on the end line, and he sent it back to me. I took two steps back while turning, dropped the ball and let it bounce, held my backswing in case I was hooked and skimmed the sliotar off the top of the ground, and it ended up in the net.'

He retired finally in 2006 after old rivals Kilkenny deprived the team of a three-in-a-row. To talk to Brian Corcoran is like watching him playing. It is impossible to escape the conclusion that he is a man of no airs but amazing graces.

20

A HURLER FOR ALL SEASONS
ÉAMONN CREGAN

Irish people have always been passionate about sport. It is said that in France you could win your country's national cycling tour seven times and walk the streets with anonymity. However, win even a stage once in Ireland and you are assured heroic status for a lifetime. Nowhere is this passion more apparent than in Limerick. As Shakespeare asked in *Coriolanus*, 'What is the city but the people?' In Limerick, sport is like a religion, touching a deep nerve in the psyche of the city's people. It is recognised worldwide as one of the great cathedrals of rugby, but it is also a powerhouse of hurling.

It is alleged that Ireland's favourite spectator sport is politics. In Limerick, politics is the favourite blood sport, but it is a mere trifle when compared with rugby, hurling and soccer. In the Shannonside city, sport is a communal obsession – as is evident in the astonishing breadth and depth of knowledge of all sports and in the highly polished and refined sense of the sporting aesthetic. Popular interest feeds on successes such as National League titles, in hurling or rugby, which in turn creates a demand for more.

From the start, hurling followers on the terraces in Limerick took to Éamonn Cregan with extraordinary warmth because of the subtlety, invention and spirit of adventure that enabled him to terrorise opposing defenders. The Limerick observers took him to their hearts because they were positive that he would willingly shed his last drop of blood for them. They knew instinctively that if defeat pained them it would hurt him even more. Allied to that were his creativity on the ball, his genius for penetration and his killing finish that commanded their respect. The fusion of great commitment and dazzling skills would be the stuff of cult status and sporting legend.

In Limerick, they appreciate style, but, equally, they are quick to see through a veneer if there is no substance to match. From Cregan's earliest games, as he lengthened his stride towards maturity, the gossip in Limerick was about how good a player he would become. Nobody had any doubt Cregan had enough class to go all the way. Reared on a diet of good – sometimes very good – players, they responded to somebody with something extra.

John B. Keane tells a story that typifies the fanaticism of Limerick supporters. He recalls meeting a supporter who was full of spirit, in more senses than one, after Limerick's defeat of Kilkenny in 1973. The man greeted Keane with a quotation from Shakespeare's *Henry V*:

> And gentlemen in England now a-bed
> Shall think themselves accursed they were not here,
> And hold their manhoods cheap whiles any speaks
> That fought with us upon Saint Crispin's Day.

He then went on to inform John B. that 'This will be worse than the Black-and-Tan War one day,' explaining that, by the end of the twentieth century, every man, woman and child in Limerick would claim to have been at the match.

In his 20-year career with Limerick – from 1964 to '83 – Cregan won three All-Star awards, but his finest hour was at centre half-back in the 1973 All-Ireland final. In a tactical masterstroke, the Limerick mentors switched him to curb the menace of Kilkenny's ace centre-forward, Pat Delaney.

'There was no way I was going to let Pat Delaney pass me and hop the ball on the ground and thunder through for scores, as he had done so often for Kilkenny. Switching me to centre-back for the final gave me a certain psychological advantage in the position. Kilkenny had never seen me line out at centre-back and were not used to my style of play, at least in that position. I had the major advantage, though, of playing in that role for my club, Claughaun.'

Three of Cregan's teammates on that All-Ireland winning side have been honoured at the Cheltenham racing festival. How does he explain this example of sporting ecumenism?

'J.P. McManus is from Limerick, and he loves Limerick hurling. J.P.'s very friendly with people who used to play for Limerick. He's called his horses after famous Limerick hurlers, like Joe Mac called after Joe McKenna – the horse that didn't win in 1998! Another horse was called Grimes [both were trained by Christy Roche], after the last Limerick man to captain an All-Ireland winning side, in 1973. A third gets his name from Limerick's great full-back, a man whose playing career was sadly ended by an eye injury, Pat Hartigan. McManus's horses race in green-and-gold colours after his beloved South Liberties club.'

Cregan would miss out on another All-Ireland medal in 1980 when Galway made the breakthrough. Noel Lane starred on that Galway team.

'We won that day because our leaders, especially Joe Connolly, stood up and were counted. We were a powerful team, and that side should have won more than one All-Ireland. It suited us that day that we were playing Limerick rather than Cork or Kilkenny, and that gave us confidence. It felt like it was for us, that day, though Limerick could have considered themselves unlucky. Éamonn Cregan gave a star performance on that day and did not deserve to lose. His goal was a clinical finish, and he got a particularly brilliant point from out the field.'

In 1994, Cregan tasted All-Ireland glory when he coached Offaly to beat his native Limerick in the final with two late goals in one of the most dramatic comebacks in living memory. It was a bittersweet day for Cregan: 'I had to separate my personal affiliation from my role of planning for an Offaly success.'

21

DALY DELIGHT
ANTHONY DALY

In decades of supreme contests, in a wide range of arenas, there have been few matches that have unleashed a greater flood of excitement and pleasure than Clare's All-Ireland hurling victory in 1995. Across the nation, enthralled listeners heard Micheál O'Muircheartaigh saying, with breathless enthusiasm, the magic words, 'We're gone 45 seconds into injury time. It's all over, and the men of Clare of '95 are All-Ireland champions.'

After 81 years wandering in the hurling wilderness, Clare had finally reached the promised land. In one of the greatest-ever All-Ireland final acceptance speeches, Anthony Daly spoke for a whole county when he said, 'There's been a missing person in Clare for 81 long years. Well, today, that person has been found, and his name is Liam McCarthy.'

During a game, communication is almost impossible on the field because of the noise. On this occasion, the Clare manager, Ger Loughnane, had to rely on his players for leadership during the white heat of battle. Anthony Daly was the natural choice to be the team's spokesman and captain. While his famous speeches and innate media skills might have seemed to be Daly's greatest attributes, Ger Loughnane chose him for his ability in the dressing-room, given his flair for helping players to cope with frustration and disappointment.

'Dalo knew moves before everybody else. I'd say there was never an occasion when Dalo didn't know who was really playing when we needed dummy teams. He was never told, but he always knew. Dalo was adept at deflecting any anger by giving his teammates a chance to air their complaints. If there ever was a grievance, Dalo would come to me. It was sorted out immediately. The players were treated exceptionally well, which was the best way of preventing grievances from arising, but if they did come up we dealt with them straight away. The fact that we had a holiday-fund committee meant that we could do things for them that other counties couldn't do.'

For the first half of 1995, Clare fans were anything but optimistic. Even when one major disappointment followed another, hopes and dreams always lived side by side in Clare. In 1995, as Daly recalls, his team were poised to react hungrily to a disappointing first half of the year.

'I think that, after the league final in 1995, 90 per cent of Clare followers felt, "That is it; we can't take any more trouncings." You couldn't blame them. Although we hadn't been trounced on the scoreboard, in hurling terms we were. Coming out after the game, one supporter said, "Kilkenny were a different class." This massacre came on the back of major defeats in the two previous years in Munster finals. When Ger Loughnane spoke about us winning the Munster final, none of the fans believed him.

'There were fewer than 15,000 fans at our first game in the championship, and most of them were from Cork. Even when we beat Cork, and the Munster final was jammed, it was mostly filled with Limerick people.'

Ger Loughnane believes that never was Daly's role as captain more clearly illustrated than before the Munster final in 1995.

'Everybody in Clare was convinced that we had no chance of winning that game, because, two weeks before, we had played Galway in a challenge match in Shannon and we bombed. It was on a glorious, sunny day, and the previous day had been the very same. When we were inside in the dressing-room, I noticed that some of our players were sunburnt and I said, "What the f*** were ye doing? Two weeks before the Munster final and ye come here sunburnt." Most of the crowd that were there went home at half-time, thinking we hadn't a chance in the Munster final. When the team came into the dressing-room, I gave them a fierce lambasting. We trained very well after that. On the day of the final, we stopped in the hotel in Cashel for a cup of tea. You could tell that morale was very good and that they were in terrific form.

'We were on the way into Thurles, and just when we came to the bridge, the place was crowded with supporters wearing the Limerick colours. A few of them shouted at us, "What a waste of time!" They were sure they were going back to the All-Ireland final. Straight away, Daly said, "We'll f***ing show ye whether it's a waste of time or not." That had a crucial bearing. It was just the sort of little spark that the players really needed to liven them up. As everybody got off the bus, there wasn't a word. As the players went out of the dressing-room, I said, "If Clare don't win today, we're never going to win anything." I was sure we were going to win. Everything was just right. The rest is history, but the incident on the bus showed Daly's sharpness of mind. Top marks to him for picking it up. A small thing like that can make a big difference.

'There was a brilliant photo taken during the All-Ireland of Brian Lohan and John Troy going for the ball. Instead of looking at the two of them, Anthony Daly was in shot looking for the loose man. It was driven home again and again, it's not the man in possession you watch but the loose man. That was how we kept Offaly down to 2–8 in that match. Daly's role was critical.'

The turning point in the All-Ireland final that year came with minutes to go. With the clock ticking, Anthony Daly, a master at the height of his powers, lobbed the sliotar into the square. Eamonn Taaffe connected, and the umpire reached for the green flag. Another long-range free from Daly gave Clare the crucial lead that they held on to in defeating Offaly. Two years later, he captained Clare to his second All-Ireland. His exceptional gifts as a player were recognised in the three All-Stars he won. After he retired from playing, Daly turned his attention to management and was an unlucky manager with Clare – particularly in 2005, when they lost out narrowly to eventual All-Ireland champions Cork. In 2008, he gave a massive lift to Dublin hurling when he agreed to manage the county team and in his first year brought them to an All-Ireland quarter-final. One memory from his playing days gives him the most contentment.

'It was great going to the schools after we won the All-Ireland in 1995 – just to witness the magic, the awe and the wonder – but to me the most special part was meeting the older people. I remember meeting my brother's father-in-law crying in Thurles after we won. He could remember back to '55 and all the catalogue of Clare's heartbreaks. At the time, I was so wound up and drained from games that I didn't fully appreciate it till later.'

22

FAMILY TIES
DESSIE DONNELLY

The Donnelly clan, from beautiful Ballycastle, are the most famous dynasty in Antrim hurling. Over a hundred years ago, in 1907, Edward Donnelly co-founded the Ballycastle McQuillans club and was its first chairman. In 1989, his great-great-grandson Dessie Donnelly won an All-Star at left full-back for his commanding performances that had carried Antrim to the All-Ireland final that year. Dessie's teammates included his brother Brian and cousin Terry, son of the legendary 'Bear' Donnelly, who hurled with distinction for club and county in the 1950s and '60s.

Dessie's older brother Eddie won a record eight Antrim senior hurling championship medals with Ballycastle and in 1970 won both a National League (Division Two) medal and an All-Ireland intermediate championship. He also played in two shinty internationals and went to the US as a replacement All-Star in both 1975 and '77. Another brother, Kevin, also played for Antrim hurlers.

In 1978, the pride of Derry, The Undertones, were singing about 'Teenage Kicks'. Dessie Donnelly's teenage kicks revolved around hurling.

'In 1977, when I was still a minor, I made my senior debut for Antrim when I came on as a sub in a league match against Westmeath in Mullingar. I scored a point and held my place after that.'

A momentous day in Antrim's history came in 1983 when Loughgiel Shamrocks won the All-Ireland senior club hurling title by defeating St Rynagh's of Offaly after a replay at Casement Park. Three years earlier, Ballycastle had lost the final to Castlegar of Galway. Twenty years on from that defeat, the game remains a very vivid memory for Dessie Donnelly.

'That was the biggest disappointment of my career – even more so than losing the All-Ireland to Tipperary, because no one really expected us to win in 1989. It was very different in 1980. The match was billed as the clash between the Connollys and the Donnellys, because there were

DESSIE DONNELLY

seven Connollys playing for Castelgar and seven Donnellys playing for us. We really thought we could do it, and it was a crushing blow when we lost.'

The year 1989 would provide Dessie with his most satisfying moment on a personal level.

'I was first nominated for the All-Stars in 1986. Although I didn't get selected, I was chosen as a replacement for the trip to America in 1987, which is the nicest consolation prize I ever got for anything. To be selected on the actual team in 1989 was, I'd say, the biggest thrill I ever got in hurling. I can't explain in words just how much it meant.'

The year 1989 also presented Donnelly with his sole opportunity to play on the highest stage within the game. Everyone was expecting the day of the All-Ireland hurling semi-finals to produce high drama – mainly because the second semi-final was between old rivals Galway and Tipperary. Eleven days previously, Galway had hammered Antrim in a challenge match, suggesting to neutrals that the northerners would be like lambs to the slaughter against Offaly.

Antrim's confidence, though, was high, because they had already beaten Offaly twice that year. Although it was an All-Ireland semi-final, the Antrim team did not think of it like that; they were conditioned to think of it as just like any other match against Offaly. Although Offaly were the form team in Leinster in the 1980s, the men in saffron and white would have been more nervous if they had been playing Kilkenny. They were mentally right for playing Offaly.

It was Offaly who made the better start, and their half-time lead was 1–10 to 1–6. It was a different story in the second half, as Dessie Donnelly marshalled the Antrim defence superbly and Antrim ran out 4–15 to 1–15 winners. Ciaran Barr assumed the playmaker role to provide ample scoring opportunities for Olcan 'Cloot' McFetridge (who, with Donnelly, won an All-Star in 1989), Aidan 'Beaver' McCarry and Donal Armstrong. It was fitting that Armstrong should be part of Antrim's finest hour, as his late father, Kevin – a dual star, Antrim GAA's most famous son and left half-forward on the Centenary Team of greatest players never to have won an All-Ireland medal – had starred in the last Antrim team to reach the All-Ireland final, back in 1943. After beating Galway by 7–0 to 6–2 in the 1943 quarter-final, Antrim had shocked Kilkenny in the semi-final, only to lose to Cork in the final.

83

In 1989, Antrim kept it 50–50 with Tipperary on the day for the first quarter of the game. They had chances, but they drove a lot of wides. Then Tipperary got a soft goal, which really deflated the northerners. It took a lot out of their play. The Antrim fans in the crowd were very demoralised by the goal.

Although Dessie Donnelly was clearly disappointed, that defeat was nothing compared with losing to Kilkenny in the All-Ireland semi-final two years later.

'That was definitely the biggest low of my career, because we had a couple of opportunities to put Kilkenny away but we didn't take them. A county like us does not get many opportunities to beat a hurling power like Kilkenny very often, so it was imperative that we took it – but we blew the chance. It was a make-or-break game for us, and after we lost, the team started to come apart and we never came that close again.'

During the Troubles, Donnelly had to contend with serious challenges.

'Thankfully, the Troubles never had a major impact on me. The only time it was an issue for me was when we were travelling for some of the Antrim matches. Of course, you have to be particularly careful when times are especially tense, like the marching season. There are quite a few places in Antrim where you wouldn't walk down the road on your own, or even in company, with a hurley stick in your hand – especially around the 12th of July.

'Back in the 1970s, our changing-rooms were bombed. The damage was superficial. I'd say that was more a matter of luck than because of careful management on the part of the bombers. There were a lot of theories floating around about who did it, as you can imagine, but I can't tell you who was responsible.'

He laughs when he is asked who was his most difficult opponent.

'As a forward, it was definitely Kilkenny's Dick O'Hara. I find it very hard to think of the words to describe what it was like to be marked by him. Let's just say it was hard to get away from him! As a back, it was Tipperary's Pat Fox. He could do things other forwards couldn't do in their wildest dreams.'

Dessie has a special place in his heart for his teammates.

'In 1989, after we won the All-Ireland semi-final, we were training hard coming up to the All-Ireland final. To get a bit of a break, Paul McKillen and I went to see the All-Ireland football semi-final between Cork and Dublin. We were having a great chat before the game, and, as the players were coming onto the field, I kind of noticed the big screen for the first time, and I said to him, "This should be a great game today." Paul looked up at the big screen and then he turned around and asked me, "Is this game live?" I nearly died laughing!'

Of the hurlers he competed against, the dream team Dessie would like to have played on is:

1   GER CUNNINGHAM (CORK)
2   SYLVIE LINNANE (GALWAY)
3   DICK O'HARA (KILKENNY)
4   DESSIE DONNELLY (ANTRIM)
5   JOE HENNESSY (KILKENNY)
6   GER HENDERSON (KILKENNY)
7   AIDAN FOGARTY (OFFALY)
8   FRANK CUMMINS (KILKENNY)
9   MICHAEL COLEMAN (GALWAY)
10 JOE COONEY (GALWAY)
11 JOHN CONNOLLY (GALWAY)
12 NICKY ENGLISH (TIPPERARY)
13 LIAM FENNELLY (KILKENNY)
14 JIMMY BARRY-MURPHY (CORK)
15 PAT FOX (TIPPERARY)

23

AT BOOLAVOGUE AS
THE SUN WAS SETTING
TONY DORAN

Tony Doran played for Wexford from 1967 to '84, winning an All-Ireland with the county in '68. One of his biggest admirers, the late Mick Dunne, former Gaelic games correspondent with RTÉ, spoke to me about this legend of the ash.

'Although Tony had the good fortune to win an All-Ireland early on in his career, he and that Wexford team were unlucky in many ways. Having said that, they beat old rivals Kilkenny in a Leinster final by 17 points in the 1970s, and that made up for a lot of disappointments. Wexford played well in the 1976 All-Ireland final, but they lost to Cork by four points.'

Galway's Iggy Clarke had a unique insight into Wexford's performance on that day.

'We drew with Wexford in a great semi-final game and lost the replay by a goal. It was an extremely hot summer. The two games were played within a week of each other, and the replay was within two weeks of the All-Ireland final. The game burned a lot of stamina. I believe if either ourselves or Wexford had won the first day that Cork would have been defeated in the final. As it was, Wexford came close that year, but I think the two games against us took a lot out of them, and they were not as fresh in the final as Cork were – and that cost them dearly. I felt a bit sorry for them that day, because they had some great players at that stage, none more so than Tony Doran. The fact that he was chosen as Texaco Hurler of the Year in 1976 is testimony to that, because it is rare for the hurler of the year to be chosen from a county that does not win the All-Ireland.'

Waterford's Tony Browne would be one of the few others to accomplish this, in 1998, and in other years only Christy Ring, Brian Corcoran and Dan Shanahan have ever emulated that achievement.

TONY DORAN

Further disappointment lay in store for Doran in 1977, as Mick Dunne recalled.

'Wexford were probably in the right place at the wrong time. They had the misfortune to come up in both years against a truly great team: the Cork three-in-a-row side. How rare is it for a team to win the three-in-a-row in either football or hurling in the modern era? There is a lot of truth in the old adage that if you win one All-Ireland you must be a good team, but to be considered to be a great team you need to win a second one. If you talk to the likes of Mick O'Dwyer or Ger Loughnane, they will tell you that. In '77, Wexford played well but probably not to their very best, and you can't hope to win an All-Ireland against a side like Cork without being at the very top of your form. Having said that, it was only a great save from Christy Keogh by Martin Coleman in the dying moments that denied Wexford that year.

'The problem for great players like Tony Doran was that it was so difficult for them to be seen in Croke Park on All-Ireland final day, because every year they had to face the most formidable opposition of all in the Leinster championship: Kilkenny, who have to be seen as the aristocrats of hurling. True to form, after "loaning" their Leinster crown to Wexford for two years, as they would have seen it, Kilkenny were back in '78 and went on to win the All-Ireland in 1979 against an emerging Galway side.

'I know Tony would feel that the All-Ireland that really got away from Wexford was in 1974, even though they lost to Kilkenny at the Leinster final stage. Wexford were going toe to toe with them but had to play the entire second half with only 14 players after Phil Wilson was sent off. Yet, true to form, Wexford hurled out of their skins, and it took Eddie Keher to characteristically win it for Kilkenny by a point with the last puck of the game. What made the defeat so galling was that Kilkenny beat Galway and Limerick very comprehensively in the All-Ireland semi-final and All-Ireland final respectively.

'Unlike today, there was no second chance for teams like Wexford, because there was no back-door system then. Also, back then the only games people saw live on television were the All-Ireland semi-finals and finals, which meant that the national audience were deprived of the opportunity to see the wonderful players Wexford had, like the Quigley brothers and Tony Doran.

'Tony was a great player, a great goal-scorer, but I think what made him stand apart was that he was such a wonderful competitor. I think a revealing insight into his personality and psychological make-up was that he once told me that the biggest disappointment of his career was not losing the two All-Ireland finals but losing to Offaly in the 1981 Leinster final. Tony was carried off in the early stages with a severe head injury and only heard the last few minutes on the radio from a hospital bed.'

No matter how high you go, there is something special about playing for your own parish or village, for the people you grew up with and for the true fans whose lives revolve around hurling – that's the heart of the GAA for giants of the ash like Tony Doran, as one of his old foes, Eddie Keher, generously acknowledges.

'Tony was one of the greats of the game. He really announced his arrival on the national stage when he scored two great goals in the 1968 All-Ireland final. The fact that they beat Tipperary, who had defeated Wexford in 1965, added to the sense of occasion. Yet it says so much for Tony that he saw the highlight of his career when he won the 1989 All-Ireland club championship with Buffers Alley at the tender age of 42, when they beat a gallant O'Donovan Rossa from Belfast in the final. It shows that the pride of the parish is everything, and that is why the GAA is so special.'

24

THE QUEEN OF THE ASH
ANGELA DOWNEY

The most celebrated incident in the late John Morley's illustrious career came in the 1970 league final clash when Mayo defeated Down. John was playing at centre half-back when a Down player grabbed him and tore his shorts. Just as he was about to put his foot into a new pair of shorts, the ball came close by. He abandoned his shorts and in his briefs fielded the ball and cleared it heroically down the field, to the adulation of the crowd.

Camogie's most famous star is Kilkenny's Angela Downey. During an All-Ireland final against Cork, Angela was goal-bound when her opponent, Liz O'Neill, made a despairing lunge at her that caused Angela's skirt to end up on the ground. Undeterred, Angela kept on running, and even when the Cork goalie, Marian McCarthy, whisked the hurley from her hands, she palmed the ball into the net and then calmly returned to collect her skirt. Even more telling was her subsequent comment: 'Even if she had pulled off all my clothes, I was going to score a goal first!'

Not surprisingly, Downey has been immortalised in folklore and is to camogie what Christy Ring was to hurling. Hurling was in her genes. Her father was the legendary Shem Downey, who starred for the black and amber in the 1940s and '50s, winning an All-Ireland medal in '47 in Kilkenny's classic triumph over Cork. Shem brought the passion he exhibited in the black and amber onto the sidelines when he watched his daughters on the camogie field.

Angela played in her first senior All-Ireland final with Kilkenny in 1972 against Cork, when she was just 15. It was to be a rare reversal for the young player, as Kilkenny lost the match, but all present that day remember their first acquaintance with Angela and say they knew intuitively that something special had arrived on the sporting scene. In the coming years, they were destined to see her often glide through bedraggled defenders, making a feast from a famine of poor possession. She appealed to the finer side of the imagination, with memory cherishing not only what she did in Croke Park and elsewhere but how she did it: with panache and elegance. Although she would be defeated in 1972, she went on to win seven consecutive All-Irelands for Kilkenny, in a team trained by Tom Ryan, from 1985 to 1991. In total she would win 12 All-Irelands; the first would come after a replay against Cork in 1974. Only Dublin's Una O'Connor, with 13, and the late Dublin star Kathleen Mills, with 15, have surpassed that achievement. Downey captained the county to All-Ireland successes in 1977, '88 and '91. In 1986, Angela became only the third camogie player ever to receive a Texaco award.

To add to Angela's joy, all her All-Ireland medals were won with her twin sister, Ann. In 2010, both were presented with the Lifetime Achievement Award at the *Irish Times* Sportswoman of the Year Awards. Sisters have formed an integral part of Kilkenny's camogie tradition. Angela and Ann's mantle was taken on by another terrifically talented twosome, Sinéad and Tracey Millea, in the 1990s.

The definitive tribute to Angela and Ann Downey comes from the star of County Down Máirín McAleenan.

'Angela and Ann Downey of Kilkenny made a fantastic contribution to camogie in the 1980s and '90s. Their longevity at the highest level is amazing and, I believe, will never be equalled, not to mention surpassed. Ann is fiery, strong, tough and was a non-stop runner. Angela was like lightning and skilful beyond belief. Camogie owes a great deal to the Downeys. *Go raibh míle maith agaibh.*'

Angela was also keenly appreciative of the importance of the club, in her case St Paul's and, later, Lisdowney. To add to her medal haul, Angela won an incredible twenty-two county titles and six All-Ireland club titles. A lot of strange things happen in club games in camogie. The strangest story must be that of a camogie club match in Westmeath in the 1970s when Cullion had a man on their team. What was stranger was that nobody noticed the difference until after the match. The headline in the local paper was 'When Is a Girl Not a Girl?'

Angela sees the club as the heart of camogie.

'Our game is not just about the winning. It's about the experience. As you get older you start to appreciate the real power of both camogie and the GAA: the sense of togetherness and community and the importance of the club. The pride of the parish is critical to what players do. There's also a great community involvement behind it. I think the GAA is so important when you are away from home. I saw in the United States the one place the community gathered was to watch a match. It is then you really see how important the GAA is for our identity of being Irish. Camogie and the GAA bring people together.'

A geography teacher at Grennan College in Thomastown, Angela's career witnessed two controversies. In 1988, just before her club faced Glenamaddy in the All-Ireland final, Angela was sensationally suspended for six months. Appropriately, St Paul's united in the face of what they saw as an injustice against Angela and won by a point with the last puck of the ball.

In February 2004, Angela boycotted the presentation of the Team of the Century in protest at the omission of her twin sister from the side. When asked to clarify her absence, Angela said, 'I don't like singling out individuals, because Gaelic games are team-based and it is teams who win and lose matches and being part of a team always appealed to me. Ann gave 25 years to camogie, has 12 All-Irelands and actually one more club title than me, because I was suspended for one final.'

The official camogie Team of the Century was:

1 EILEEN DUFFY-O'MAHONEY (DUBLIN)
2 LIZ NEARY (KILKENNY)
3 MARIE COSTINE-O'DONOVAN (CORK)
4 MARY SINNOTT-DINAN (WEXFORD)
5 BRIDIE MARTIN-MCGARRY (KILKENNY)
6 SANDIE FITZGIBBON (CORK)
7 MARGARET O'LEARY-LEACY (WEXFORD)
8 MAIRÉAD MCATAMNEY-MAGILL (ANTRIM)
9 LINDA MELLERICK (CORK)
10 SOPHIE BRACK (DUBLIN)
11 KATHLEEN MILLS-HILL (DUBLIN)
12 UNA O'CONNOR (DUBLIN)
13 PAT MOLONEY-LENIHAN (CORK)
14 DEIRDRE HUGHES (TIPPERARY)
15 ANGELA DOWNEY (KILKENNY)

25

FIELDS OF BLUE AND GOLD
JIMMY DOYLE

In the closets of Jimmy Doyle's mind as a boy, all his dreams were consumed by thoughts of playing in an All-Ireland final. Like so many of his generation, he was converted to Gaelic games by the GAA's answer to St Paul, Micheál O'Hehir. O'Hehir's conversions did not take place on the road to Damascus but from the 'magic box' on kitchen tables throughout the country. Doyle grew up in an era when Micheál O'Hehir was at the height of his extraordinary career, in the days of wet batteries and communal radios. For hundreds of thousands of Irish people he was the only mediator. A phenomenon never to be emulated, O'Hehir alone had the power to bring Gaelic games to the people. And he did. It was he who made Doyle aware for the first time of the unlimited potential that Gaelic games have for excitement, drama, tension, spectacle, elation and heartbreak – all packaged together in the ebb and flow of the enthralling broadcasts of the man with the golden voice. As one of the greatest forwards in the history of hurling, Doyle would weave his own magic into the lush tapestry of the GAA.

The 1950s was a golden era for hurling because there were great teams like Cork, Tipperary and Wexford. Not only that, but these teams had five or six great players competing for each position. In an era of outstanding defenders such as John Lyons and Willie John Daly of Cork, Diamond Hayden of Kilkenny, and Billy Rackard and Nick O'Donnell of Wexford, it was going to take a formidable talent to shine, but Jimmy Doyle lit up the hurling pitch like a Christmas tree. He could get scores from left or right. However, it comes as a shock that such a classy forward should have started and finished his career as a goalkeeper: his Tipperary career was bookended by an appearance as goalkeeper on the losing side in the All-Ireland minor final against Dublin in 1954, when he was just 14, and a stand-in appearance in goal against Waterford in 1973.

Even when early childhood memories are fading, almost every boy can recall his first football or hurling match. He can remember the score, who got a great goal and who had a bad miss. But mostly he remembers his father. And that is the magic of the GAA. Hurling was part of Jimmy Doyle's family tree. His father, Gerry, was sub goalie when Tipperary won All-Irelands in 1937 and '45, and his uncle Tommy was one of the legends of Tipperary hurling, winning five All-Irelands.

As a result, Jimmy grew up almost from the cradle hearing stories about Tipperary teams who had featured some of the greatest characters in the game, such as Mick 'Rattler' Byrne, who was a small man but, pound for pound, the toughest man you could ever meet. He would mark guys from Wexford three or four stones heavier than him, but he would never be beaten. He was a great corner-back for Tipp but also a wonderful storyteller. He did not have much time for all the talk players have today about their injuries, especially about their 'hamstrings'. He always said that the only time in his playing days he heard anybody talking about hamstrings was when they were hanging outside a butcher's shop.

One day, Byrne went to New York with Tommy Doyle, who was making his first flight and was very nervous. He sought comfort from the Rattler, who told him, 'Don't be worrying, Tommy. There are two parachutes under the seat. You put one on, jump out, count to ten, press the button and you jump to safety. What could be simpler?'

'But what happens if the parachute doesn't open?' asked Tommy.

'Tha's easy,' answered the Rattler. 'You just jump back up and get the spare one.'

Having won three minor All-Ireland medals, Jimmy Doyle went on to win six senior All-Ireland medals in 1958, '61, '62, '64, '65 and '71, captaining the teams in '62 and '65. He also won six National League medals and seven Railway Cups. The ultimate accolade came for Doyle when he was chosen at right corner-forward on both the Team of the Century and the Team of the Millennium.

It helped that his Tipperary team were a well-oiled machine with outstanding players like Babs Keating, Donie Nealon and, of course, Tony Wall, who was one of the greatest centre-backs of all time. For Babs Keating, Jimmy Doyle was a great role model.

'Long before players were handed out gear for free, we were very conscious of the importance of equipment. Jimmy Doyle was one of the best hurlers I ever saw. He would always arrive in the dressing-room with five spare hurleys. I learned from him the importance of proper preparation.'

Doyle enjoys the humour of hurling, such as the story of the former hurler who is in an accident and is rushed to hospital. Two men are in the ward with him. One dies almost immediately, then the second. The player, in panic, screams when the consultant appears: 'Doctor, doctor. Get me out of here quick, and stick me in the backs. Things aren't going well in the forwards.' Another example was the headline in the *Tipperary Star*: 'Death of hurling immortal'.

An essential element of the appeal of Gaelic games, that extra quality that distinguishes them from all other sports in Ireland, is the tribalism on which the structures are based. No other sports enjoy the intense rivalry that exists in the GAA between clubs. From time to time, this creates problems, but in the main it generates a sense of community that has been all but lost in contemporary Irish society. Despite the intensity of the rivalries in hurling, Jimmy Doyle is particularly proud of its tradition of sportsmanship. One parable that illustrates this came in the 1958 All-Ireland semi-final between Tipperary and Kilkenny, when he scored eight points off Paddy Buggy. After the match, a Kilkenny supporter asked Paddy, 'What happened? Why didn't you hit him?'

Buggy replied, 'Why should I? He didn't hit me.'

26

HELL'S KITCHEN
JOHN DOYLE

Sex, say the Italians, is the poor man's opera. That is utter nonsense. Anyone with half a brain knows that hurling is the poor man's opera. Although there is no question that sex is nicer than watching hurling – because there are no bad wides, no annoying referees and you are warm and reasonably dry, as a norm – it does not engender the feelings that are brought about by winning an All-Ireland. Nobody has experienced the joy of winning All-Irelands more often than Holycross's John Doyle.

For Doyle, 1949 was a never-to-be-forgotten year.

'I will always cherish the excitement of winning our first Munster final. We all came home from Thurles on our bicycles, with the boots, togs and socks strung over the handlebars. Our captain, Pat Stakelum, tied the cup to the bicycle as well. Nobody now would believe that. Of all the All-Irelands I won, the first one, in 1949, stands out. All the others were special in their own way, but the first one was magical. We were playing Laois, who were captained by a fella called Ruschitzko, who was of Polish extraction. I was too young to be really nervous. Still, when a Croke Park official came in and told us we had ten minutes to be on the pitch, the seriousness of the situation suddenly hit me. Laois did not do themselves justice, and we won, rather easily, on a score of 3–11 to 0–3. I was thrilled that I had won an All-Ireland senior medal at 19 years of age. When we arrived home, the whole county seemed to be there to greet us. Thurles was jammed with people and bicycles. We went on then to win three-in-a-row, beating Kilkenny and Wexford respectively in the following years.

'Nostalgia can be a dangerous pastime when it clouds the memory and impedes our ability to recall accurately the strands of the past. I am sometimes criticised, when offering opinions about hurling today, that I am for ever harking back to the past and to the great Tipperary team that I played on. Maybe I do, but I still think the team I played on was pretty exceptional. We were a good team. It is all that needs to be said.'

Tipperary's 1960 full-back line of John Doyle, Michael Maher and Kieran Carey rejoiced in the name of 'Hell's Kitchen', given to them for their tenacious defending. Their collective motto seemed to be, 'Thou shalt not pass.'

Hopes rise; hopes are crushed. It will always be thus. But there is one abiding, redeeming feature that all sports share. New every morning, the hopes are there. Motivation, though, becomes tougher after success. It is like climbing Mount Everest: once you have reached the summit, it is very hard to motivate yourself to do it again. Motivation is not something that happens five minutes before a big game. The motivation to win a first All-Ireland is obvious. Getting the team to draw from the well a second time is a whole new challenge, but the old seductive dream of gaining glory came knocking on Doyle's door again.

'I suppose we are all selfish really. When you win one, you want to win a second, and then you need to win more. But it was never just about the medals; it was about doing everything you could to bring honour to the parish and to the county jersey.'

In 1967, Doyle stood on the cusp of history. Having equalled Christy Ring's record of eight senior All-Ireland medals, Doyle lined up against Kilkenny to win a record ninth, but it was not to be. Doyle is philosophical.

'It would have been lovely to win it, but I think of players like Clare's Jimmy Smyth, who was one of the greatest hurling artists I ever met, who did not even win a Munster medal, let alone an All-Ireland. It was time to give up hurling, as I had been training regularly for 18 years. I needed to concentrate more on my home and farming life.'

Doyle looks back with affection on the glory days rather than the ones that got away.

'I was so lucky to be on such a great team. During the '60s, the competition for places was so intense that the Tipperary substitutes were nearly the second best team in Ireland!'

After retiring from the game with eight All-Ireland medals, eleven National Leagues and eight Railway Cups, Doyle continued to have some great moments as a fan of Tipperary – none greater than the 1987 Munster final replay when Tipp beat Cork and their captain, Richie Stakelum, said the immortal words, 'The famine is over.' It was a momentous occasion for all Tipp fans but particularly for Doyle, as his son Michael scored two crucial goals. The undiminished status of the Munster final has withstood all assaults on its uniqueness since it was first contested over a century ago, but this victory was all the sweeter because it meant that hurling order had been restored. Few would accept that the evening need ever end. The occasion had so much life force it could kill the heedless. Doyle had experienced many great moments as a player, but a few magic moments as a fan could trump them.

Doyle was adept at the psychological aspects of the game. His lengthy career has left him a treasure chest of memories from which he can quietly plunder pleasures for himself. According to folklore, Doyle was patrolling the line in a very tight club match when his team were on the attack. In order to distract the rival goalie, he screamed, 'Jaysus Christ. Look out. The bull is coming!' Terrified, the goalie looked behind him. Just as he realised he was being duped, the ball crossed the line beside him for the winning goal.

27

EARLEY RISER
DERMOT EARLEY

Dermot Earley was a precocious talent. News of young Earley's performances reached the ears of the Roscommon minor selectors. He was picked for a challenge match against Westmeath minors in 1963, when he was just 15. His opponent was running rings around him and scoring at will. At one point in the game, a high ball came into the Roscommon square. Earley lunged desperately for it, accidentally striking his tormentor in the solar plexus with his elbow. His opponent went down like a sack of potatoes and was knocked out cold.

The Roscommon minor selectors were happy with Earley's performance. Even though he had been completely outclassed, at least he had the capacity to 'look after' the main threat to the Roscommon goal. Accordingly, he was retained for the Connacht minor semi-final against Leitrim. After their final training session before the game, the team congregated in a café in Roscommon. Father Pat Brady, whose brother Aidan is rated as one of the greatest goalkeepers of all time, was the team coach, and he gave a lengthy talk on tactics for the game. He made extensive use of the blackboard to illustrate the main points of his instructions. Father Brady's final words took the team by surprise.

'I am living up there on the Leitrim border, and I am sick to death hearing what Leitrim are going to do to Roscommon next Sunday. When ye have beaten Leitrim by five goals and sixty-five points, would ye ever kick the skitterin' football up their skitterin' arses.'

There was stunned silence. This was very avant-garde language from a priest in 1963. After what seemed like an eternity, somebody laughed. Within 30 seconds, the whole team had collapsed with laughter. Somebody whispered, 'By God. He is an awful man.'

Having made his senior debut for Roscommon in 1965 as a 17 year old, Earley learned a lot when he won his first Railway Cup medal for Connacht in 1967.

'I later asked Johnny Geraghty, the Galway goalie of the three-in-a-row team, how he knew that side was crumbling. He replied, "I remember coming into training one day, and one player did not have his boots polished. I put that down as the beginning of the end." I learned that the preparation that was required was total. When that did not happen, the team went downhill.'

Earley won All-Stars in 1974 and '79. However, it is another trip to America, rather than his trips with the All-Stars, that stands out for him.

'Long before Cork made striking fashionable in the GAA, we were the first to threaten to use player power. We were in New York to play Kerry in the Cardinal Cushing Games over two matches. We beat them initially in a 13-a-side in the first game. We had been promised money from John Kerry O'Donnell, who was "Mr GAA" in New York. We knew for a fact that Kerry had been paid, but we got nothing and we were running short of money. A council of war was held by the Roscommon players. The word was sent back to John Kerry: no money, no playing. As far as I know, we were the first county to threaten to strike!

'Another memory I have of the trip is that we were invited to a formal reception hosted by the Mayor. It was a real big deal for the county board. The problem was that the heat was almost unbearable. One of the lads brought down a keg of beer to keep himself distracted from the heat! The late Gerry Beirne went so far as to take off his shirt, which was a major breach of protocol. The message quickly came down from the top table, from the county chairman, Michael O'Callaghan, to get it back on quickly.'

The American influence was soon felt in an unexpected way in Roscommon, when team coach Seán Young asked the players to kneel down and say a prayer before running out onto the pitch.

Earley won a National League medal in 1979 but, unusually, had found himself embroiled in controversy in 1977 in the All-Ireland semi-final against Armagh. With the score tied at Armagh 3–9 Roscommon 2–12 as Earley faced up to a long-distance free – the last kick of the game – the Armagh trainer, Gerry O'Neill (brother of former Celtic manager, Martin), ran across the field in front of him and shouted something at him. The kick sailed high and wide. There was much press comment on the O'Neill–Earley incident in the following days. In his column in the *Evening Press*, Con Houlihan offered two All-Ireland tickets to the person who could tell him what O'Neill had said to Earley. However, the Roscommon star had not been unduly distracted.

'I had no idea what he said to me that time. I wasn't even aware that he was talking to me. All I wanted to do was drill the ball over the bar.'

Roscommon won the All-Ireland under-21 final in 1978 and had picked up some class players from that side: Tony McManus, Seamus Hayden, Mick Finneran and Gerry Connellan.

'The spine of the team was very experienced, but the new lads brought another dimension. Tom Heneghan had come in as our manager. He was ahead of his time as a coach. With Tony, Mick and John O'Connor in our forward line, we had three guys who could get you scores. Their worth was really shown in the All-Ireland semi-final in 1980 against Armagh, when, after failing in four previous semi-finals, we finally qualified for the All-Ireland. Tony Mac's goal that day typified what our forward line was capable of. Tom once said to us, "Our tactics are very simple; get the ball fast into the forwards." There was none of the passing to the side or even backwards that you see today.

'It was just incredible to reach the All-Ireland final in 1980. Tom had us really well prepared. He arranged for us to get two weeks off work, and for those two weeks we trained twice a day: at noon and in the early evening. By night-time you couldn't wait to get to bed. We had Kerry reeling early on, but we lost the game because our fear of losing was greater than our desire to win.'

Since his retirement in 1985, Earley has watched his son Dermot score a goal in the 1998 All-Ireland final and win two All-Star awards, and his daughter Noelle become a top inter-county ladies' footballer. Unfortunately, illness caused Dermot to step down from his job as head of the defence forces in April 2010.

Earley's dream team from his playing days, excluding Roscommon players, is:

1   BILLY MORGAN (CORK)
2   ENDA COLLERAN (GALWAY)
3   JACK QUINN (MEATH)
4   TOM O'HARE (DOWN)
5   PÁIDÍ Ó SÉ (KERRY)
6   NICHOLAS CLAVIN (OFFALY)
7   MARTIN NEWELL (GALWAY)

DERMOT EARLEY

8   JIMMY DUGGAN (GALWAY)

9   JACK O'SHEA (KERRY)

10 MATT CONNOR (OFFALY)

11 DENIS 'OGIE' MORAN (KERRY)

12 PAT SPILLANE (KERRY)

13 MIKE SHEEHY (KERRY)

14 SEÁN O'NEILL (DOWN)

15 JOHN EGAN (KERRY)

28

TIPP TOP
NICKY ENGLISH

In a poll for RTÉ's *Sunday Game* in 2009, Nicky English was voted the greatest Munster hurler of the last 25 years. Hurler of the year in 1989, he won six All-Stars and two All-Irelands as a player and went on to coach Tipperary to All-Ireland glory in 2001. However, it was none of those All-Irelands that provided English with his finest moment.

'Winning the 1987 Munster final was my greatest day in hurling. The fact that we beat Cork after extra time in a replay added to it. Tipperary hadn't won a Munster final since 1971, so that's why Richie Stakelum's comment, "The famine days are over," struck such a chord. The emotion our victory unleashed was unreal. Nothing has ever matched that feeling.'

In both 1987 and '88, Galway deprived English and Tipperary of All-Ireland titles. Galway's Noel Lane feels Tipperary did not deploy English most effectively in those years.

'In '87, in the All-Ireland semi-final, we were up against Tipperary. When they won the Munster final, their captain, Richie Stakelum, said, "The famine is over." That was the motivation we used to beat them. We had lost All-Ireland finals in '85 and '86, and there was no way we were going to lose three in a row. The '88 final is one of the great All-Irelands. There was great rivalry and great duels. One of the decisive factors was that our full-back, Conor Hayes, had Nicky English in his grip. If they had moved English, we would have been in trouble. I think the captaincy played on Nicky.'

The ever-helpful side of Sylvie Linnane's nature was revealed shortly before the end of the 1988 All-Ireland, when Nicky English asked, 'How much time left, Ref?' Linnane quickly interjected, 'At least another year for Tipperary!'

The backdrop to the 1989 showdown between Tipperary and Galway in the All-Ireland semi-final was the infamous 'Keady affair': Galway's Tony Keady had been suspended for playing illegally in America before the game. Keady had been hurler of the year in 1988. The Galway camp were angry about the suspension because there were hundreds of footballers and hurlers going to play in America at the time but Tony was the one that was made a scapegoat. After he had been suspended for a year, there was an appeal, which he lost 20–18.

Before the game and the appeal, there had been a lot of discussion about whether Keady would play or not. In the end, in an ill-tempered game, Tipperary made the breakthrough and went on to beat Antrim in a one-sided final, with English setting a new record of 2–12 in the game. However, the most revealing insight into English's character and his belief in the importance of team spirit came – with Antrim dead and buried, largely due to English's own efforts – when he offered to come off the field to give a sub a run. Although they lost their crown to Cork in 1990, Tipperary would win another All-Ireland in 1991.

By then, injuries were starting to catch up with English. Given the toll on English's body, Babs Keating once said to him, 'Nicky, if I had legs like yours, I'd be wearing nylons.'

English unwittingly created controversy in the 1993 Munster final, when he was alleged to have insulted the Clare fans. Ger Loughnane is able to set the record straight that the reality was otherwise.

'I marked Nicky English a few times. I thought he was a really fantastic player. Sometimes, though, Nicky's too honest and too open. There is no deviousness about him. What happened in '93 was something I used subsequently to motivate Clare.

'I went to see Clare beat Limerick in the league in April 2001 as an ordinary fan, with my son Barry. On the way in, he asked, "Do you remember the last Clare match we went to together?" It was the '93 Munster final. Barry was only 11, but he remembered it as well as could be. It shows how much the trouncing we got that day was on the mind of every Clare person. It wasn't just a trouncing. It was a total and utter embarrassment.

'Walking out after the match, I saw Seán Cleary – who was the principal in the school that I had been teaching in and whose son Eoin was playing that day – was just ahead of me. I didn't want to catch up with him. I didn't want to have to talk to him, because what could I say? The whole thing was a disaster. Clare were beaten out of sight.

'Tipperary had effectively beaten us after ten minutes. I decided to stay on until the end of the game. English scored a point, and he went out and had high-fived Pat Fox with this big smile across his face. It wasn't that English was laughing at Clare, but it encapsulated the whole scene of what was wrong with Clare. They were nothing. These guys didn't matter.

'Why do I still remember where I was sitting in the stand that day? Why would Barry still remember that day? Why would all Clare supporters remember that day? They all remember the trouncing by Tipp, but what left an indelible memory on their mind was Nicky English's gumshield. I can still see it, years later. It was unfair to say it was English. It was the total annihilation, but what symbolised it was English's gumshield, and that was the thing that really hurt. Every Clare person felt that "snub" keenly. English didn't mean it in that way. That defeat had to be avenged. That was what drove us all on.

'I knew he would be a success as a manager. In 1999, in the Munster semi-final against Tipperary, we should have lost, but we scrambled a draw with a last minute penalty from Fitzy [David Fitzgerald]. Nicky English's tactics that day were brilliant: draw Clare out and play the ball in fast behind them, and it almost worked. The replay was set for the following Saturday, and we produced our best ever performance to win it. I knew then that it was only a matter of time before Nicky guided Tipperary to an All-Ireland, and it only took him two more years to do it. He deserves all the plaudits he has ever got as one of the greatest forwards in the modern game and as a very intelligent manager.'

29

A WATERFORD WONDER
JIM FIVES

Waterford's sole representative on the Centenary Team of greatest players who never won an All-Ireland medal is Jim Fives, right full-back on the hurling team. It was as a forward, though, that he first made his name with Waterford and his club, Tourin. The club was founded in 1940, and his family played a prominent role in its development. He was the youngest of five brothers who all played senior hurling with their native county. Apart from the club and his family, another influence was his school, Lismore CBS, who had had a strong team in the 1930s.

Fives's heroes were the Waterford hurling team who won the All-Ireland title in 1948, particularly centre half-back John Keane, who hit the headlines for his fine performances against Limerick in the late 1930s. Although Jim had played for Waterford minors in 1947, he was too old to play for them the following year, when they went on to win the All-Ireland. With his substantial physical presence, the six-footer played for the county at minor, junior and senior levels.

In 1949, Fives made his senior debut for Waterford against Wexford. It was a baptism of fire, as his immediate opponent was no less a player than Billy Rackard. Waterford's defeat that day was to be an omen of things to come. The memories of that time still sting Fives.

'The biggest disappointment of my time with Waterford came when we lost to Tipperary by two points in the Munster championship in 1951. They were the big power then, and we were so close. We never put it together after that.'

Why did Waterford have such little success?

'The Waterford team that won the All-Ireland in 1948 was a relatively old team, and the team broke up straight after that. We had a poor team while I was there. You have to remember that it is a small county and that the number of clubs playing the game is small. Another problem was that we had not the right management structures. We had far too many selectors, and this led to a lot of "political" selection decisions, with selectors sometimes more interested in having players from their club on the team than having the 15 best players. Of course, that was not a problem unique to Waterford, but at the time we couldn't afford to be going out with a weaker side.'

After cadet school, Fives was transferred to Renmore in Galway. For four more years, he continued to play for Waterford, even though he was playing club football and hurling in Galway. He won a Galway county championship medal with the army, playing at midfield, and played for two years with the Waterford senior football team, although the closest he got to winning a county hurling medal came in 1955 when they lost the county final.

In 1955, Fives made the difficult decision to forsake his beloved Waterford and declare for Galway.

'It wasn't near as easy then to move around from Galway to Waterford as it is now. I was also often caught between the club and county. The club wanted me for a big match, but Waterford would want me on the same day for a league match or a tournament game. Really, for practical reasons, the only option for me was to switch to Galway, although I was very sorry not to be playing for Waterford any more.

'The hardest part was the two times I had to play for Galway against Waterford: in the All-Ireland semi-final in 1957, and in 1959, when we played them in the Munster championship – because Galway were "in Munster" then. It's a very, very difficult thing to do to play against your native county.'

As had been the case with Waterford, Fives was on the Galway team during lean times. The highlight was winning the Oireachtas final by a big score over Wexford in 1958. There were also a couple of good performances in the Railway Cup: notably, a draw with Munster in 1957 and a victory over Leinster in the 1959 semi-final. That year, the final was delayed until Easter Sunday due to renovations on the Hogan Stand, but Munster were to win it.

The move to Galway coincided with Fives's switch from the forwards to the backs.

'I was anxious to play in the backs, because I always liked to be facing the ball. The thing about forward play is that you always have to turn once you get possession.'

A serious back injury caused Fives to step down from senior inter-county hurling in 1959. Two years later, he was transferred to the barracks in Castlerea and came out of retirement to play junior hurling for Roscommon. Among his teammates was legendary footballer Gerry O'Malley. Although Roscommon won the junior hurling All-Ireland in 1965 – finally giving O'Malley his long-awaited All-Ireland medal – Fives had actually been transferred to Castlebar the previous year. Having played football for one county and hurling for three, Fives came within a whisker of playing for a fourth. He had hardly arrived in Castlebar when he was asked if he would be willing to play for Mayo the following Sunday. The old back injury had returned, and Fives was forced to decline the offer, unable to cross the fitness threshold.

Fives glows affectionately as he recalls some of the more unusual incidents in his career with the wonder of a baby counting his toes.

'In 1948, I played a senior club match in Waterford. It was a very niggly game, and there was a lot of moaning to the referee, the great Limerick player Garrett Howard. At half-time, he brought the two teams together and said, "Let's have no more of this whingeing. Hurling is a man's game. It's not tennis. Be men and take your challenges and your punishment. Go back out there, and play like men not mice." We took his advice to heart and went out and played like men possessed. Nobody held back, and there were some fierce challenges and an awful lot of sore limbs the next day!

'I was playing a junior hurling match for Tourin against Ballyduff in Lismore. Our full-forward "manhandled" their goalie, and a melee developed around the goal because they tried to lynch him, and he ran. Everyone got involved. What made it unusual was that all of us ended up against the railing of the pitch first, and then things got so hot and heavy that we all ended up in the next field. It was the most bizarre sight I ever saw on a hurling pitch – actually not on the pitch! Finally, the referee restored order, and the match restarted as if nothing happened.'

Fives's dream team from the players of his era is:

1   TONY REDDAN (TIPPERARY)
2   BOBBY RACKARD (WEXFORD)
3   NICK O'DONNELL (WEXFORD)
4   JIMMY BROHAN (CORK)
5   SEAMUS CLEERE (KILKENNY)
6   JOHN KEANE (WATERFORD)
7   IGGY CLARKE (GALWAY)

100 GAA GREATS

8   JOE SALMON (GALWAY)

9   JACK LYNCH (CORK)

10 JOSIE GALLAGHER (GALWAY)

11 MICK MACKEY (LIMERICK)

12 CHRISTY RING (CORK)

13 PADDY KENNY (TIPPERARY)

14 NICKY RACKARD (WEXFORD)

15 JIMMY SMYTH (CLARE)

30

A STAR IS BORN
DICK FITZGERALD

They do things differently in Kerry. In 1979, Pope John Paul II came to Ireland. In every diocese in the country, except one, they arranged a collection to defray the expenses of the trip. The exception was in Kerry, where they had to defer the collection because it clashed with one for the Kerry training fund. The fact that this was necessary is an indication of the importance of football to the county, a tradition shaped over the generations by many great players – none more so than the first star of Gaelic football, the master of the swerve, Dick Fitzgerald. He won five All-Ireland championships and became the first man to captain a county to consecutive All-Irelands, in 1913 and '14.

Although Limerick won the first All-Ireland in 1887, Gaelic football really came of age in 1903 when Kerry won their first All-Ireland. They beat Kildare in a three-game saga that grabbed the public's imagination. Kerry won the first game, but the match had to be replayed because Kerry had been awarded a controversial goal. So intense was the second game – which finished in a draw – that the referee collapsed at the end. On the third occasion, Kerry were comprehensive winners by 0–8 to 0–2.

The following year saw the first taster of what would become one of the great rivalries in the GAA when Kerry beat Dublin to claim their second All-Ireland. By now, Dick Fitzgerald had emerged as the first true star of Gaelic football, most notably when he appeared to defy the laws of physics during one of the Kildare games by pointing a late free only yards from the touchline.

Like many men of the time, Fitzgerald was active in the IRA as the movement for Irish independence gathered momentum. After the 1916 Rising, he found himself interned with Michael Collins in Wales. No sociologist can ignore the power of Gaelic games to harness the communal values of loyalty, self-discipline and sacrifice – and all for the glory of the parish. The games epitomise the importance of respect for place. Fitzgerald saw football in very spiritual terms, creating a team ethic, a feeling of kinship that goes beyond professional loyalty and a camaraderie that overcomes differences of age, sex and even previous fallings-out. This was particularly important in Kerry in the 1920s and '30s, when memories of the civil war lingered very powerfully. Neighbours who had shot at one another in the war displayed a greater desire to forgive and forget when gathered around the goalposts than when gathered around the altar. Fitzgerald's philosophy was that love of a country draws its strength and vitality from love of neighbours, fellow parishioners and fellow countrymen and women. The traditions, culture and way of life associated with one's home, place of origin, club or county provided a sense of importance, belonging, identity, shared goals, a pride and a purpose. His ethos was not to talk the talk but to walk the walk.

Fitzgerald was not influential simply because of his achievements on the playing field. He was pivotal to the decision that Kerry should wear green and gold. He organised street leagues, trained Clare to an All-Ireland final in 1917, refereed two All-Irelands and acted as a delegate to Congress.

Tragedy darkened his door in 1929 when his beloved wife, Kitty, died. Success in Gaelic football is about geography and history – about being in the right place at the right time. Fitzgerald was the right man for his time and was destined to remain one of the chosen few whose names live on after their stay on this earth has ended. He died prematurely at the age of forty-six in 1930 when he fell from the roof of Killarney courthouse, a short distance from where he was born. The incident happened just two days before the All-Ireland final. On the Sunday, thousands kneeled outside the church for his commemorative Mass. It was a spontaneous, marvellously unforced gesture that typified the Kerry fans. Fitzgerald had been a selector with the Kerry team the year of his death, and at the All-Ireland final between Kerry and Monaghan, the Artane Boys' Band played Chopin's 'Funeral March' before the national anthem. Kerry did what the occasion demanded and routed Monaghan by 18 points.

The most obvious reason for Kerry's success has been the team's phenomenal array of fantastic footballers, from Dick Fitzgerald to Paddy Kennedy and Séamus Moynihan. Dick's name lives on in Fitzgerald Stadium in Killarney, which was opened in 1936. His legacy was to make the green and gold synonymous with Gaelic football.

As the son of Dan Spring, who captained Kerry to All-Ireland glory in 1940, former Tánaiste Dick Spring is intimately acquainted with the county's illustrious tradition.

'As a boy, my father's hero was Dick Fitzgerald, probably one of the greatest Gaelic footballers of them all. In Kerry, we have taken and applied the words of the Olympic motto, "Higher, faster, stronger", for our sporting heroes. As has been said of the Jesuits, "We are top in everything, including modesty." But modesty is not something Kerry people have had much opportunity to experience.

'I still follow even club football in Kerry. Like the progress of Laune Rangers. Someone said they are the best side in Kerry since Tonto was their manager. This reminds me of the Galway wit who described an old Corinthians team as being the best since St Paul wrote to them! But when we look back, we see that perhaps no Kerry footballer had the seminal influence that Dick Fitzgerald did. Were it not for him, the Kerry football story would have been thinner, definitely in his generation and possibly even in subsequent generations. He blazed the trail that so many other great players followed.'

31

MIGHTY MAURICE
MAURICE FITZGERALD

Genius has an indefinable quality. Samuel Beckett was once asked to clear up the mystery of the missing protagonist in *Waiting For Godot*. Beckett dismissively replied, 'If I knew that, I would have put it in the play.' Whatever that indefinable quality we understand as genius, Maurice Fitzgerald had it in abundance. His mesmeric wanderings totally flummoxed defences and neutralised countless tactical plans drawn up to sabotage Kerry's domination. You can teach a player many things, but there is something you cannot transmit. It is natural talent. It is a mystery that only the player and God can really know about.

Maurice's effortlessly exquisite touch, killer swerve and the fluency of his every movement unfailingly troubled opposing defences. He was a forward who consistently promised to fill the minds of football fans with glittering memories and delivered on that promise with a series of sublime performances. He is destined to be remembered for ever for the All-Ireland quarter-final in Thurles in 2001, when his magical long-range sideline drew the match. Mickey Ned O'Sullivan said of Fitzgerald, 'If he had played in the Kerry team of the 1970s, he would probably have gone down in history as one of the greatest forwards of all time.'

Even as a boy, young Maurice's exceptional talents were evident to all shrewd observers. His father, Ned, had played for Kerry, and the family were close friends with the legendary Mick O'Connell. Maurice won the first of three All-Star awards in his teenage years in 1988, having scored ten points in the defeat to Cork in the Munster final. It would be another nine years before Fitzgerald would win his first All-Ireland medal, when Kerry beat Mayo, their first All-Ireland in eleven years. After such a period of plenty in the 1970s and '80s, the lack of an All-Ireland title since 1986 seemed unnatural. Some are obliged to work hard for their place in the sun. Others have greatness thrust upon them. In the 1997 All-Ireland final, Maurice wrote his name into the national consciousness, regularly breaking through with

Mayo defenders falling around him like dying wasps and kicking ten incredible points from all angles. On foot of that performance, he was chosen as footballer of the year.

Peter Ford was a selector on the Mayo team for that game.

'Maurice Fitzgerald scored three points from play that day. Pat Holmes did what any good defender is told to do in these situations. He forced him out to the sideline, and normally there would be no danger, but Maurice could kick points from there. It's very hard to find anybody to mark any player that good in that sort of form. It's almost freakish.'

The then Mayo manager, John Maughan, has never been able to forget what happened that day.

'I took a lot of flak after the game for the way we didn't replace Dermot Flanagan directly but made a series of switches – and above all for leaving Pat Holmes on Maurice Fitzgerald. The best man to have marked Maurice would have been Kenneth Mortimer, but we needed him up in the forwards. With the benefit of hindsight, we maybe should have put someone else on Maurice with ten or fifteen minutes to go, but we felt then it was best to stick to our guns.'

In 2000, Maurice would win his second All-Ireland medal. This time, though, he was cast in the role of super-sub. Enda McNulty observed him at close quarters when his Armagh team lost an All-Ireland semi-final replay to eventual champions Kerry.

'We knew we were good enough to beat Kerry that time, but I'd say we just weren't smart enough. I think if we had had a bit more cuteness on the pitch we would have won either of those games. The master Maurice Fitz created all sorts of havoc when he came on as sub in both games. Looking back, if he had been there in 2002 when we beat Kerry in the All-Ireland final, he could have done something special, either a score or a pass, to win the game for Kerry.'

The later years of Fitzgerald's career were overshadowed by the controversy created by his relationship with the team manager. Pat Spillane watched the storm that unfolded between two of the giants of Kerry football.

'The wheels came off the wagon in the 2001 All-Ireland semi-final when Meath beat Kerry by no less than 15 points. Kerry went through a 29-minute spell in the first half without scoring and then could only muster a single point from substitute Declan Quill in the second half. Inevitably, when a Kerry team loses by 15 points in Croke Park, serious questions were asked, particularly when Páidí refused to start Maurice Fitzgerald.

'Maurice is very quiet. However, some of the people surrounding him liked publicity. The people advising him had Maurice's best interests in mind but not necessarily the best interests of Kerry football, although they purported to have the good of Kerry football at heart. He had two very high-profile people backing him in the media, GOAL's John O'Shea and the editor of the *Sunday Independent*, Aengus Fanning.

'You can argue that Páidí was right or wrong. At the end of the day, Páidí was proved right. There is a very thin line between success and failure, and on the basis of your decisions, you have to be judged on whether you were right or wrong. Páidí was proved right in 2000. Maurice was most effective as an impact sub. It was a big gamble, but it delivered an All-Ireland.

'I was looking forward to reading Páidí's autobiography because I thought it would be the perfect opportunity for him to finally tell us what his problem with Maurice was, but on the single issue that most exercised Kerry people he said absolutely nothing. Ronan Keating was wrong. You do not say it best when you say nothing at all. Along with Mike Sheehy, Maurice was the most skilful player I ever played with in the Kerry jersey.'

32

THE GREEN AND RED OF MAYO
SEÁN FLANAGAN

Seán Flanagan captained Mayo to All-Ireland titles in both 1950 and '51. He was selected at left corner-back on both the Team of the Century and the Team of the Millennium.

Even as a teenager at St Jarlath's College, Flanagan showed his true colours on and off the field. Having captained the school to its first junior championship only to discover that there was no cup to be presented, he improvised and borrowed a golf cup from one of the priests in the college. When he played for Connacht Colleges in 1939, he was involved in an early example of player power. The team suffered a bad beating, and the manager, a priest, thought they had disgraced the province and refused to give them their jerseys. The players staged an immediate revolt on the basis that they had tried their best and held a sit-in in the team hotel until they got their way. When the priest said, 'I give you my word of honour as a priest,' one of the players, showing, for the times, an untypical lack of reverence for the clergy, replied, 'We need your word of honour as a man.' Victory went to the players, at least in the argument.

Things were also tense when Flanagan began to play for Mayo. Relations with the county board were less than harmonious. Such was Flanagan's frustration with the incompetence of the board that he resigned from the team in 1947. The county secretary, Finn Mongey, wrote back to say he had placed Flanagan's letter before the board, who asked him to reconsider and make himself available for the 1948 season. The league was beginning in Tralee, but Flanagan said he would not travel. Following intense moral pressure from his friend and teammate Eamonn 'George' Mongey, he was eventually persuaded to go. When the team reached Tralee, Flanagan was addressed by a man who asked him what position he played in. When Flanagan told him he was a corner-back, the man said in a strong Kerry brogue, 'Aren't you a bit small to play full-back? Kerry always have great backs, big, strong men.' Flanagan's blood was boiling, and he retorted, 'Mayo came here in 1939, and we beat the lard out of you. We propose to do the same to you tomorrow.'

The incident did not so much light a flame under Flanagan as a powder keg. All his hesitancy was vanquished. The Kerry game had become a do-or-die issue for him. Although Mayo had only 15 players, they drew with the Kerry men, who had contested the historic All-Ireland final the previous year in the Polo Grounds in New York. So desperate were Mayo that the only subs they could tog out were the county secretary and the rather rotund team driver. The situation could not be left unchallenged. Flanagan and the established players on the team drafted a letter that left no room for ambiguity.

The letter described, in no uncertain terms, the players' disappointment with the county board and, in light of the events in Tralee, called for immediate action to avoid the death of football in Mayo.

Two Connacht titles were secured, but Mayo failed to win the All-Ireland. A view emerged within the more progressive elements of the county board that Sam would not return to Mayo until Flanagan was made captain. The problem was that Flanagan 'only' played for a junior team. This required a change of rule at the GAA Convention, giving the captaincy of the senior team to the person nominated by the county champions. Flanagan duly repaid the county board for their benevolence by immediately banning them from any contact with the team until after they had won the All-Ireland! He did make an exception for the chairman of the county board and for the county secretary, Finn Mongey. One other member, a man of the cloth, thought he should be an exception and paid a visit to the team during their collective training. Flanagan went over to him immediately and coolly informed him, 'Get out, and I'll see you when I have the Sam Maguire.' While this did nothing for his popularity, winning the next two All-Irelands did surmount any residual problems in that area.

It is immediately apparent in conversation with Seán's son Dermot, a twice All-Star, that he has intimate knowledge of the innermost workings of his father's mind and his thoughts on the team. He is privy to the secrets of its success.

'Eamonn Mongey did everything to a very high standard and had a single-minded approach. Paddy Prendergast mightn't have been the tallest full-back, but he had a spring in his step, like Willie Joe Padden, and could soar in the air. Mongey and Padraig Carney had a tremendous partnership. The entire team were great players individually who would all be superstars today, and collectively they were a wonderful unit. When the going got tough, they had ability to come through really difficult games. They never knew when they were beaten. For them it wasn't just about football. Times were tough. They really wanted to do something that transcended the harshness of life and give Mayo people something they could never get in ordinary life.'

Likewise, Dermot is keenly aware of his father's place in the drama.

'He was part of a great full-back unit. Mongey and my dad were very big on strategy and tactics. Dad was always thinking ahead. Before the 1951 All-Ireland, for some reason the Meath players had to walk through the Mayo dressing-room in Croke Park. Dad had warned his players that none of them were to make eye contact with the Meath lads, because he wanted to make a statement that Mayo meant business.'

Seán Flanagan's dream team was his Mayo team of 1950 and '51:

1 SEÁN WYNNE
2 JOHN FORDE
3 PADDY PRENDERGAST
4 SEÁN FLANAGAN
5 PETER QUINN
6 HENRY DIXON
7 JOHN MCANDREW
8 PADRAIG CARNEY
9 EAMONN MONGEY
10 MICK FLANAGAN
11 BILLY KENNY
12 JOE GILVARRY
13 MICK MULDERRIG
14 TOM LANGAN
15 PETER SLOAN

33

THE FLYING FLYNN
JIMMY FLYNN

Jimmy Flynn was at the centre of the most successful period of Longford's history. Longford's only previous success at national level had been in the All-Ireland junior championship of 1937. In 1968, Flynn helped Longford to take their only Leinster senior title. His towering performances in midfield helped Longford to beat the famous three-in-a-row All-Ireland-winning Galway team in the National League final in 1966. Flynn retains a great admiration for that Galway team.

'They had great players individually, but they were also a great unit. The great teams like that Galway side and, later, Mick O'Dwyer's Kerry were teams without a single weakness. Having said that about the Kerry lads, the first man I would have on a team of all-time greats would be Galway's Seán Purcell. The teams that are most successful are the teams that mould as a team. If a team has one or two great players, you can always blot them out and you can take them, but you can't blot out six class forwards. You couldn't single out any one player on either that Galway or Kerry side. They were a team of stars from the great Johnny Geraghty in goal to Enda Colleran, Noel Tierney and Martin Newell in the backs right through to John Keenan at top of the left. If we kept Mattie McDonagh quiet, someone like the young Liam Sammon would pop up to get the scores.'

Flynn made his senior debut for Offaly in 1963 as a 19 year old marking Larry Coughlan. That same year he won a Dublin championship medal with UCD in a side made up almost entirely of inter-county players, such as Westmeath's Georgie Kane ('a lovely footballer', according to Flynn), Kerry's Paudie O'Donoghue, Longford's Bobby Burns and Seán Murray, who also doubled up as team manager. To complete a memorable year, Flynn also won a Longford championship medal with Clonguish. It was one of eight county titles with his native club. Sadly though, all his medals were stolen in a burglary of his family home.

Longford had reached their first Leinster final in 1965, losing out to Dublin by 3–6 to 0–9 after missing a penalty at a crucial stage. That September they won their first senior tournament of note when they defeated Kildare to take the O'Byrne Cup. A turning point in Longford's fortunes came when three-times All-Ireland-winner Mick Higgins of Cavan agreed to become county trainer in 1965.

The New York-born Higgins found that management was a more frustrating experience than playing. He often told the story of taking charge of Cavan for a championship match against Armagh. As the match reached its climax, Cavan's dominance was threatened when Armagh took control over midfield. Corrective action was required urgently, and Higgins decided to send on a sub, big Jim O'Donnell, whose high-fielding prowess was just what Cavan needed. Jim, though, didn't seem to realise the urgency of the situation. After going onto the pitch, he strolled back to the sideline seeking a slip of paper with his name on it for the referee. Moments later, O'Donnell was back again seeking a pair of gloves. Higgins forcefully told him to get back to his position immediately and not to mind about the gloves. A minute or two later he was back a third time to ask, 'Mick, would you ever mind my false teeth?' As Jim calmly handed the manager his molars, Higgins's blood pressure hit record levels.

Higgins, at one stage during his time with Longford, also managed Cavan. A conflict arose when both counties qualified to meet each other in the league semi-final, which was played at Carrick-on-Shannon. Mick's first loyalty was to Cavan, causing Seán Murray and Brendan Barden to take temporary charge of Longford for the semi-final. Flynn is keen to acknowledge the role of the Cavan man in Longford's success.

'To win the league was a great achievement for a small county like Longford, and although there was a lot of dedication on the part of the players, I think Mick Higgins has to take a lot of the credit for it.

'Mick often told us a story from his days with Cavan. He captained them to an All-Ireland final victory in 1952. The first match ended in a draw. It was the first time the GAA brought the two teams together for a meal after the game. When Mick and some of the Cavan boys got to the hotel, they ordered drinks – just bottles of ale and a mineral. Mick went to pay for it, but the barman said it was on the GAA. Mick double-checked if he had heard correctly. Quick as a flash, once this was confirmed, one of his colleagues said, "Forget about the ales, and get us brandies." For the replay, though, there was no free drink!'

Who was Flynn's most difficult opponent?

'Andy Merrigan from Wicklow. He was very strong and a real slogger. It was like hitting a brick wall clashing with him. He was an iron man. They talk about Paddy McCormack, who was very tough all right, but not in comparison with Andy Merrigan. Wicklow had great players in Gerry O'Reilly and Jim Rogers.'

Who were the players Flynn admired most after he retired?

'Colm O'Rourke was a great forward. He could give it and take it. I would have to mention Matt Connor. He was in a league of his own. We're good friends and meet often. I was always a great admirer of Martin Furlong. Roscommon's Dermot Earley was something special. He was certainly one of the greatest players never to win an All-Ireland medal.'

Jimmy Flynn's dream team is:

1   PADDY CULLEN (DUBLIN)
2   JOHN EGAN (OFFALY)
3   JOHN O'KEEFFE (KERRY)
4   TOM O'HARE (DOWN)
5   PÁIDÍ Ó SÉ (KERRY)
6   KEVIN MORAN (DUBLIN)
7   SEÁN MURPHY (KERRY)
8   JACK O'SHEA (KERRY)
9   BRIAN MULLINS (DUBLIN)
10 JIMMY KEAVENEY (DUBLIN)
11 SEÁN PURCELL (GALWAY)
12 SEÁN O'NEILL (DOWN)
13 MIKE SHEEHY (KERRY)
14 EOIN LISTON (KERRY)
15 COLM O'ROURKE (MEATH)

34

LETHAL WEAPON
PAUL FLYNN

Waterford's former ace forward and sharpshooter Paul Flynn is one of the greatest hurlers never to have won an All-Ireland medal. Flynn was one of the most prolific scorers of modern times.

Waterford almost made the breakthrough in 1998 under Gerald McCarthy. Even though Clare were leading all through the Munster final, Paul Flynn got a late goal and then had a chance to win the game from a long way out, but he put the ball wide.

There is a story told about two grasshoppers who came onto the field before the 1998 Munster final replay, as the pulling and dragging started between the players on both teams. One said to the other, 'We're going to be killed here today. Do you feel the tension?' The other replied, 'I do. Hop up here on the ball. It's the only place we'll be safe!'

In one of the most infamous games in living memory, in which the intense aggression began even before the match, Clare came out on top after an explosive start that saw a lot of 'incidents' on and off the ball. The match spawned the infamous 'Colin Lynch Affair', which led to the Clare midfielder being suspended for three months.

In 2002, Flynn was one of the chief architects of Waterford's first Munster title in 39 years, beating Tipperary in the final. Over the next five years, the Cork–Waterford rivalry would light up hurling and produce some of the finest games in recent history, notably Waterford's triumph in the classic 2004 Munster final. Under Justin McCarthy, Waterford re-emerged as a major power. While Waterford won a third Munster title and the National League in 2007, the Liam McCarthy Cup would prove elusive. Babs Keating has a firm view on the reasons for their failure to go all the way.

'I would say the Waterford team of recent years was very unlucky. Waterford had three massive players: Tony Browne, Ken McGrath and Paul Flynn. On the crucial days, they never got the three of them to play well on the one day. If you take 2004, Paul Flynn got 13 points in the All-Ireland semi-final against Kilkenny. If he had got any help at all, they would have won, but neither Browne nor McGrath backed him up properly. That was their undoing. They were so dependent on those three. They were like the Waterford team of the late '50s and '60s. They were just short of two or three players.'

Flynn downplays his own importance to the team.

'A big part of Waterford's game was creating space, and the way our forwards switch around and move about also makes it very hard for defenders to contain us. So the other lads are very good at opening up space for players like me. This makes it hard for backs to hold their shape and stop all ball getting in to me.'

Disappointingly, Flynn found himself on the subs' bench that summer when Waterford reached their first All-Ireland since 1963, only for the Déise to be humiliated in a 23-point defeat. Before the match, Kilkenny's Christy Heffernan was asked if he thought the Waterford players would be fit enough. He replied, 'They should be fit enough; they've been training for 45 years!'

GAA pundits are the people we love to hate – except on those rare occasions when their prejudices resonate with ours – yet they have become an integral part of the sporting landscape and folklore. Since his retirement in 2008, Flynn has become a pundit on *The Sunday Game*. For media bosses, the temptation to plunder the thoughts of former star players and successful managers, and to benefit from their judgements, is overwhelming. For those personalities who have retired, media involvement affords the platform to continue their happy addiction to the small and large dramas created by hurlers on the pitch.

As a pundit, Flynn draws on the depth and authenticity of his own playing experience. He knows the mood of the players, the way they speak and what is important to them. He can read faces. He can appreciate the subtle difference between a player blinking in acknowledgement and the moment when the lashes touch for a fraction longer, suggesting encouragement. Then there are the smiles: sometimes bonhomie, but sometimes a strain betrays itself in a smile, like the smile of a deaf person afraid of showing incomprehension. Above all, he is constantly alert for glances that are veiled and hostile when the story is told in the silences. As a pundit, Flynn raised eyebrows himself when he was critical of Davy Fitzgerald's management of the Waterford team, particularly of the types of drills done in training. While acknowledging that Flynn was one of the greatest hurlers of modern times, Davy's riposte was, 'While the training was up to speed, I am not sure Paul Flynn was.'

Flynn left the game with many happy memories of his former teammates. A case in point is that of Dan Shanahan, an employee for an oil company who went into a shop one day in 2007. At that stage he had become hurling's supreme goal machine. He had just starred in Waterford's triumph over Cork in the All-Ireland hurling quarter-final and had scored eight goals and eight points in his four games that year, bringing his championship score to an incredible nineteen goals and thirty-six points.

A little lady of mature years eyed Shanahan up slowly. Suddenly, a smile of triumph came over her face. 'I know who you are now,' said the woman.

'That's good,' said Big Dan politely.

'You're the oil man!' the woman replied with a flourish.

35

GALWAY BOYS HURRAH
JOSIE GALLAGHER

Josie Gallagher has legendary status in Galway. At a time when Galway hurling had been in the doldrums, great hurlers like Gallagher and Seánie Duggan emerged in the 1950s and laid the foundations for modern-day hurling in Galway. They won a National League and a Railway Cup, which was a big deal back then.

Seán Duggan particularly enjoyed the Oireachtas final victories of 1950 and '52. However, the 1951 National League final against New York at the Polo Grounds is his happiest memory.

'We were one point up with a few minutes to go, and New York were awarded a 21-yard free. Up stepped Terry Leahy – great hurler, master scorer. My mind was very uneasy: would it be defeat all over again? Leahy bent, lifted and struck, but his shot was saved and cleared. Then the late, great Josie Gallagher sealed our victory with two more points.

'To have won at home against an up-and-coming Wexford team, and to win a major national trophy before 30,000 exiles at the Polo Grounds, is still clear and vivid and pleasing; and, of course, a trip to New York in 1951 – when many people never went outside their own county – was the treat of a lifetime.

'Down the decades when Galway had some great men and very fine teams, games were lost through lack of competition. That vital edge was missing in close finishes; it cost us several games, and possibly titles, over the years. If we had had a few more Josie Gallaghers back then, we would have hit the big time. Actually, Josie was so good that just another one like him would probably have been enough. He was as good as any hurler I ever saw.

'He never wanted to shirk anything. If you told him, "Jump over a wall," he'd say, "Which wall?" He wouldn't go around it. He would go through it. He was brilliant. Put him in a gap, in the most tense situation, and nothing would get to him. He was ice cool. He was a player driven not by the thought of medals or fame but by his love for the game. He lived for those moments when he could lose himself completely in the action and experience the pure joy of competition. Hurling was not primarily about beating someone else, for Josie, but to search out the best in yourself.'

Josie Gallagher died in 1998 aged 75. He always said that if you can't meet a man afterwards and shake his hand then there is little point in playing the game. Josie first came to prominence when he played senior club hurling at the age of 15. Like so many players featured in this book, his career could be summed up by the words 'so near yet so far'. In his thirteen-year career as a senior hurler, he experienced the heartbreak of losing three All-Ireland semi-finals by a point and another by just two points.

In 1944, against a powerful Cork side seeking a four-in-a-row at Ennis, Galway lost by 1–10 to 3–3. Josie starred against Kilkenny in the 1945 All-Ireland semi-final in Birr. Galway were completely in control of Kilkenny in the first half and led by 2–9 to 2–1 at the interval, only to lose to a late rally from the Noresiders. In 1947, the same two teams met at the same stage and at the same venue, with the exact same result. In 1951, Josie put Galway ahead with just five minutes remaining against Wexford in the All-Ireland semi-final, but the men in the purple and gold snatched victory in the dying moments. In 1952, the catalogue of misery continued when Galway lost to Cork at Limerick by 1–5 to 0–6.

There was further heartbreak in 1953. This time, Galway had beaten Kilkenny in the All-Ireland semi-final and qualified to play the Christy Ring-led Cork side in the final. Galway had the game for the winning but failed to take off Mick Burke, despite his obvious concussion. What made their inaction all the more inexplicable was that Burke was marking the great Christy Ring. The bruising battle on the day ensued from the fact that a large section of the Galway crowd had booed Ring throughout the game and that Galway appeared to have targeted the Cork legend for 'special treatment'.

Josie's widow Mary Colette (Maisy) retains a keen interest in hurling matters and speaks authoritatively on the details of his career.

'Josie's proudest moment was when the Galway team that represented Connacht in 1947 beat a Munster side that was filled with stars like Christy Ring, Jackie Power, John Keane and Tommy Doyle. After he retired, Josie became a referee and felt honoured to referee the league final in 1958.

100 GAA GREATS

'The game has changed a lot from his time, but I think what would please him most today is the sight of so many children around the town here wearing Galway jerseys.'

Before he died, Josie had been invited to select his dream hurling team. It was:

1 SEÁN DUGGAN (GALWAY)
2 BOBBY RACKARD (WEXFORD)
3 NICK O'DONNELL (WEXFORD)
4 JIM TREACY (KILKENNY)
5 JIMMY FINN (TIPPERARY)
6 PAT STAKELUM (TIPPERARY)
7 JIM YOUNG (CORK)
8 PADDY GANTLEY (GALWAY)
9 MICK RYAN (TIPPERARY)
10 CHRISTY RING (CORK)
11 MICK MACKEY (LIMERICK)
12 JACKIE POWER (LIMERICK)
13 JIMMY DOYLE (TIPPERARY)
14 NICKY RACKARD (WEXFORD)
15 MATT NUGENT (CLARE)

36

MAGIC MOMENTS
CIARA GAYNOR

In the unforgiving world of boxing, there is a term of endearment for quitters. A fighter who turns his back in the heat of combat is labelled 'a dog'. As the old sages would say, when the going gets tough the dog will out. Tipperary's Ciara Gaynor was one camogie player who never quit in the heat of battle.

It is often said, usually by Tipperary people, that Tipperary is the home of hurling. In the last decade, Tipperary has also become one of the powerhouses of camogie, as the county has won three consecutive senior camogie All-Irelands. One of the stars of the team was centre half-back Ciara Gaynor. For Ciara, the fascination with camogie arrived – like talking – too early to remember.

'I can't recall when I actually started playing camogie. Back home, my sisters and I would be playing around the yard. My interest developed further when I got to primary school. Our principal, Albert Williams, won an All-Ireland club hurling medal in 1986, and he was a big influence. I went to St Mary's Secondary School in Nenagh. We had great success winning junior and senior All-Irelands.'

No camogie player of the present has more right to vanity, or ever showed less trace of it, than Ciara Gaynor. Being cursed neither with arrogance nor with pride, she is selfless in pursuit of improvement and never above seeking advice. From the outset, though, there was one voice whose whisper was worth more than the shouts of most other critics: no one is more attuned to the nuances of the game than her father, Len Gaynor. He won three All-Ireland senior hurling medals, trained both the Clare and Tipperary senior teams and took Tipp to the All-Ireland senior final in 1997.

'When I was young, Dad was still playing at inter-firms level. When he got into management, then, with Clare and Tipperary, we'd all head off with him when he was going to training or to matches. As a result, hurling was always talked about back home, and I suppose that was part of the reason why I became so passionate about camogie.'

There is one jewel of a memory from the sport's greatest theatre that outshines all others for Ciara. She lurches into nostalgia about a victory that left bubbles of pleasure that will never disappear.

'The highlight of my career was winning my first All-Ireland in Croke Park in 1999. The buzz was great in winning each of the three All-Irelands, but the first one was really special.

'I suppose it was a bit of a fairy tale really. We are only playing at senior level for four years, and we've won three All-Irelands. The team has been building for many years. A lot of us played together at minor and junior level in the '90s. The junior team won an All-Ireland in '92. The talent was there, and it was just a question of getting the blend right. Then Michael Cleary, who had been a great hurler with Tipperary, got involved in training us, and he was the biggest influence of all. He put the emphasis on the skills.'

Ciara's immense stature in camogie rested on her capacity for jealously guarding possession of the ball and passing it with a finely balanced combination of patience and penetrative aggression. She always played with intelligent industry and a rich, combative spirit. Those qualities do not come without sacrifices far away from the clamour of Croke Park.

'You have to be disciplined in a lot of areas: diet, keeping fit, getting plenty of sleep and so on. There's no point in me going down to training for an hour and a half and then going in for a burger and chips or going drinking or heading off to a nightclub. My job as a Garda involves shift work all the time, so I had to take a lot of time off work, which ate heavily into my own holiday time. Camogie takes time, money and effort, but it's worth it in the end.'

In autumn 2001, a major controversy developed when it emerged that a huge sum of money had been provided to enable the Tipperary hurlers and their partners to take a two-week holiday in South Africa. Meanwhile, the camogie players were not getting any tangible reward, even though they had just won a historic three-in-a-row. Is Ciara annoyed by the obvious inequality?

'It doesn't bother me at all. I was at the hurling All-Ireland, like all the Tipperary camogie players, and we were delighted to see the hurlers win. I think it's great that they went to South Africa and that their wives and girlfriends were going with them, because they made a lot of sacrifices too. After our second All-Ireland, we got a week's holiday in Lanzarote. It was great, but in all honesty I'd prefer it if we

Marching to glory: Jimmy Murray leads the victorious Roscommon team, while Paddy Bawn Brosnan leads Kerry, before the 1944 All-Ireland final. (© John Murray)

Giants of the ash: The Munster Railway Cup team in 1955. Back row (from left): Phil Purcell (selector), Pat Stakelum, John Doyle, John Lyons, Gerry O'Riordan, Des Dillon, Tony Reddan, Johnny O'Connor, Jim Barry (manager), Mick Mackey (selector). Front row (from left): Dónal O'Grady, John Hough, Jackie Greene, Willie John Daly, Josie Hartnett, Jimmy Smyth, Christy Ring, Vin Twomey. (Photo courtesy of Jimmy Smyth)

Supermacs: Roscommon legend Tony McManus is presented with yet another award by former Galway star and GAA president Joe McDonagh. (© John Murray)

Glory days: Seán Flanagan (near right) leads 'the Flying Doctor', Padraig Carney, in the parade in Croke Park. (© Dermot Flanagan)

My ball: Mayo full-back Paddy Prendergast grabs the ball from Meath's Jimmy O'Reilly in the 1950 National League final. On the right is 'the Man in the Cap', Peter McDermott.

The fruits of victory: Jimmy Murray with the match ball and the Sam Maguire cup after the 1944 All-Ireland.
(© John Murray)

The stamp of approval: Enda Colleran (right) and Mick O'Connell (far left) are presented with commemorative stamps after their selection on the Team of the Millennium in 1999. (Photo courtesy of Ann Colleran)

He ain't heavy. He's my captain: Donal Keenan (kneeling) gives a rest to Jimmy Murray in the build-up to the 1943 All-Ireland final. (© John Murray)

Over the bar: Donegal captain Anthony Molloy (left) takes the Sam Maguire on tour after the county's only All-Ireland triumph in 1992. (© John Murray)

Sporting heroes: Willie McGee (left) meets Kildare great Larry Stanley (centre).

Simply the best: Dermot Earley tackles George Best in a charity match.

Bless me, Father: Jack Lynch presents Iggy Clarke with his All-Star award in 1979.

The breaking ball: Mick Bermingham, with the hurley at his toe, awaits developments. (© *Irish Press*)

Goalmouth action: Umpire Nicky Rackard (far left) watches as Seán Duggan (on his knees) and Mick Burke are on the defence against Cork's Christy Ring and Liam Dowling in the 1953 All-Ireland.

Primrose and blue: Pat Lindsay leads the Roscommon team before the 1979 Connacht final against Mayo, followed by John McDermott and Harry Keegan.

The clash of the ash: The rivalry between Tipperary and Galway illuminated hurling in the 1980s. (© *Connacht Tribune*/Joe O'Shaughnessy)

Bringing home Sam: Former All-Ireland football winning captains gather to remember Sam Maguire, including in the front row Larry Tompkins (third from left), Mick O'Connell (fourth from left) and Jimmy Murray (second from right). Former GAA president Seán Kelly is third from right. (© John Murray)

Don't cry for me Argentina: Jim Fives visits Iguazu Falls in Argentina.

got the basic things, like a cup of tea and a sandwich after training and proper travelling expenses for training and matches, rather than a holiday.'

For Ciara, the rewards of camogie are largely spiritual: its true function is to inspire, absorb and reflect deep emotions. Victory belongs to everyone. It provides a collective shroud, a communal safety net, and brings out feelings that go beyond words when words are patently inadequate. It creates a personal connection between the players and the fans and rare moments when worries about medals seem irrelevant.

'The biggest achievement we had was not to win All-Irelands but to play as well as we could. That was the ultimate ambition. I think the biggest compliment we got is that in Tipperary now camogie is very strong with young girls, and a lot of them are now swinging hurleys for the first time. We know that, whatever happens, the future of camogie in the county is secure.'

37

THE PURPLE AND GOLD
LIAM GRIFFIN

Managing a county team requires commitment. Of course, so does insanity. Wexford's Liam Griffin is one of those brave souls who have taken on the challenge of balancing the pressures of a career with the needs and demands of managing his county team, home life, family and personal interests.

In 1996, the charismatic Griffin made Wexford the home of 'the Riverdance of sport', steering them to their first All-Ireland since 1968, when, captained by Martin Storey, they had beaten Limerick by 1–13 to 0–14. Griffin brought inspired management to one of the sleeping giants of hurling with innovative new techniques, such as camping out with the team as a bonding exercise – and, of course, everyone heard about his masterstroke of having the team walk across the county border between Wexford and Wicklow on the way to the All-Ireland final in 1996.

Griffin believes that hurling is a game for warriors, and he wanted Wexford to win the All-Ireland the hard way. After the Leinster final, he said, 'If we're going to win the All-Ireland, I want to do it in a year when we beat Kilkenny, Dublin, Offaly, Galway and Limerick.' His dream came true.

Griffin often said that he had not the 15 best hurlers in Wexford but the 15 who most wanted to win. He thought that previous Wexford teams had lost because of a lack of belief. Griffin devised a training programme that would cater for the psychological and emotional elements as well as the fitness. Before the All-Ireland in 1996, he told the team to believe in the game plan, to believe in each other and to keep working – even if the team were 15 points down. His man management is probably best illustrated in his dealings with one of the veterans of the team, Tom Dempsey. Griffin asked him if he was prepared to 'shed 500 beads of sweat to win the All-Ireland for Wexford'. When Dempsey answered in the affirmative, Griffin's response was, 'Make that 1,000 beads.' Dempsey went on to score a critical goal and three points in the final and to win an All-Star.

Former Wexford star Martin Quigley is ideally placed to explain why the Yellow Bellies won the All-Ireland that year and not earlier.

'Expectations were low in 1996 because we had been beaten in the league semi-final. To me, the key match in 1996 was not the All-Ireland final but beating Offaly in the Leinster final. That really set them up as a team of winners. I think the supporters played a huge part in Wexford's win – almost as much as the team itself. It was fascinating to see the way the support snowballed in the county throughout the championship. It was said there were 8,000 Wexford fans at the Kilkenny match, but there were 40,000 there for the final.

'I think there were two crucial factors to explain why Wexford won that year. Firstly, there was Liam Griffin and the passion, motivation, organisation and leadership he gave to the team. Secondly, there was Damien Fitzhenry. I don't want to cast any aspersions on anybody, but Wexford had been waiting for a long time for a goalie up to that standard. He was the best goalie in Ireland in my opinion. If I had to pinpoint one player on the pitch who meant the difference between victory and defeat in 1996, it would be him – combined with Griffin's influence off the pitch. When the history of hurling in Wexford is written, there will be a special place for Liam.'

Griffin is imbued with the ethos of Gaelic games. At grass-roots level they are based on volunteers giving far more than they take, though whether time – and the corporate boxes in Croke Park – will sustain that remains open to question. They are rooted in a sense of community that enables so many to give so much, in purely material terms, for so little. Neville Cardus was talking of his beloved cricket when he observed that 'a great game is part of the nation's life and environment; it is indeed an organism in an environment . . . as our great game is inevitably an expression in part of our spiritual and material condition as a nation and a people, it must go through metamorphoses; it must shed skins and grow new ones . . .' Cardus could have been writing about hurling in the early years of the third millennium.

One of the media's annual rituals every Christmas is to publish the sports quotes of the year. Liam Griffin stole the honours in 2000 with his comments on the GAA: 'I have never seen an organisation so hidebound by bullshit.' Not content just to talk the talk, Griffin became one of the leading lights of the Hurling Development

Committee. He was determined to bring the stubbornly conservative sporting organisation face to face with the realities of its current situation – because, it often seemed to him, the most important things in the GAA, like underage coaching, are those that are least talked about – and in the process won the admiration of fellow committee members like Ger Loughnane.

In the last 20 years, Liam Griffin has become hurling's greatest evangelist. With his extraordinary passion for the game, he is a one-off. My fear is that we will not see his like again. He has experienced some strange moments during his association with the beautiful game. At one of his first meetings with the Wexford panel, he gave them a questionnaire to fill in. It had a number of questions, such as, 'Where would you prefer to train?' At the bottom was an additional query: 'What is your favourite position?' Most players answered in the obvious way: 'full-back', 'centre half-back', 'full-forward' etc. The exception was Larry O'Gorman, the joker from Faythe Harriers, who gave Griffin information he did not really need. His reply was, simply, 'On top.'

38

A GOOD HARTE IS HARD TO FIND
MICKEY HARTE

'Character is what you really are. Reputation is what other people consider you to be.' Applying Mickey Harte's dictum to his own career, he is universally recognised as one of the greatest managers of all time, masterminding Tyrone to three famous All-Irelands. Harte has helped Ulster football to make up for the lean years of the 1970s and '80s, when it had little success. After Tyrone's All-Ireland victory in 2003, Harte said, 'We had to work very hard for this. It took 119 years for us to get it. Did you ever hear, "One Day at a Time, Sweet Jesus"? Before yesterday there were no All-Irelands in Tyrone; now there's one.'

Harte is a very astute, shrewd manager who is most meticulous in his preparation. The great managers are often not easy men. They are driven by an endless quest to avoid the inevitable, to minimise risks and to maximise potential. Management is a process of replacing one anxiety with one another, and Harte is noted for his attention to detail. His record as a manager at minor and under-21 is unrivalled, and the final part of his CV was written when he delivered Sam Maguire to Tyrone. With that kind of track record it is very hard to find flaws in Harte's game.

Harte thinks very seriously about the tactical side of the game and is a stickler for statistics. What draws people to him is something intangible. He surprised many a few months later with provocative comments in his autobiography about Seán Cavanagh's involvement in that game. Cavanagh was largely absent in Tyrone's League campaign in 2010, when the team were relegated. Liam Hayes went so far as to describe Harte as 'the most cantankerous manager' in the league. Yet he is fuelled by a fierce energy and drive, despite the calm exterior he maintains on the sideline.

In 2009, Harte's biggest challenge was to get his Tyrone team to rekindle the appetite, work rate, commitment and hunger that had so epitomised their success the previous year. Against Cork they just could not reclaim that intensity, and they lost the All-Ireland quarter-final to a hungrier team.

Harte's daughter Michaela has become a well-known face in the GAA because of her devotion to the Tyrone team and her frequent appearances in the media. In 2004, she was a finalist in the Rose of Tralee competition. She, too, shares her father's strong faith and has a great devotion to Padre Pio in particular. Before the historic 2003 All-Ireland, she presented each member of the Tyrone team with Padre Pio medals and rosary beads.

The Tyrone manager has shown himself to be a genius and a tactical master. He innovated a new style of football that nobody had seen before. His towering gifts as a manager – the priceless 'feel' for players and commanding urgency of his voice, the cold nerve and iron determination, the judgement that springs a sub at precisely the right moment to suit his capacities – have never been better exemplified than in his icily patient delivery of the injured Peter Canavan in the 2003 All-Ireland final.

Harte guided Tyrone to glory that year using controversial new tactics. In this approach, nothing was left to chance. Tyrone's success was based on a platform of defence and safety first: keep possession, keep mistakes to a minimum and play in a manner that allows skilful opponents only the least bit of room and time to do their thing. It appeared Tyrone football subscribed to the belief that victory is based on getting defences right, on players funnelling back and on slowly but surely choking individuality.

After Kerry lost to Tyrone in the 2003 All-Ireland semi-final, Séamus Moynihan incisively observed, 'The midfield area was like New York City, going down Time Square – crazy.' While such a tactical approach was, in the eyes of many, ugly and horrible to look at, it was both deadly effective and legal.

Pat Spillane was its most vocal critic and famously called it 'puke football'.

'I am not going to use the "P" word again, but at its worst Gaelic football is like watching Tyrone beat Kerry in the 2003 All-Ireland semi-final. A perversion of the beautiful game like that is like measles; it is something you should get over young, not at my stage of life. Football should leave you looking frenzied, looking mad with joy. That type of football simply left me looking mad. It is watching muck like this that is causing me to grow old disgracefully. Having said that, Harte brought a more expansive style to Tyrone in 2005, when they deservedly beat Kerry to win the All-Ireland, playing some great football.

'Before Tyrone played Dublin in the All-Ireland quarter-final in 2008, I was ready to write their obituary. I know many people will be surprised to hear me saying this, but in short they played football the way it should be played. Even my beloved Kerry could learn from them on that performance, and they would prove that when they beat the Kingdom in the final that year. Although they have some great players, a lot of the credit for Tyrone's success must go to Mickey Harte, but I was still glad when Kerry won the All-Ireland in 2009 and pipped Tyrone as Team of the Decade. When Tyrone were relegated in 2010, people were again speculating that they were finished. I think we all will be curious to see how Harte handles the task of replacing players like Brian Dooher in the coming years.'

Joe Brolly is a huge fan of Harte's achievements as a manager.

'In '05, Mickey Harte had been working on the team for three years and had a harmonious blend between defence and attack. Although Kerry got off to a great start in the All-Ireland final that year, Tyrone wiped the floor with them and played beautiful football and showed they had some great players. Harte's tactical genius was again showcased in 2008, when, against the odds, he led Tyrone to another All-Ireland at the expense of red-hot favourites Kerry, having earlier crushed the highly fancied Dublin side in the All-Ireland quarter-final. He's the best around.'

39

HEFFO'S HEROES
KEVIN HEFFERNAN

Tempora mutantur, nos et mutamur in illis (Times change, and we change with them). One of the biggest changes in the world of the GAA over the last 30 years has been the prominence of the manager. It began in the 1970s with Kevin Heffernan and Mick O'Dwyer. Without Heffernan or O'Dwyer, who knows what Gaelic football management might have been, and without the rivalry between their two counties that ignited the GAA in the 1970s, it is doubtful whether Gaelic games would enjoy the profile they do today.

Heffernan initially came into the limelight as one of the finest players in the history of the game. As a consequence, he was selected at left full-forward on the Team of the Century in 1984 and on the Team of the Millennium in 1999. The tactical acumen he would later showcase as Dublin manager was already evident in his playing days, when he pioneered the role of the roving full-forward. The high point of his playing career came when he captained Dublin to a 2–12 to 1–9 victory over Derry in the 1958 All-Ireland final. He also won three league medals and seven Railway Cups. He scored no fewer than 52 goals and 172 points in his career with the Dubs. Heffo was central to St Vincent's dominance of club football in Dublin when they won an astonishing 13 consecutive senior championships from 1949 to '62.

Those of us who watched Dublin's unconvincing win over Wexford in the opening round of the Leinster championship in 1974 could not have dreamed that we were watching the future All-Ireland champions. Heffo's transformation of Dublin was Gaelic football's equivalent of the Eliza Doolittle story in *My Fair Lady*. The ingredients of his success were simple.

'What I set out to do was to try to get a team that could win. We had a poor record in the preceding years, and morale was at a very low ebb. What we wanted to do was simply start games again. To start off we got a fairly large group of players together, many of whom we knew from earlier days and many of whom were recognised as good footballers but had no success at county level. It was critical for the success of the project to get a reliable free-taker, and so I persuaded Jimmy Keaveney to come out of retirement. He always had the skill, but getting him fit was a little more difficult. But, fair play to him, he really put in the work, and without him we would not have won those three All-Irelands in 1974, '76 and '77.'

One of the stars of that team, Gay O'Driscoll believes credit is due to Heffernan because of his ability to adapt to changing circumstances.

'Tactics didn't come into it in '74. The only instruction the backs were given was to win the ball and get it quickly to the forwards. Their instruction was to win the ball. I would kick the ball straight down to Anton O'Toole. After losing to Kerry in '75, tactics came in the following year and a more professional approach, like watching videos of our opponents. I remember we watched a video of Kerry beating Cork in the Munster final and picked up one of Kerry's key tactics. They tried to pull out the opposing full-back line and pump the ball over their heads and get their forwards to turn around and run in. We countered that by keeping either Robbie [Kelleher] or myself back to act as a kind of sweeper.'

Surprisingly, Heffo's managerial style was to play a significant role in the philosophy of Ger Loughnane.

'In 1974, Clare were playing Dublin in a National League hurling match in O'Toole Park. When we arrived, the Dublin footballers were already training, and we watched them. It left a lasting impression on me. The Clare players went out on the sideline. There was a match going on between two teams of footballers. On the sideline was a man in an anorak. He came down along the field, and you could see he was serious about what was going on. There were no words spoken, but, as he came down, everyone instinctively started to move back, because this man in the anorak had the teams out on the field in a mental grip. The exchanges were absolutely savage, physically. But you knew that the man in charge was the man in the anorak. Kevin Heffernan taught me that day the greatest lesson of all time for a coach. When you are coaching a team, YOU are in charge. Players don't want a committee. They always want a man in charge. There must be one central voice.'

Having returned to manage Dublin to All-Ireland success in 1983 against Galway, Heffo went on to enjoy one of his proudest moments in the Compromise Rules series against Australia. The series really entered the popular consciousness in 1986 following a major controversy. One of the Irish players on that tour was Pat Spillane.

'There was controversy before we went to Australia when the Dublin coach Kevin Heffernan was appointed as tour manager ahead of Mick O'Dwyer. Micko is the most successful Gaelic football coach of all time, and he has never managed the International Rules team, which is extraordinary.

'The GAA owes Heffo a lot. Gaelic football was not fashionable before his Dubs came on the scene, but they did a massive PR job for the game, as was seen in the number of Dublin jerseys being worn at the time, which later spread to jerseys of the other counties – generally when they had a taste of success. Heffo's Dublin team made Gaelic football sexy because of the hype they generated.

'Heffo's Dublin team had great players on that team and great characters, notably the late Mick Holden. Coming up to an All-Ireland final, Kevin Heffernan spoke to the Dublin team about diet and proper preparation. He told them if they had any problems sleeping before the final they should get tablets from Pat O'Neill. The first person in the queue was Mick Holden.

'Heffo said to Mick, "I never thought you'd have any problems sleeping."

'Holden answered, "Oh, these are not for me. I sleep like a baby. These are for my mother. She can never sleep the night before a big match!"'

40

MONAGHAN'S MAESTRO
NUDIE HUGHES

Monaghan's most famous footballer, Eugene 'Nudie' Hughes, is part of an elite few who won All-Star awards as a forward and a defender, winning three Ulster senior football championships in 1979, '85 and '88, as well as a National League title in '85.

In any list of the greatest players never to have won an All-Ireland medal, Nudie's name features prominently. Asked about the greatest players he came across, Nudie is keen to pay tribute to players who do not always get as much of the limelight as their talents deserved.

'I saw so many great performances from Dermot Earley. I remember Galway's Johnny Hughes telling me that he drew on a ball in the 1977 Connacht final, making contact with Dermot's hand and almost taking the top off his four fingers. His reaction was to get his hand patched up and play one of the games of his life, and it had no effect on their friendship. Dermot was very sporting, but he was tough. I remember him leaving one of our defenders on the flat of his back another day. That's the way the game should be played: everybody giving their maximum. I never minded anybody trying to go through me. The only thing I hated was off-the-ball stuff, which I consider very cowardly.

'I often said if there had been a transfer system in Gaelic football and we could get Dermot, Tony McManus or Mickey Kearins, we would have won maybe not one but three All-Irelands. All three would have stood out in any company. Connacht probably produced more great backs, like Harry Keegan, than great forwards in my time.'

Who was the greatest player he ever saw?

'I've often been asked that question, and I've always answered by saying that there were many great players but the one I respected most was Offaly's Matt Connor. And I'm certainly not saying this because of sympathy, because I said the same when he was playing. When the chips were down, he rose to the occasion. Some players, like myself, could do it when you're winning by 20 points, but I saw him in a Railway Cup final in Breffni Park in 1983 when it was gone. Ulster seemed to have won it, and they needed a goal. He manufactured a goal from his own 21-yard line and finished it by scoring it at the other end. His free-taking ability and point-taking from play with either foot was something else.

'Apart from Matt, another player I'd have to mention is Kerry's Maurice Fitzgerald. I saw him play for Kerry. He scored so much so often, including points from play with both feet. He could also catch some magnificent balls in the centre of the field and defended well. He could hit phenomenal passes with both feet.

'Playing against Jack O'Shea was great, because he was probably the complete player – maybe the most complete player in the history of the game. Brian Mullins was a great player to play against, because he would play his own game, but then if the notion took him, he could stop you playing.'

Nudie was well able to hold his own in any company. One player who gave him a lot of problems, though, was Kerry forward John Egan. Ulster were playing a Railway Cup match against Munster, and Nudie was marking John. They were standing talking, because Nudie always talked to opponents even though he would be told not to. At one stage, John said, 'What's that man writing down on that piece of paper? He's a right looking eejit, isn't he?' As Nudie turned to answer, John was sticking the ball into the net.

In 1988, Nudie used that same trick on Cavan's Damien O'Reilly. He was marking him in the Ulster final. At one stage in the game, Nudie said, 'Jaysus, there's an awful lot of people up on the hill. How many people would you say is up there?' As Damien looked up to make his guess, the ball came in between them and Nudie caught it without any obstruction and stuck it over the bar. O'Reilly was taken off him immediately.

Nudie also made his mark on foreign shores. He played in England, but one day a club game with Round Towers in New Eltham was cancelled. A few enterprising men came up from Bristol and got Nudie to play against Gloucester in a league final, totally illegally. He was the last brought on and about to hand his name, 'Brian Murphy', to the ref. The official from Bristol called him back and said, 'I'd better change that, as the other two I sent in were Brian Murphys, and the ref would surely spot it.' They changed it to Aidan Dempsey and went on to win the match.

Nudie has seen some bizarre things in games he played.

NUDIE HUGHES

'Monaghan were playing against Clare in a league match in Ennis. Some young lads started throwing stones at our goalie, Bubbles McNeill. True to form, Bubbles started throwing stones back at them. The only problem was that he got so caught up with the stones that he completely forgot about the match. A Clare forward pumped a hopeful ball in from midfield, and it went into the empty net. Monaghan lost the match by a point.'

Since his retirement, Nudie has become a distinguished pundit on Northern Sound radio. As a player, he won three Railway Cup medals with Ulster. He chose the Ulster team of 1984 as his dream team:

1   BRIAN MCALINDEN (ARMAGH)
2   JOEY DONNELLY (ARMAGH)
3   GERRY MCCARVILLE (MONAGHAN)
4   TONY SCULLION (DERRY)
5   CIARAN MURRAY (MONAGHAN)
6   PADDY MORIARTY (ARMAGH)
7   JIM REILLY (CAVAN)
8   JOE KERNAN (ARMAGH)
9   BRIAN MCGILLIGAN (DERRY)
10 GREG BLANEY (DOWN)
11 EUGENE MCKENNA (TYRONE)
12 PETER MCGINNITY (FERMANAGH)
13 MARTIN MCHUGH (DONEGAL)
14 FRANK MCGUIGAN (TYRONE)
15 NUDIE HUGHES (MONAGHAN)

41

THE MAN WHO COULD KEEP UP WITH THE JONESES
IGGY JONES

Many a prodigious talent has been evident as a minor, but that in itself does not guarantee a player a place in the football immortals. As the distinguished writer Peter Woods insightfully observed:

> What passes for good football at underage level can notoriously dissipate in the years afterward, and not just because of lack of interest. The boxing adage that a good big 'un will beat a good little 'un holds also for Gaelic football – not always, but enough times so that it counts – the good big 'un being likely to weigh the odds in his favour by crippling his opponent.

Iggy Jones was great as a little 'un and as a big 'un. He first came to prominence on the national stage in 1946 in the inaugural All-Ireland Colleges final, when his three goals helped St Patrick's College, Armagh, make a great fightback to snatch the title from St Jarlath's College, Tuam. The northerners, who also had Eddie and Jim Devlin in the team, trailed at half-time by 2–3 to 0–6, with Jones having scored four of those points. In the second half, Jones scored three goals, the best of which came from a solo run when he spread-eagled the entire defence, having collected the ball deep in his own half, before unleashing a rocket of a shot into the Tuam net. The Galway side were powered by the great Seán Purcell.

Previously, Colleges football had been played only at inter-provincial level. Indeed, by 1946 Iggy had played for Ulster Colleges for four years and for the Tyrone senior team for two years. The following year in the Colleges final the results were reversed, with Seán Purcell dominating. By that stage Iggy had left school. He was too old to play on the Tyrone minor team who won the Ulster minor championship in 1946. It was the start of a great period in underage football in the county, as they won the minor All-Irelands in both 1947 and '48. Barney Eastwood, later to find fame as the manager of Barry McGuigan, was corner-forward and free-taker on the 1948 team.

Strangely, the burning ambition of the young Iggy Jones was not to play for Tyrone but to play at senior level for his club, Dungannon Tomás Ó Cléirigh. In the course of a radio interview in 1992, he said, 'I always felt there was no higher ambition than to play for my club. When I did wear the county jersey I would have died for it, even though we won very few matches in the early years. I find it very strange today when I hear about players who have to be motivated before playing games. To me just pulling on either my club or county jersey was all the motivation I needed.'

As he revealed in the same interview, Iggy's introduction to championship football was not the happiest one.

'My championship debut was against Down. The first time I got the ball I passed it to a teammate and raced on to take the return pass, but instead he booted the ball two miles in the air! I knew then that I was not going to have a big influence on that match.'

Iggy Jones came onto the scene at a time when Cavan were the superpower in Gaelic football. Cavan's success left Jones with mixed feelings.

'You could say I was a half-Cavan man, because my father was from there. As Tyrone weren't doing well, we supported Cavan. When an Ulster team goes to Croke Park, the neutral Ulster fans will always back the team from their province. The only problem I had with Cavan's success was that they completely dominated the Ulster team, and they were a very clannish bunch, so that the rest of us never got much of a look-in. I would have been happier to have played with Ulster when the great Down team came along, because my game would have been more suited to their style. The only thing was that when we finally made the breakthrough in 1956 and won the Ulster final, we beat Cavan. That really made the whole occasion for us.'

Tyrone had stepped up their preparations in the run-up to the Ulster final, doing an hour and a half of training every night for two weeks in Pomeroy. There were none of the lavish facilities that top-class players enjoy today. If they were lucky, they got a cup of tea and a sandwich. After the training session, they washed themselves from a galvanised basin that was placed on the sidelines.

Despite missing a first-half penalty, Louth beat Tyrone in the 1957 All-Ireland semi-final by six points, thanks in no small measure to the lethal boot of Kevin Beahan. Like so many of his generation, Jones had left Erin's shores in 1956 but was back for the semi-final. He considered that match to be the biggest disappointment of his career.

'There was a lot of discussion about whether I should play or not. I was fit, but I wasn't match-fit. In the end it was decided I should play. The line of reasoning was that I would at least stop Stephen White from coming up the field and scoring for Louth as he had been doing all year. We felt Galway were the team to beat that year and if we could beat them we would win the All-Ireland.

'Our reign in Ulster didn't last the third year. We thought all we had to do against Down was turn up. Over-confidence beat us, but that Down side were an up-and-coming team and went on to win two All-Irelands.'

Iggy offered a surprising perspective when asked about the reason Tyrone did not win the All-Ireland in the late 1950s.

'We should have put all our eggs into the one basket and devoted all our energies to winning it. The problem was that our officials were too honest. When we were invited to play in a tournament, no matter how unimportant, they insisted on putting out our strongest team, because they thought people were entitled to see the very best. That was very noble, but we paid a high price in terms of wear and tear and injuries when we could have benefited from a rest.

'I remember one such tournament match when I had a bad clash of heads with Noel O'Reilly and the blood was pumping out of me. By any stretch of the imagination, I should have gone off – especially considering there was nothing at stake. It would have been different if it was an All-Ireland or even an Ulster final. I needed stitches afterwards, but I didn't come off. One of our mentors came on and said to me, "Look at our subs' bench. Do you see any player there good enough to take your place?"'

Iggy's dream team was:

1 DAN O'KEEFFE (KERRY)
2 ENDA COLLERAN (GALWAY)
3 PADDY O'BRIEN (MEATH)
4 SEÁN FLANAGAN (MAYO)
5 SEÁN MURPHY (KERRY)

IGGY JONES

6   JOHN JOE O'REILLY (CAVAN)

7   STEPHEN WHITE (LOUTH)

8   MICK O'CONNELL (KERRY)

9   JIM McKEEVER (DERRY)

10 SEÁN O'NEILL (DOWN)

11 SEÁN PURCELL (GALWAY)

12 PADRAIG CARNEY (MAYO)

13 PADDY DOHERTY (DOWN)

14 TOM LANGAN (MAYO)

15 KEVIN HEFFERNAN (DUBLIN)

42

THE SLIGO SUPREMO
MICHEÁL KEARINS

Con O'Meara was playing midfield for Sligo versus Roscommon in the FBD League. Before the throw-in, the referee noticed there was no ball and shouted to the Sligo dugout, 'Sligo, Sligo. FOOTBALL, FOOTBALL.' To which Con replied, 'Ah, come on, Referee, everybody knows there is no football in Sligo.'

One Sligo player, though, put the county team on the map: Micheál Kearins. As a boy, Kearins's hero had been the great Sligo full-back Nace O'Dowd. Kearins first played for Sligo minors in 1960, losing out in the Connacht championship to a Galway side – powered by Noel Tierney and Johnny Geraghty – that went all the way to win the All-Ireland. The following year, he made his competitive debut being marked by Gabriel Kelly against Cavan in a league game in Ballymote, and he played for the county at all three levels that year. He played in 17 successive championship seasons with Sligo from 1962 to '78.

Kearins's introduction to championship football in 1962 would be the first of many bitter disappointments. In the Connacht semi-final, Sligo led by a point against the reigning champions, but Roscommon stole victory with a goal in the last kick of the game and went on to contest the All-Ireland final.

Football was in Micheál's genes as his father had played a lot of club football and had lined out a few times for Sligo – beginning something of a Kearins dynasty. Not only did Micheál and his brother James play for Sligo, but, a generation later, Micheál's son Karl also lined out for the county.

Micheál's place in the lore of Gaelic football is made additionally secure by his phenomenal scoring feats: a record that has no equivalent in the past and is likely never to find an echo in the future. He was Ireland's leading marksman in competitive games in four different years: 1966, '68, '72 and '73. In the drawn 1971 Connacht final, he scored a record fourteen points: five from play and nine from placed

146

balls, including two forty-fives and one sideline kick. He won two Railway Cup medals in a thirteen-year career with Connacht, in 1967 and '69. In 1973, he scored twelve points for Connacht against the Combined Universities in the Railway Cup, all from placed balls. With the Combined Universities leading by 3–9 to 0–17, Connacht got a line ball 45 yards out in the dying seconds and Kearins calmly slotted it over the bar to earn Connacht a replay.

Kearins was a natural, rather than a manufactured, talent. Although he ranks, with stars like Ollie Campbell, among the greatest place-kickers in the history of Irish sport, he did very little actual practice in that area.

'Especially in the early years, I did a lot of physical training on my own. I would run a few miles early in the morning, maybe four times a week. I never bothered much practising my free-taking, not even taking a practice one in the kickabout before a match.'

Despite the longevity of his career, Kearins was always the focus of the county's hopes. It was a heavy burden to carry.

'I was always nervous before a game, knowing Sligo were depending on me. To slot the first free between the posts was always very important to help me to relax.'

Kearins won an All-Star award in the inaugural year of 1971 at left half-forward. In 1972, he was also a replacement All-Star: a major controversy had ensued when he was omitted from the original selection. He also played in three losing National League semi-finals with Sligo and three Connacht senior football finals, losing to Galway in 1965 and '71 before finally winning the title in '75.

With a Cinderella county like Sligo, it was inevitable that Kearins's career would be marked by pain: the anguish of seeing his team lose so often and the horrible certainty of defeat. But his is also a story of hope and dreams that sometimes, just sometimes, come true. Dreams such as the once-in-a-lifetime ecstasy of winning the Connacht final: the joy is even greater because you have known the pain of losing. It's about being willing to accept a lifetime of frustration in return for one day of utter wonderment. The fact that Kearins scored 13 points in the Connacht final helped to make the occasion all the more memorable for him. Surprisingly, though, he does not see this as the climax of his playing days.

'Winning the Connacht championship in 1975 was a great honour, but it was not the highlight of my career. Winning the senior county championship with St Patrick's, Dromard, in 1968 was my best moment in football.'

A cattle dealer, Kearins has been a familiar sight at many a cattle mart down the years. After his retirement from playing, he became a referee. Kearins did not have to think too deeply when asked about his most difficult game to referee.

'It was an All-Ireland semi-final between Cork and Dublin in 1989. I had to send Keith Barr off that day. He had got involved in an incident five minutes earlier, and he ran thirty or forty yards to get involved in a second incident. There was an awful lot of off-the-ball stuff that day, and it's very hard to manage those games.'

In fact, the tension escalated to such an extent that Kearins publicly pulled the captains, Dinny Allen and Gerry Hargan, aside before the start of the second half and instructed them to warn their players about their behaviour. He didn't exactly get the response he hoped for from Allen, who, when quizzed by the Cork lads about what the referee had said, claimed Kearins had simply wished them well for the second half and said that he hoped the awful weather would improve.

Kearins's dream team is:

    1   JOHNNY GERAGHTY (GALWAY)
    2   DONIE O'SULLIVAN (KERRY)
    3   NOEL TIERNEY (GALWAY)
    4   TOM O'HARE (DOWN)
    5   PAÍDÍ Ó SÉ (KERRY)
    6   GERRY O'MALLEY (ROSCOMMON)
    7   MARTIN NEWELL (GALWAY)
    8   MICK O'CONNELL (KERRY)
    9   JIM MCKEEVER (DERRY)
    10 MATT CONNOR (OFFALY)
    11 SEÁN PURCELL (GALWAY)
    12 PAT SPILLANE (KERRY)
    13 MIKE SHEEHY (KERRY)
    14 SEÁN O'NEILL (DOWN)
    15 PADDY DOHERTY (DOWN)

43

BAREFOOT IN THE PARK
BABS KEATING

The GAA is part of Michael 'Babs' Keating's DNA.

'Coming from where I was in rural Tipperary, we all had the dream of wearing the jersey, of walking behind the Artane Boys' Band and playing in Croke Park. The one thing we had was the confidence that if we got to an All-Ireland, we would win it because of the power of the Tipp jersey. Football was in my blood. My granduncle, Tommy Ryan, won two All-Irelands with Tipperary. He was playing in Croke Park on Bloody Sunday and helped remove Michael Hogan from the pitch after he had been shot by the Black and Tans. I played football for ten consecutive years with Munster. The fact that I came from a football background came easier to me. I could play football just by togging out because I was brought up with a football, whereas with hurling I had to work a bit harder.

'I had huge disappointments at underage, losing four All-Ireland finals at minor and intermediate level. Then, having won an intermediate All-Ireland in 1963, three of us arrived on the Tipp senior team for the first league game against Galway and played in the most games in the league, but of the three new boys I was the most vulnerable, because the Tipp forwards were so strong.

'The highlight for me was playing in my first All-Ireland against Kilkenny in '64. Seamus Cleere was the hurler of the year in '63, and he was an outstanding wing-back. The one thing about that Tipp team was that they had the forwards thinking like backs, and the backs like forwards. Seamus Cleere had scored a couple of points from the half-back line in the final the previous year. When you have a half-back scoring like this, he's a seventh forward. My role was to stop Seamus. Lucky enough, the first ball that ran on between us, I got it and scored a tricky point. I made a goal for Donie Nealon, as well as doing my own job, so I ended up as Sports Star of the Week and on a high. The hype at home then was as big as it is now. The only thing was that the media coverage wasn't anything like as intense as it is now. I was back at work on the Tuesday morning. There was no such thing as banquets here, there and everywhere. Having said that, there was a better atmosphere in Croke Park then, because you were closer to the ground.'

For Babs, the 1971 All-Ireland final has special significance.

'Long before players were handed out gear for free, we were very conscious of the importance of equipment. I had the very best pair of football boots, but the night before the final, my bag was stolen with the boots in it. I got a spare pair, but they didn't suit the conditions, so I took them off. Micheál O'Hehir famously described me in his commentary as "barefoot in the park". I was marking Fan Larkin, and guys like Fan and Ted Carroll were not the sort of fellas to be walking around without some sort of protection. Fan never stood on my feet. He tried it a few times, but I was gone before he could make contact!'

Having won every honour in the game, including hurler of the year, Babs turned to management after his playing days ended.

'I was invited to coach Galway by Father Jack Solon in the late '70s. He was a great golfer. I was welcomed by the players and to this day retain great friendships with them. I was basically a coach and had no role as a selector.

'We got to the All-Ireland final in '79, where we lost to Kilkenny. I remember waking up that morning feeling very depressed because it was raining heavily. We had a flashy team with the Connollys, Noel Lane, P.J. Molloy, Bernie Forde – who were dry-ball players. I believe that bad, wet conditions suit an experienced team more than an inexperienced team. Kilkenny were very experienced. We weren't. I believe the wet day cost us two of Kilkenny's goals.'

In 1986, Babs was appointed Tipperary manager after a rare barren period in the county's fortunes. His unique magic worked quickly, and in the 1987 Munster final replay his Tipperary team defeated Cork in one of the most memorable matches between the two old rivals. Babs glows at the memory.

'It was one of the days of our lives. You could have cut the atmosphere with a knife. We had huge confidence going into the Munster final, even though Cork were the hot favourites. We had come from nowhere in Division Two and had twelve new personnel. We had money behind us. When we travelled away for big matches, we stayed in five-star hotels. I will never forget the first game we played against Cork. Both of us got to the ground at the same time. Our bus was in the Tipperary colours. The Cork players were in their jeans and jumpers. Our lads looked like film stars in their blazers. Richie Stakelum said it was worth five points to us.'

Galway would deprive Tipperary of All-Irelands in 1987 and '88, but Babs marched the team to the Liam McCarthy Cup in 1989 and '91. After his spell ended in Tipperary, he later managed Offaly and Laois and had a second spell with Tipperary, but without the same success.

With the obvious exception of Ger Loughnane, few hurling managers have inspired as many quotes as Babs, such as Tom Humphries's observation.

'The miracle of Babs is his tongue. You can be expelled from the NUJ if you are within half a mile of Babs when he speaks and you don't record it. Babs loves microphones. If he could grow them in his garden, he'd be out there all the time talking to them like Prince Charles to his daffodils.'

44

BACKS TO THE WALL
HARRY KEEGAN

During his 17-year inter-county career, Harry Keegan was a pillar of the Roscommon defence. Despite his toughness, he only got one booking in his playing days. Yet his career almost perished before it had begun.

'I made an inauspicious debut for Roscommon in a league match in 1972 against Kilkenny. A few months later, we played Galway in the Connacht semi-final in Roscommon. We were leading by 12 points at half-time, and the perception was that the referee gave everything to Galway. John Tobin kicked frees for fun, and the match ended in a draw. The crowd were incensed and broke through the fences to attack the referee. It was a real mob scene. John Morley was on duty that day and stood in front of the referee, and only for that he might have been killed or certainly very badly injured. The ref was struck though, and Martin Silke and myself were accused of hitting him. Martin was a sub for us that day. In fact, the ref was hit – but by another Roscommon sub. We were brought up before the Connacht Council. It was very serious for Martin, as he was a Garda, and if he had been found guilty of assault, it would have had major repercussions for his career. Likewise, I had just begun my nursing career in St Ita's [Hospital], Portrane, and if a finding of assault was upheld against me, it would have been very damaging professionally.

'The maddening thing was that when the incident happened I was 30 yards away. I had been marking Seamus Leydon that day, and he wrote a letter to the Connacht Council. The night of the inquiry, Seán Purcell spoke on my behalf as well. The frustrating thing was neither the referee nor the umpires turned up. We were put through all that stress for nothing.

'We beat Galway in the replay in Tuam. Tom Heneghan was put on John Tobin that day, and Tobin didn't get a smell of the ball. Heneghan was the perfect man to put manners on a player like Tobin.'

HARRY KEEGAN

The All-Ireland semi-final that year proved significant for Keegan.

'I got my right ankle injured that day, and the injury was to persecute me for the rest of my career. I had to go off, and we were badly beaten. We trained very hard for that game but left our fitness on the training ground. We were really flying two weeks after.'

Keegan is the only Roscommon player to have won three All-Star awards. He is very appreciative of the role played by the Roscommon County Board, though their methods were unorthodox.

'They always looked after us, even if the money wasn't too generous. One incident stands out for me. After a Connacht final in the '70s, I went to one of the top officials in the county board and told him that I needed money for expenses. He brought me out to his car, opened the boot and pulled out a £100 note from a green Wellington and handed it to me. He then told me to send in the docket for it.'

In 1977, Roscommon played Armagh in the All-Ireland semi-final. Surprisingly, it is not the loss in the replay that most irks Keegan today.

'Everybody keeps talking about the Kerry–Dublin semi-final that year, and it's regularly shown on TV, but people forget that we produced two great entertaining games, which almost 100,000 people came to watch. Yet neither of the games is ever shown on television. The other so-called "classic" was really a game of rugby league; there was so much hand-passing. We played Armagh again in the 1980 semi-final, and that was a very entertaining, high-scoring game, but it is never shown on TV, whereas our final in 1980 is shown, even though it is a much poorer game.'

Keegan has one particularly strong memory of playing Armagh.

'We played them in a fierce match in the league at the height of the Troubles. There was a skirmish and a lot of "scelping" in that match. They beat us by a point. We were delighted they beat us, because there were rocks and stones raining down on us after the game in the dressing-room. What would they have done if we had won! It was not one of my favourite places to go, as they were one of the few crowds I found abusive. I'm sure the Troubles did have an impact on them, but I couldn't understand why they took it out on Roscommon above any other team.'

Despite his long service to the county, Keegan missed out on the county's national title in that era.

'I was a mere bystander in the National League in 1979 because of a hamstring injury. Hamstrings were the bane of my life. During training I would have to hold myself back to try and protect them, but I gave it my all in the games. I really had to mind myself, and there was no drinking, especially because I was living and working in Dublin and I had a lot of travel to deal with.

'I was surprised we beat Cork so easily in that league final. Cork had a team of stars, including Jimmy Barry-Murphy, who was lethal from 12 yards, but Tom Heneghan had him in his pocket that day. I didn't tog out, which was a mistake because I didn't feel like part of the squad. The only time the team went up the steps of the Hogan Stand to collect a cup, I was in the stand.'

A more crushing disappointment came in 1980 when Roscommon lost the All-Ireland to Kerry by three points, having raced to a good lead early on. The reaction to that Kerry victory is still a bone of contention in Roscommon today, as Keegan's teammate Tony McManus recalls with feeling.

'Kerry used their power in the media to convince everyone that Roscommon used dirty tactics on the day and that we didn't attempt to play football. Tyrone and Armagh have suffered similar fates in latter years at the hands of the media after Kerry objected to the way they play. Tyrone and Armagh beat Kerry at their own game in recent years, and Kerry didn't like it one little bit. What a lot of people do not realise is that Kerry have huge power in the national media, which is not good for the game in general.'

In 1986, Keegan almost single-handedly won a Connacht title for Roscommon with a vintage display. An injury late in the game saw him leaving the pitch, and his immediate opponent took advantage of the situation to score a late winning goal for Galway.

'I always hated marking Stephen Joyce, because he was so small! That day, though, he wasn't giving me any problems. The really annoying thing about that game was that I had warned the county board that someone would get injured because there was a hole in the pitch, but nobody did anything about it. In the end, it was me who ran into it and busted my right ankle. The pain was horrific, and I had to go off, and Stephen won the game for Galway, but it could have been avoided.'

HARRY KEEGAN

Former All-Star full-back Pat Lindsay played alongside Keegan for most of his career. His summation of Keegan's career is the most authoritative.

'Harry was the real deal. He was one of the finest corner-backs of all time.'

A league match against Dublin provided Keegan with the most amusing moment of his career.

'The week before, I had played against Charlie Redmond in a club match, and he was sensational. Charlie, though, did not like close attention. He was a big man but was a bit soft and didn't like the physical stuff. If you gave him a yard, he would destroy you. I managed to get a clatter in on him, and he went down like a sack of spuds. One of his own players came running up to him and said, "Get up you f***er, he didn't hit you half hard enough."'

Keegan's dream team is:

1   CHARLIE NELLIGAN (KERRY)
2   JIMMY DEENIHAN (KERRY)
3   MICK LYONS (MEATH)
4   ROBBIE KELLEHER (DUBLIN)
5   KEVIN MCCABE (TYRONE)
6   KEVIN MORAN (DUBLIN)
7   LIAM CURRAMS (OFFALY)
8   JACK O'SHEA (KERRY)
9   BRIAN MULLINS (DUBLIN)
10 MATT CONNOR (OFFALY)
11 DENIS 'OGIE' MORAN (KERRY)
12 PAT SPILLANE (KERRY)
13 JIMMY BARRY-MURPHY (CORK)
14 JIMMY KEAVENEY (DUBLIN)
15 JOHN EGAN (KERRY)

45

STEADY EDDIE
EDDIE KEHER

Hurling is to Kilkenny what films are to Hollywood: a country-wide obsession that sets a pecking order, discussed endlessly and by everyone, complete with its own arcane laws and rituals. Pubs are the churches of this strange sporting religion. Hurling-talk is no idle gossip here but a crucial element in the county's psyche, to which business, love, the land and the weather regularly take second place.

One incident that illustrates the passion hurling generates in the Marble City came in the 1970s when the great Dublin football team travelled down to Kilkenny for what they expected to be a meaningless fixture against the county side. When they got to the ground, they were very gratified to find a huge crowd was in attendance to see what was spoken of then as the greatest team of all time. The warm-up match was a club minor hurling championship fixture. When the mighty Heffo's army took the field, their pride took a mighty dent. The ground was virtually empty because the majority of the crowd had gone home as soon as the hurling match was over.

Kilkenny are the aristocrats of hurling, and one of their greatest princes was Eddie Keher – because of his skill, dedication and attention to detail. He was hurler of the year in 1972 and won six All-Ireland medals, nine Railway Cups and five consecutive All-Stars, from 1971 to '75. Keher played senior for Kilkenny for the first time in 1959, having starred in the minor All-Ireland final that year. The senior final ended in a draw, and he was drafted on as a sub for the replay. He was still playing for the seniors in 1977. That he remained at the top for so long is proof of his stature in the game. A prolific scorer, he amassed a grand total of seven goals and seventy-seven points in All-Ireland finals alone.

Keher's Kilkenny team of the early 1970s is considered one of the greatest of all time, with players like Pat Delaney at centre-forward, Frank Cummins in midfield, Pat Henderson at centre half-back and Noel Skehan in goal. They won the All-Ireland in 1972, '74 and '75 and lost the final in '73 against Limerick. Significantly, Keher was injured for that game.

One victory ranks highest in Keher's memory bank.

'The honour that meant most to me was my first ever All-Ireland senior medal in 1963. Beating Tipperary in the '67 final was also very important, because we hadn't beaten them at that level for 40 years, I think. There was an attitude then that you'll never beat Tipperary in a hard game. Although we always play a certain type of game in Kilkenny, I think we toughened up a bit for that game, and it made for a very satisfying victory, particularly as we proved our critics wrong.

'Nineteen seventy-one was very satisfying from a personal point of view, and things went well for me on the day in the All-Ireland final, and I scored a then record score in an All-Ireland final of 2–11 – a record which was broken by Nicholas English in 1989. I rang him up a few days later to congratulate him on the record. Coincidentally, it was Tipp who beat us in the final in '71, and we can't have complaints with that because they had so many great players, like Babs Keating, who was hurler of the year that year.'

Keher did have some disappointments along the way.

'In 1966, Kilkenny lost the All-Ireland to Cork, although we were red-hot favourites. Cork won by 3–9 to 1–10. The papers the next day were full of talk about "the year of the sleeping pill". It was the first year players had taken them before an All-Ireland final. There were a lot of smart comments afterwards that we took them too late, because we hadn't fully woken up until after the match!'

In 1979, Keher was manager of the Kilkenny team who defeated Galway in the All-Ireland final when the westerners made a present of two soft goals to the men in amber and black, as Keher recalls.

'Kilkenny were spurred on by the defeat at the hands of Cork the previous year and didn't want a second successive defeat.'

For a perfectionist like Keher, routine is everything. You have to get the little things right. A famous incident occurred in the 1974 Leinster hurling final when the sides were tied. With seconds to go, Kilkenny's legendary corner-forward had an opponent tread on his foot, and his lace was broken. Almost immediately, Kilkenny were awarded a free. As a meticulous player, Keher knew he wouldn't be able to score with the lace not attended to, so he bent down and tied it. The Wexford fans thought he was engaged in gamesmanship and running up the clock, and let him know with a chorus of booing, but Keher kept his concentration and slotted the sliotar between the posts to win the match.

Eddie is a big admirer of the current generation of hurlers.

'The present Kilkenny team is the best I have ever seen. If you can have perfection in hurling it was the All-Ireland final against Waterford.'

Kilkenny hurling has sired many characters, and Eddie Keher has seen plenty of them.

'Ollie Walsh was a wonderful character. After we lost the All-Ireland in 1966, we came home from Dublin on the train. At the station, Ollie got on board the luggage car and started driving it around the platform. It's a wonder he wasn't arrested!

'Fan Larkin was a wonderful player and a great character. On an All-Star trip to America, someone challenged Fan Larkin to a race, the whole length of the pitch, and Larkin famously said, "Be the Lord save us, you won't. But I'll tell you what – I will race you to the 21-yard line. That is as far as I have to go!"'

When I asked Eddie to pick his dream team, he asked for dispensation to pick two goalkeepers, because he could not separate them:

1   OLLIE WALSH/NOEL SKEHAN (KILKENNY)
2   FAN LARKIN (KILKENNY)
3   NICK O'DONNELL (WEXFORD)
4   JOHN DOYLE (TIPPERARY)
5   MICK ROCHE (TIPPERARY)
6   PAT HENDERSON (KILKENNY)
7   MICK JACOB (WEXFORD)
8   FRANK CUMMINS (KILKENNY)
9   THEO ENGLISH (TIPPERARY)
10   JIMMY DOYLE (TIPPERARY)
11   PAT DELANEY (KILKENNY)
12   FRANKIE WALSH (WEXFORD)
13   CHARLIE MCCARTHY (CORK)
14   TONY DORAN (WEXFORD)
15   CHRISTY RING (CORK)

46

WE NEED TO TALK ABOUT KEVIN
KEVIN KEHILY

Kevin Kehily first sprang to prominence as a 17 year old in 1967 when he played for the Cork minors. The Cork junior championship, which he should have won in the same year, was postponed to the following March, when the final, delayed by an outbreak of foot-and-mouth disease, was finally contested. In 1971, he won an intermediate championship medal courtesy of a victory over St Finbarr's, who had an emerging talent – by the name of Jimmy Barry-Murphy – to draw on. Like the famous JBM, Kehily was a dual star. He won a Fitzgibbon medal with UCD, two Cork senior hurling medals and even played hurling for the Cork seniors.

It was in football, though, that he won his two All-Star awards: in 1980 at full-back and in 1982 at right full-back. The magic of sporting competition was memorably highlighted when Offaly beat Kerry to win the All-Ireland in 1982. The following year, the Kerry team, ranked by all the experts as the greatest team of all time, sought an unprecedented nine-in-a-row Munster titles. The match provided Kehily with his proudest moment in the Cork jersey.

'The game that stands out the most for me was the Munster final in 1983 when the long period of frustration at the hands of Kerry ended and we snatched the game in the last minute with Tadhgie Murphy's goal. What I remember most about the day was going in to visit my teammate, the late Tom Creedon, in hospital, with some of the rest of the players. There was horrific thunder and lightning as we were walking in the corridors of the hospital, and we wondered if the game would go ahead. In fact, though, the weather turned out to be quite good in the afternoon.'

If 1983 provided Kehily with his greatest memory, it also provided him with his biggest disappointment.

'Losing to Dublin in the replay of the All-Ireland semi-final by such a big margin was a real downer, especially as we were playing in our own backyard.'

However, another event was to help put the defeat into perspective.

'I got a call afterwards from Ray Cummins, and he told me that Tom Creedon had died. Tom and I were very close friends, and our wives were also very good friends too. Tom had been critically ill after an accident with his Hiace van. It was a tragic loss for his wife and young family and really put sport in perspective.'

Kehily has noticed significant changes in the game since his retirement.

'I'd say the big difference is that the game is much faster now. As a back, you are finished unless you have speed. The other change is that there is much less emphasis now on staying in your position. Backs turn up in the forwards and vice versa, but the single biggest change is the speed of the game. On the downside, I don't think you see as much high fielding in the game as you used to.'

The identity of Kehily's most difficult opponent will come as no surprise to keen fans of the game.

'Eoin Liston. He came on so much from his early days. I played on him at the start of his career, and there was no comparison between the player I marked then and the guy I marked a few years later. He was very imposing physically, and yet he was surprisingly mobile. He was a great man to lay off a ball, which was bad news for any team playing Kerry, because he had wonderful forwards to pass to anywhere he looked. So even if you kept a few of them quiet, there would always be one of them that could hurt you. He really was a very effective link man. The only thing I will say about the Bomber, though, is that I found it much easier to mark him whenever Jack O'Shea wasn't playing. Jacko always gave him a wonderful service, and Eoin wasn't as dangerous when he wasn't getting perfect balls in to him all the time.

'I marked Jimmy Keaveney a few times. He was a very different player to the Bomber, but you could never give him an inch because he would really do damage. He was deadly accurate, and you could never relax for a minute playing on either of them.'

The Beatles may have been 'the Fab Four' of music, but according to Kevin Kehily, Cork football had its own 'Fab Four'.

'The great characters of Cork football were Dinny Allen, Jimmy Kerrigan, Davie Barry and Tadhgie Murphy. Each of them was great fun in the dressing-room, and you need guys like that, especially when you are losing to Kerry every year! Fellas like that are great to lift a team, and just to have them around gives a boost to the morale of a side.'

Throughout Kehily's career, his Cork colleagues always kept him in laughs.

'When I was finishing playing football, it was the era of the roving full-forward. I was the last of the traditional full-backs who marshalled the square, and it was a big culture shock for me to have to start running halfway out the field and running back in again for the whole match, and it was tough on the body. Billy Morgan was always winding me up before a match, saying, "Kevin, keep close to the goal today. I didn't bring any oxygen!"

'After we won the Munster final, I rang Tadhgie Murphy a few days later, and he said, "I'm sorry, Kevin. I can't talk to you now 'cause I've somebody with me. Ring me back in ten minutes." I did, and when I rang I got Tadhgie's answering machine. The message was, "This is Tadhgie Murphy here. The man with the golden boot. Kevin, without me you wouldn't have won a Munster medal!"'

Kehily's dream team from the men of his era is:

1   PADDY CULLEN (DUBLIN)
2   NUDIE HUGHES (MONAGHAN)
3   JOHN O'KEEFFE (KERRY)
4   ROBBIE KELLEHER (DUBLIN)
5   PÁIDÍ Ó SÉ (KERRY)
6   PADDY MORIARTY (ARMAGH)
7   MARTIN O'CONNELL (MEATH)
8   DERMOT EARLEY (ROSCOMMON)
9   JACK O'SHEA (KERRY)
10 ANTON O'TOOLE (DUBLIN)
11 KEVIN KILMURRAY (OFFALY)
12 PAT SPILLANE (KERRY)
13 MIKEY SHEEHY (KERRY)
14 EOIN LISTON (KERRY)
15 MATT CONNOR (OFFALY)

47

THE ORANGE REVOLUTION
JOE KERNAN

Much of the credit for Armagh's success in the noughties must go to Joe Kernan. Joe is a larger-than-life individual and a great raconteur but also possesses an exceptional footballing brain. He was the final piece needed in the jigsaw to bring a first All-Ireland to Armagh in 2002. To many observers, it seemed he had inherited an Armagh team close to the end of the line when he took over the side the previous year. He reinvigorated them and got what looked like a tired team back on the track to ultimate glory.

As a player, Joe had been one of Armagh's finest, starring in the county's All-Ireland final defeat to Dublin in 1977 and winning All-Stars in '77, '80 and '82. Failure can be a self-perpetuating misery chain, but equally it can be a tremendous motivator for success. Joe was determined that the ultimate disappointments he had experienced as a player were not going to be replicated once he became a manager – and that his team were going to win by whatever means necessary. In 2009, he would make another tilt for glory when he was appointed manager of Galway.

As a manager, Joe first came to prominence thanks to his superb record at club level with Crossmaglen, guiding them to club All-Irelands in 1997, '99 and 2000. As a county manager, Kernan changed the footballing culture. Colm O'Rourke famously said of his team, 'Armagh are hard in every sense of the word. They live a bit on the edge, blocking runs for return passes, staying in the dressing-room at half-time and feigning injury at times.' The All-Ireland quarter-finals in 2003 were an illustration of this. Armagh kept Laois waiting for an age in Croke Park before they returned for the second half. Apparently, the reason they were so late is because they were analysing the statistics.

Armagh's style of football at that time was not to the purist's taste. Statistics reveal that the 2003 All-Ireland football final, when Armagh met Tyrone, had a mere 58 kicked passes during the match, compared with 227 hand passes. But the biggest change Joe made was to take the team on a trip abroad to a training camp in La Manga before the 2002 championship. The team started wearing arm bracelets with mottos to keep them focused, and Kernan used inspirational speeches, like those of Al Pacino in *Any Given Sunday*, when speaking to his team before the play-offs. All of these innovations were signs that, in terms of approach, a new era of professionalism had begun.

Big Joe's emphasis on diet was not always to his players' tastes. Armagh's pre-match breakfast menu provided their goalkeeper, Benny Tierney, with a classic quote.

'It used to be a good old Ulster fry before matches, but we've changed that now to muesli – which tastes a wee bit like what you'd find at the bottom of a budgie's cage.'

As an Armagh defender of the glory days, Enda McNulty is ideally equipped to evaluate Kernan's importance to the team as Armagh manager.

'The biggest thing that Joe brought to the table was belief. When Joe walked into the Canal Court Hotel in December 2001 for his first team meeting with us, he had already won All-Irelands with Crossmaglen. So, when he sat down with us, you knew you were in the presence of a winner in Croke Park. Allied to that, he had already played for Armagh in an All-Ireland final. Of course, when Joe walks into the room, he brings a great presence because of his physique. All he said was, "Get me to Croke Park, and I'll ensure ye'll win." You believed him. We knew we were on the edge of winning an All-Ireland and believed that Joe was the final piece of the jigsaw – and he was.

'We played Louth in the league in 2002, and Louth are always tough to play against in the league. I think we were level at half-time. I remember vividly Joe saying to us at the break, "Do you think that just because I have won an All-Ireland with Crossmaglen that I have a magic wand? Boys, there's no magic wand. You have to make more blocks than you ever made in your life. You have to kick the ball in to the forwards better than you ever have in your life. It's not about anything that I can say. It's about what ye do. It has to do with what ye do in the middle of the game." That struck a chord with me.

'In 2002, before the Ulster championship, Armagh went on a training week in the sun, which was very innovative then, though everybody does it now. We were walking up the hill in Clones like an army before the Tyrone game. Everyone knew we had been on the trip to the sun, and one of the Tyrone fans shouted at us, "I don't see any suntan, lads!" When Joe got us in the dressing-room, he used that incident and said, "We'll show them a f***ing suntan before the end of the match." That was the spark we needed.'

McNulty believes that Kernan's finest moment came in that year's All-Ireland final, when Armagh went in at half-time trailing the mighty Kerry.

'Joe came in, and he started talking: "Listen, boys, we aren't playing well. I played in the 1977 All-Ireland final, and I remember going home on the bus crying and with all the boys crying. Do ye want to be like f***ing me?" It wasn't really what he said next but the impact of him physically throwing his loser's medal from that game against the shower and it rattling all over the wall. And it shattered into little pieces, and the plastic broke, and the coin, or whatever, was rolling all over the floor. I again vividly remember looking around and seeing the body language change immediately. Before that, everybody was sitting kind of slumped, and suddenly everybody was sitting up, as if we were all saying, "That's not going to be us." To use a term from sports psychology, we all went up into a "peak state". It was as if we were all saying to each other, "Jesus, boys, we're going to win this." We did win, and Joe has to get great credit for that fact.'

Perhaps the definitive assessment of Kernan's career came from his wife. Asked to sum up her husband on the *Late, Late Show*, after careful consideration, she replied, 'He's some man, for one man.'

48

KING STEPHEN
STEPHEN KING

As a youngster, Stephen King had always been a precocious talent.

'When I was 14, I played under-16 for the county. When I was 16, I played for the county minors, and when I was minor, I played under-21 for the county. When I was 18, I played my first match for Cavan seniors against Meath in a challenge match in Kells, and I never really looked back after that.'

For 17 years, King's career progressed without any real success at inter-county level. He had the consolation, though, of winning four Railway Cup medals.

'The Railway Cup was hugely important to me, particularly in the 1980s. At the time, Ulster football was in the doldrums. The Railway Cup allowed us to rub shoulders with players from the great Kerry team and match ourselves with many of the greatest players of all time. Ulster, probably more so than the other provinces, always took the competition very seriously, and it paid off with the success we had.'

One of the highlights of King's career was playing for Ireland in the Compromise Rules against Australia. Despite the disappointments with Cavan, King's zest for the dramas of the game was undiminished.

'It probably wasn't as difficult as people might think to keep going. I got great enjoyment from playing, and it was a great way of meeting people. Having said that, it was hard to lose Ulster championships year after year. You would ask yourself, "Why am I doing this to myself?" Then, a few months later, the league started, and after you won a couple of matches the hunger came back as strong as ever.'

The longevity of his career saw King playing under a number of different managers. He admired them all, but one stood out for him.

'I would have to say they were all very good; people like Gabriel Kelly and P.J. Carroll were very committed. Eugene McGee came with a big reputation, having won an All-Ireland with Offaly, and he certainly was a very deep thinker about the game. Martin McHugh was definitely the best of them all. He was the first to really adapt our style of football to the modern era and really move us up with the times in terms of taking us away from a catch-and-kick style of play and to a faster style.'

Apart from the change of style, and Martin McHugh's influence, why did Cavan make the breakthrough and win the Ulster title in 1997?

'Ulster is such a minefield that it is very hard to win the title. In Martin's first year in charge of us we got to the Ulster final. We could have won it, but we were too naive on the day. In 1997, we were a mature outfit, and for a few players like me it was the end of the line, so it was do or die. We got out of jail to snatch a draw with Fermanagh, and I think we knew then that it was going to be our year.'

Cavan's victory in the Ulster final prompted celebrations the likes of which had not been seen in the county since the glory days of John Joe O'Reilly. The local media and radio station, Shannonside Northern Sound, celebrated the win as the major news story of the year.

'Everyone in Cavan went haywire. I'll never forget the scene in Clones after we won. You couldn't see a blade of grass on the pitch because of the sea of blue and white.'

The year 1997 would bring both joy and heartache to King.

'Definitely the low point of my career was losing the All-Ireland semi-final to Kerry. As a team, we didn't perform to the best of our abilities on the day. We missed the boat. It was all the more galling because I still believe we would have won the All-Ireland that year had we beaten Kerry.'

Having climbed the mountain in 1997, Cavan football went into something of a decline afterwards. King sees it more as a transition than a crisis.

'The change of management probably had something to do with it. Then there were players like myself who stepped down so that a new panel had to be developed, and it takes time for things to settle.'

Major controversy erupted when Martin McHugh's successor, Liam Austin, was forced to resign as Cavan manager because of so-called 'player power'. King was the punters' favourite to take the job, but he declined to run for the post.

'I had just started up my own pub in Killashandra at the time, so there was no way I could even consider taking the position.'

How does King feel about player power?

'In general, I think it's a bad thing. The one thing I would say, though, is that players should be properly looked after by the GAA, because it is the players that generate the big crowds and the revenue for the Association. Once that happens, I think players should concentrate on playing and not get involved in politics, if that's what you want to call it.'

When asked about his favourite character in the game, his answer is immediate.

'Anthony Molloy from Donegal. He's got such a great way with people and is so friendly. It's no wonder he's such a popular guy.'

He is equally emphatic when asked about the greatest players he ever saw.

'Jack O'Shea and Brian Mullins. They would have made a fantastic and unbeatable combination if they had played for the same team.'

Stephen King is a strong believer that Gaelic football must rid itself of its thuggish element.

'The GAA has had a lot of controversies in recent years, with violent incidents on the pitch, and they must do something about it. Probably the most worrying thing is that some of these incidents have taken place in underage and college matches. I have no time for the off-the-ball stuff that's spoiling the game. We have to face up to some hard choices if we are to stamp this out.

'I also feel that we have to have a long hard look at the rules of the game. I think football is being killed by the stop–start way in which the games are being played. It's ruining the game, because the pace of the game is so slow now. When you contrast it with hurling and the speed of that game, football is playing catch-up.'

King's dream team is:

1   BILLY MORGAN (CORK)
2   ROBBIE O'MALLEY (MEATH)
3   MICK LYONS (MEATH)
4   TONY SCULLION (DERRY)
5   PAIDÍ Ó SÉ (KERRY)
6   PADDY MORIARTY (ARMAGH)
7   JIM REILLY (CAVAN)
8   JACK O'SHEA (KERRY)

100 GAA GREATS

9   BRIAN MULLINS (DUBLIN)
10 MARTIN MCHUGH (DONEGAL)
11 GREG BLANEY (DOWN)
12 MATT CONNOR (OFFALY)
13 PETER CANAVAN (TYRONE)
14 COLM O'ROURKE (MEATH)
15 JOHN EGAN (KERRY)

49

THE LIMERICK LEADER
GARY KIRBY

Hurling, like entertainment, is in the business of fantasy. The celebrated English actor Ralph Richardson summed up acting in the phrase, 'At three minutes past eight, you must dream.' Hurling dreamers are for ever assuring themselves that the truly great player is on the horizon, but, like the skyline, he never seems to come any closer. He is always just out of reach. Limerick's Gary Kirby was to change all that. He will always be one of the legends of hurling, even though he never won the game's ultimate honour.

Kirby first came to prominence in 1984, winning an All-Ireland minor medal with Limerick and taking his first senior medal with Patrickswell. Three years later, he helped Limerick to an All-Ireland under-21 title and captained the Irish under-21 shinty team. In 1986, he made his senior debut for Limerick, and in 1991 he won the first of his four All-Stars. In 2009, he was chosen at centre half-forward on the Munster team of the last 25 years, and he ranks among the greatest hurlers never to have won an All-Ireland senior medal. The high point of his hurling career came in the Munster final in 1994.

'My greatest and fondest memory would have to be looking down on the Thurles field, seeing it full with Limerick people waving their green and white and, as captain, lifting the Munster Cup after we beat Clare. There was a huge sense of excitement because it just meant so much to the fans because hurling means so much to Limerick. Although we had won the match, the significance of the occasion didn't sink in for a while.'

The All-Ireland hurling final that autumn was one of the most dramatic matches in the history of the game. Limerick outplayed Offaly throughout the match and, with just minutes remaining, had an apparently unassailable five-point lead. Then Offaly's Johnny Dooley scored a goal from a free. Within a minute, Pat O'Connor had a second goal. Limerick floundered, while Offaly players suddenly looked as though they could score points at will. A new joke was born. Why are Limerick magic? Because they can disappear for five minutes.

Kirby had won a National League medal in 1992, when Limerick made a dramatic comeback against Tipperary to snatch a one-point victory in injury time. What was it like to be on the opposite end of the experience?

'It's a feeling I wouldn't wish on anyone. With seven minutes to go, I felt I would be going up to be presented with the Liam McCarthy Cup. Then, all of a sudden, it was gone. Something happened in the last five minutes. You can't analyse it. It was a huge disappointment.'

Two years later, Limerick again won the Munster final after snatching victory from All-Ireland champions Clare in the final minutes of the semi-final. Limerick went all the way to the All-Ireland final again that year, but it was to be Liam Griffin's Wexford that claimed the title. The match itself was a personal disappointment for Kirby.

'I got a broken finger in the first five minutes. I remember going over towards the Cusack Stand to take a free from near midfield. I was trying to stop the bleeding before I took it, but as I took the free I felt a searing pain go up my hand.'

Kirby has played under a number of high-profile managers, all of them with different styles.

'Tom Ryan had a strong presence about him and knew what he wanted. He related that to the players, and everyone knew where they stood. Éamonn Cregan was a different type who got more involved in the training of the team. He got players trying to play a more open type of game. While they are great managers, the one I really enjoyed was Phil Bennis. Phil coached both our minor and under-21 sides that won the All-Ireland. He also trained our club, Patrickswell, and seems to understand every player individually and what his strengths are. He had a great understanding with the players.'

The year 2007 was one Kirby will never forget, as he was on the Limerick backroom team who reached the All-Ireland final against Kilkenny.

'I remember, just before we took the pitch, our manager, Richie Bennis, came into the dressing-room, and he said Kilkenny were just after running out to a silent Croke Park and that we'd run out to a massive roar. "Prepare for it, lads," he said, but you couldn't be prepared for that. I couldn't believe the roar. Brian Cody and his players were very clever. They don't have so many All-Ireland medals in their pockets for nothing. Every one of them was flying and buzzing the same day. There was no space at all. All their hits were hard. Our lads could hardly catch their breath there sometimes.'

His experiences in management have made Kirby more philosophical about his own playing disappointments.

'Missing out on the All-Ireland hurling finals in 1994 and '96 were probably the low points. Yet, at the same time, I did not allow myself to get shattered by the whole thing. I had to go on with my life. Looking back, they were great years for hurling. Although we lost the Munster final to Clare in 1995, it was obvious that it meant so much to Clare people. Those years brought new life to hurling and really brought a whole new popularity to the game and won a new audience for hurling.'

For Kirby, selecting his dream team was difficult, particularly having to exclude players like Brian Whelahan, Brian Corcoran and Leonard Enright. His team is:

1   TOMMY QUAID (LIMERICK)
2   SYLVIE LINNANE (GALWAY)
3   BRIAN LOHAN (CLARE)
4   MARTIN HANAMY (OFFALY)
5   PETER FINNERTY (GALWAY)
6   GER HENDERSON (KILKENNY)
7   TOM CASHMAN (CORK)
8   FRANK CUMMINS (KILKENNY)
9   JOHN FENTON (CORK)
10 D.J. CAREY (KILKENNY)
11 JOE COONEY (GALWAY)
12 NICKY ENGLISH (TIPPERARY)
13 JIMMY BARRY-MURPHY (CORK)
14 RAY CUMMINS (CORK)
15 ÉAMONN CREGAN (LIMERICK)

50

DOWN BUT NOT OUT
MICKEY LINDEN

'Joy cometh in the morning,' says the Bible. For much of the 1970s and '80s, Ulster football was in the doldrums. Down's All-Ireland triumph in 1991 would change all that. That victory was the fulfilment of a promise of life as it was meant to be lived for an entire province. The unthinkable had become the thinkable. For fans, the memory of that match lingered long into the night, only to be stopped gently by sleep like a candle that has been pinched out. Yet a flame had been lit that day that would fuel an entire generation. The following morning, the football world settled into the rhythms of a new life. The haunting echoes of failure were finally banished from an entire province and a new era of unprecedented success was ushered in, as Joe Brolly recognises.

'If Down hadn't won that All-Ireland, you could have forgotten about Derry winning an All-Ireland, you could absolutely forget about Donegal winning an All-Ireland and there wouldn't be Tyrone or Armagh All-Irelands. All of those titles were grafted on the back of Down's '91 win. Donegal realised they could win an All-Ireland, and there was a sense of inevitability that Derry would win the All-Ireland in '93 – and Down came back to win another final in '94.

'We had nearly beaten them in '91 in a titanic game in the Athletic Grounds. We were a point up at the end when they got a free 60 yards out. I was close to the ball at the time, and I heard Ross Carr saying to Enda Gormley, "I'm going to drive this over the bar." Enda told him, "Wise up, you f***ing eejit." But Ross sent it over the bar, and they went through instead of us, but when they won the All-Ireland it inspired us, because it made us realise how close we were.'

At the heart of that Down team was Mickey Linden, who is widely recognised as one of the great forwards of our time. A goal poacher par excellence, his speed, skill and stamina set him apart. Although he was not tall for a forward in the modern game, he proved the veracity of President Truman's comment about size: 'When it comes down to inches, my boy, you should only consider the forehead. Better to have a spare inch between the top of your nose and the hairline than between the ankle and the kneecap.'

Linden starred in Down's 1–16 to 1–14 All-Ireland victory over Meath in 1991 and again in their 1–12 to 0–13 win over Dublin in the 1994 All-Ireland final. His performance in that match would secure his selection on the All-Star team in 1994. After his retirement from inter-county football, he continued to produce quality performances for his club, Mayobridge, into his 40s.

The widespread admiration for that Down team is shared by Armagh's Enda McNulty.

'Mickey Linden was a class player. I played with him in an ex-All-Stars match in '08, and he was still in better shape than 90 per cent of players I have come across in the last five years. He was unbelievably quick, and he was 42 years of age.

'He was fortunate in that he had some great players around him on that great Down side of the 1990s. I would be a massive fan of Greg Blaney. The amount of balls he put into Mickey Linden's hands was incredible. I would be a big fan of James McCartan, too, who I would say was one of the greatest players of all time because of his ability to lose a player, his ability to tackle, his ability to score and his ability to catch a high ball even though he was only 5 ft 6 or 7.'

As Ireland's best-known sports psychologist, Enda was also interested in Linden from a psychological perspective.

'Motivation is a big thing for footballers. Some players get fired up by a fire-and-brimstone approach, but for someone like Mickey Linden the motivation is internal. Yet even the most motivated player can respond to inspiration. When I think of players like Mickey, I recall the story of the Notre Dame American football team. Their fortunes had declined enormously, and their playing standards had reached rock bottom. The school decided that the team was not worthy of wearing the traditional Notre Dame colours. For years, they played in the second strip. Then a team came together and qualified for a minor final. In accordance with the custom in American football, the team went out and were introduced to the crowd. Then they went back into the dressing-room for their final instruction. There, hanging on every player's peg, was the traditional jersey of Notre Dame. The coach told them to throw away their old jerseys and put on the traditional colours. When the team left the dressing-room, they felt like kings. Mickey Linden is the type of player who would have responded to a gesture like that and would have gone out to produce a sensational performance.

'The will to win is easy, but the will to prepare to win is more problematic. What singles out the great players like Mickey Linden is their willingness to give everything for the cause and to prepare in every way possible. By having adversity in life, we can see in others and in ourselves who quits and those who won't quit, and in the end adversity will make winners of those who won't quit. Early in his career, Mickey Linden, like most teams in Ulster, went through many a dark day, but that did not stop them from thinking they could reverse that trend and bring the Sam Maguire back over the border. It was guys like Mickey Linden who inspired guys like me, and, I am sure, boys in Tyrone, to bring the All-Ireland to our counties for the first time.'

51

SIMPLY THE BEST
BRIAN LOHAN

Brian Lohan, not a man but a giant, is the greatest hurling full-back of the modern era, winning All-Stars in three consecutive years from 1995 to '97 and again in 2002. In their halcyon days of the 1990s, nothing ignited the passions of the Clare crowd more than the distinctive red helmet of Lohan soaring up to grab the ball then thundering down the pitch to magisterially clear it and turn defence into attack.

When Lohan flexed that indomitable amalgam of strength and leadership, resilience and courage were never going to be a problem for Clare. With incredible teamwork, they were able to prevent other sides with superior firepower. The players admired Lohan because he was not only the impregnable fortress on the Clare back line but also as tough as iron and steadfastly loyal. His athletic body generated astonishing power, but even more impressive was his strength of his spirit, as Ger Loughnane was all too aware.

'In the All-Ireland semi-final against Galway in 1995, Brian Lohan damaged his hamstring. He was on Joe Cooney, and Cooney had got a couple of points off him. I went down to the sideline and looked at him. I did more than look at him, I needn't tell you! He started to hurl out of his skin. Lohan said afterwards, "I saw Loughnane coming down the sideline and decided it was time to start hurling!"

'In the All-Ireland final that year, with about 20 minutes to go, he pulled a hamstring and he gave a signal. We had built up such an understanding that, at any time, whether it was in a dressing-room or out on the field, a look was all it took. There was no need for words most of the time. It was the look and, especially, how you sent the look that sent the message, especially with players like [Anthony] Daly, Seánie [McMahon], Lohan and Doyler [Liam Doyle]. It showed the terrific understanding there was between everybody, and that applied with the selectors as well.

'Our physio, Colm Flynn, said to me, "Jesus, his hamstring is gone." I replied, "Tell him he's not f***ing coming off!" I turned my back and walked in the other direction after Lohan called me to inform me of his distress. Colm went in and broke the news to Brian. No reaction whatsoever. He just got on with it and pretended nothing was wrong with him. When you talk about mental toughness, what Lohan did in the All-Ireland was out of this world. It would never happen in soccer. If a player pulls his hamstring in soccer, the stretcher is brought in and there's a big exit.

'In the last 20 minutes, he used his head, stayed goalside of John Troy and whoever else came on him and played away with a torn hamstring. He wasn't able to train for three months afterwards. For those last 20 minutes, he held out by sheer guts. For a Clare player to do that in an All-Ireland final was incredible and said everything about the difference between the team I played on and the team I managed. There's no way I'd have done that when I was playing.

'He got through it by cutting down the angles. It was a measure of his courage and his intelligence. He used his head to survive with a torn hamstring. He was willing to go through the pain barrier because the team needed him to do so.'

In training, Loughnane was like Shania Twain: difficult to impress.

'I drove Brian Lohan to distraction in training. When I wanted to improve a forward like Barry Murphy, I always put them on Lohan in training. Indirectly, I was giving him the line that he "cleaned" Lohan. Then I'd say, "Barry, move around. He's slow. He won't be able to keep up with you." Lohan would be growling. Then I'd say something like, "Don't let him forward. Drive him back. He's not able to hit the ball when he's going backwards." All the time I was giving messages to Lohan. I never told him directly what his weaknesses were. Any message I wanted to give him was via somebody else, and then he'd go out and prove me wrong.

'To Conor Clancy I'd say, "Catch the ball. Lohan can't catch it. He's no use in the air." Brian would be fuming inside, but he'd never say anything. He is one of the most loyal people you could meet. I just can't find the words to praise him enough. We'll never see his like again. Lohan will become a legendary character, even more so than he already is. The characteristics he showed, the nerve for the big occasion, the intelligent play meant that I've never seen a full-back like him. In all aspects of his life he's ambitious. He's driven to succeed, but he is a totally calm, calculating person. His good points are too numerous to mention, but anyone who's seen him play knows what they are. He is simply the best.'

For his part, Lohan is keen to give Loughnane praise, albeit in more muted terms.

'He just dictated everything that you had to do, and you did it or else you stood outside and watched other people doing it. So it was very simple: his way or no way. Nobody would have dared question it. Loughnane constantly did things that were to the benefit of the players, and everything was for the benefit of the team. He was brutal, but he was very honest. He didn't allow you to have feelings for him. You did what he asked you to do because of pure respect for him. When we did what he asked us to do, we were winning matches – so that's why we kept doing what he said.'

52

THE MAN FROM CLARE
GER LOUGHNANE

Those who make history can afford to ignore it. In 1994, when he became Clare manager, Ger Loughnane could not have known that his name would become the most instantly identifiable and, in several senses, the most emotive in the recent mythology of hurling. His is a fame shot through with many subtleties of feeling.

In his 16 years as a player, he became Clare's first All-Star in 1974 and won another in '77. He won two league medals, in 1977 and '78. Having been on the losing side in five Munster finals, he was determined to buck that trend when he started managing the team. To do this, he was going to have to do things differently.

'In 1997, Colin Lynch was not named for our Munster championship clash against Cork. I knew that Colin was very upset by this, but we weren't sure if he had the temperament for the big occasion. He went to Anthony Daly, and his basic theme was: what more did he have to do for us to be selected for Clare?

'One night shortly after, in Cusack Park, I gave the panel a lecture about trust. I looked everybody in the eye, especially Colin Lynch, and I said, "We won the All-Ireland in '95 because ye trusted what we did. Never doubt a decision we make. Here there is total trust. We have total trust in ye. Ye have total trust in us. Anybody who hasn't that attitude is out the gate." I looked Lynch straight in the eye. You could hear a pin drop. There was no more complaining. Everybody knew who I was speaking about. The players were as close as could be. They all knew the slightest move in the camp. It was the same rules for everybody. That's the way we all are. We all trusted each other.

'By chance, Lynch did play, and he was brilliant. He was outstanding in the Munster final and in the All-Ireland final and won an All-Star that year, but even brilliant players have to understand the message that you fall into line or else.'

Loughnane was one of the great innovators of hurling.

'In '98, the Munster semi-final against Cork was always going to be a crunch game for us. We drove home the message to the players beforehand that we couldn't let Cork beat us. That was the game we played our first real dummy team. I can still see Tom Cashman and Jimmy Barry-Murphy looking out at the field, looking at their programme, looking at the numbers on the players' backs and trying to figure who exactly was playing and who wasn't. They were totally confused!

'We wore Cork down physically, and in the last 20 minutes we completely outhurled them with speed and skill and everything you'd want to see in your team. At one stage, Brian Corcoran got the ball. He turned to his right, and P.J. O'Connell was there. He turned to his left, and Jamesie [O'Connor] was there. Jamesie took it off him and put it over the bar. Corcoran looked out at Jimmy Barry-Murphy and threw his arms up in the air. It was like he was asking, "What can we do?"'

In 1995, the outcome of the All-Ireland final seemed clear-cut. Managers are selected for winning matches, certainly not for the quality of their post-match interviews. They have no obligation to produce either profundity or entertainment for the microphones and notebooks that cluster round them in the half-time interval. Yet, at half-time, Loughnane had boldly told the television audience, hungry for direct evidence, that Clare were going to win: 'We're going to do it.'

Cockiness is no crime, especially in a world where undue reticence is a recipe for being left behind, but Gaelic games is one of the areas where the penalties for overdosing on self-approval are especially severe. With five minutes to go, the manager's confidence had apparently been exposed as the creation of a romantic and deluded imagination. As the historic contest entered its decisive final minutes, Offaly were travelling so smoothly that it seemed they would win as easily as a nun gets to heaven. Twelve months earlier, Limerick had outplayed Offaly throughout the All-Ireland final and held a five-point lead with just minutes remaining, but then they were caught by the Dooleys. Back-to-back titles now seemed inevitable for the Midlanders, but the Clare team had a morale so tough that railway sleepers could be broken across it. People who witness miracles, even minor ones of the sporting variety, are wont to carry around for ever afterwards a potent cocktail of reminiscence, and any hurling fan who wants to avoid a long monologue on the 1995 hurling final had better steer miles clear of Clare.

'When we got back to the dressing-room, we put the cup on the table and everybody chatted away. There was no jumping up and down. It wasn't like beating Tipp in '97. There wasn't that ecstatic feeling. It was nearly a feeling of wonder. Then we went out on the bus, and with the cup up on the front we headed for the Berkeley Court. From then on, we knew we were All-Ireland champions.'

In 2006, Loughnane began an unsuccessful two years as Galway manager, where he had a jaundiced view both of some of the county's hurling officials and the training facilities.

'I was on the Hurling Development Committee, which tried to persuade Galway to come into the Leinster championship. When we met them, one official fell asleep at the end of the table. That's a fact. Another official's only concern was that the kitchen was closing at 9 p.m., so the meeting had to be over then so that he'd get his meal. They weren't the slightest bit interested.

'Ballinasloe is like a sheep field. Loughrea is an absolute disgrace: a tiny, cabbage garden of a field. Athenry is the worst of all. I asked myself what were these people doing in the 1980s when they had all this success? It was Pearse Stadium they concentrated on – the stand, not the pitch. Because the pitch is like something left over from famine times, there are so many ridges in it.'

After Galway, Loughnane returned to reclaim his status as hurling's most high-profile and controversial pundit.

'From the time Clare won the All-Ireland in 1995 to my retirement in 2000, it seemed that every Tom, Dick and Harriet with access to a word processor was writing about the Clare team and giving their "expert opinions" about the team in general and me in particular. Leaving aside what was said about me – which was rather a lot – I often found myself wondering what team they were writing about. How could so many people who wrote about us with such certainty get it so badly wrong so often? Eventually, I was persuaded that the time had come for me to set the record straight, particularly about the many controversies that marked my terms as Clare and Galway manager. My philosophy is to tell it as I see it. Mind you, that is not to everybody's taste!'

53

THE LYNCH MOB
JACK LYNCH

The late Jack Lynch is credited with having changed the rules of the Catholic Church. In 1945, he lined out at top of the right in the All-Ireland football final against Cavan. According to folklore, at one stage he was 'roughed up' by the late John Wilson – the former Tánaiste – who was a clerical student at the time. Wilson was booked for his troubles. The hierarchy were embarrassed by the incident and introduced a new rule whereby priests and clerical students were no longer allowed to play for their clubs and counties – to prevent scandal and to avoid men of God being contaminated by the ways of the world. In a uniquely Irish solution to an Irish problem, the footballing men of the cloth got around the rule by playing under assumed names. A case in point was the late Father Michael Cleary, who metamorphosed into Mick Casey.

Jack Lynch had the unique distinction of winning All-Ireland senior medals in six consecutive years, from 1941 to '46: five in hurling and one in football in 1945. A personal highlight came when he captained the hurlers to All-Ireland glory in 1942. He also won three National League medals and ten county championships with the famed Glen Rovers. His status within the game of hurling was reflected in his selection at midfield on both the Team of the Century and the Team of the Millennium.

After his great success in sport, Lynch went on to achieve even greater success in politics. He was first elected to the Dáil in 1948, having initially been approached to contest the election by Clann na Poblachta. He was appointed Minister for Finance in 1965, and the following year he became the first Taoiseach of the post-civil-war generation. His finest hour came in 1977, when he led Fianna Fáil to a general election victory with a 20-seat majority.

When I asked him about the high point of his career, he came up with an unexpected answer.

'It may be paradoxical, but the games of which I have the most vivid memories are the ones we lost. Of these, I remember best the first All-Ireland hurling final in which I played. It was Cork versus Kilkenny on 3 September 1939. I was captain of the team and hopeful of leading Cork out of a comparatively long barren spell. Cork had not won a final since 1931, when they beat Kilkenny in the second replay of the final.

'The match I refer to has since been known as "the Thunder and Lightning Final". We had all kinds of weather, including sunshine and hailstones. It was played on the day that the Second World War commenced. I missed at least two scorable chances – of a goal and a point. I was marking one of the greatest half-backs of all time, Paddy Phelan, and we were beaten by a point scored literally with the last puck of the game. I can remember more facets of that game than almost any other in which I played.

'Although I was lucky enough to play in many All-Ireland finals, all the Munster finals were special. It was always about more than sport. It was a social occasion where men drank in manly moderation, but probably more than any other moment in the calendar it defined our identity. Looking back, there was a lot of hardship in those days, with rationing and so on. To take one example, both Tipperary and Kilkenny were excluded from the 1941 hurling championship because of an outbreak of foot-and-mouth disease. Yet no matter how bad things were, like Christmas, the Munster final was always guaranteed to put a smile on people's faces.

'I especially remember the finals during the Emergency years when petrol was rationed. People thumbed lifts on lorries bringing turf to the city; others walked and set out days beforehand. Some would cycle through the night to get there.'

When asked his opinion of himself as a hurler, Jack Lynch was understandably reticent.

'I would prefer to leave this assessment to people I played with or against or who saw me play.'

However, he was much more forthcoming with his opinion of other great players. Inevitably, the analysis began with Christy Ring.

'Christy Ring was the greatest hurler that I knew. I know there are some who will contend that others were better – Mick Mackey, for example. I think Mick Mackey was the most effective hurler that I played against. Mackey was great, but in my opinion Ring's hurling repertoire was greater. He was totally committed to hurling, perhaps more so than any player I have ever met.'

Lynch was also associated with one of the biggest-ever sporting occasions held in GAA headquarters. On 19 July 1972, it took Muhammad Ali eleven rounds to defeat an ex-convict from Detroit, Al 'Blue' Lewis, at Croke Park. The fight itself was unremarkable, but it was a wonderful occasion, particularly after Ali announced that his maternal great-grandfather, Abe Grady, had emigrated from County Clare over a century before. As part of the build-up to the fight, Ali met the Taoiseach, Jack Lynch, who informed the pugilist that despite his busy schedule he hoped to make it to the fight the following Wednesday. Ali replied, 'Since you're a busy man, I guess I'll get it over quickly.'

'Ah sure, that would spoil it,' Lynch retorted.

The last word, as always, went to Ali: 'Well, in that case, I'll let Lewis stay in the ring for more than one round.'

It was with the greatest reluctance that Jack Lynch picked what he termed his 'hypothetical dream team' for me. It was:

1   TONY REDDAN (TIPPERARY)
2   BOBBY RACKARD (WEXFORD)
3   NICK O'DONNELL (WEXFORD)
4   JOHN DOYLE (TIPPERARY)
5   JIMMY FINN (TIPPERARY)
6   JOHN KEANE (WATERFORD)
7   IGGY CLARKE (GALWAY)
8   FRANK CUMMINS (KILKENNY)
9   JOE SALMON (GALWAY)
10 CHRISTY RING (CORK)
11 JIMMY LANGTON (KILKENNY)
12 JIMMY DOYLE (TIPPERARY)
13 JIMMY SMYTH (CLARE)
14 NICKY RACKARD (WEXFORD)
15 EDDIE KEHER (KILKENNY)

54

THE PLAYBOY OF THE SOUTHERN WORLD

MICK MACKEY

'Nothing is permanent but change.' So said Heraclitus, Greek philosopher, in 500 BC. The world of Gaelic games is constantly evolving and changing, but the one constant is that each generation produces its own legends and iconic names. Limerick's Mick Mackey was both an extraordinary hurler and a great character. He had an immense physical and social presence. Few people could match him for charisma.

Nicknames are not part of the culture in the GAA, unlike in rugby. There is no question that this is a good thing. There have been a few exceptions, like Antrim manager Liam Bradley, who is known as 'Baker' because back in the 1970s he always wore a white sports jacket. One current inter-county hurler is nicknamed 'Butter' on the basis that butter is found 'in bread' – and that his father married his first cousin. What makes Mick Mackey unique among the giants of Gaelic games was that he had three nicknames. He was often described as 'the Laughing Cavalier', occasionally as 'the King of the Solo Run' but most often as 'the Playboy of the Southern World'. He always seemed to have a smile on his face – both on and off the field. He was one of those exceptional talents who made the crowd come alive with his swashbuckling style, and the higher the stakes the better he performed, which is a sure sign of greatness.

Mackey was also renowned for his shrewdness. In a senior hurling game between his club, Ahane, and Thurles Sarsfields, the established practice was for a prominent clergyman to throw in the ball to start the game. Sometimes it served as the real throw-in and the match started, but other times it merely acted as a ceremonial throw-in. For this match the local parish priest was given the honour of throwing in the ball. With typical mischievousness, Mick shouted, 'Go easy there, lads. This is not the real throw-in.' The opposing team fell for the trick and made no attempt to go for the ball, allowing Mackey to swoop in unchallenged and race for goal with one of his trademark solos, securing the opening point.

One of Mackey's finest performances came in the 1936 Munster final against Tipperary. He had suffered a bad knee injury before the game and, knowing he was likely to 'have it tested' by his opponents, wore a massive bandage – on his healthy knee. He scored five goals and three points that day. In the heady aftermath of the triumph, the Limerick fans were ready to acclaim Mackey as a new hero, a player who had reached his zenith on that occasion. They were enthralled by his almost irresistible aggression, which mixed animal drive with a keenly appreciated mastery of the fine skills. His armoury included seemingly lightning speed on the solo run, staying power and limitless heart.

Mackey captained Limerick to the All-Ireland title that year, defeating Kilkenny in the final by 5–6 to 1–5, and again in 1940, having won his first All-Ireland in 1934. He made his debut for Limerick in 1930 and over his seventeen-year career also won five National League medals and eight Railway Cups, many in the company of his brother John. He also won fifteen county senior hurling championships with Ahane and five county football medals. One of those football titles came in 1939, when Ahane won by a single point. Nothing unusual in that at first glance, but what made that point unique was that it was the only score in the match.

The Munster final is one of the last genuine folk festivals left to us. There is no lens wide enough or screen big enough to take in its uniqueness, the ritual, razzmatazz and throbbing public excitement of it all. Who could resist its rustic charm? In all sport, there is no arena to match it. Mackey was to stamp his genius all over it. Although, ultimately, he did not reap the reward his dazzling performance deserved, one of his finest hours came in the 1944 Munster final, which has gone down in history as 'the Bicycle Final'. It occurred during the Emergency, when private cars were off the road because of rationing during the war effort led by Seán Lemass. People arrived in Thurles in their droves on bicycles. The fact that the match was against old rivals Cork added to the lustre of the occasion. One of Mackey's most valuable contributions was to temporarily challenge the traditional established order of the 'big three': Cork, Tipperary and Kilkenny.

· When he died in 1982, such was Mackey's reputation that the funeral cortège was three miles long. He lives on in the Mackey Stand in the Gaelic Grounds in Limerick. He won the Hall of Fame award in 1962 and a Bank of Ireland special All-Star award in 1980. His place in folklore is assured by the many incidents that set him apart on the pitch. A case in point was when Limerick played Kilkenny in the 1940 All-Ireland final. Mackey fired in his first shot, and it was saved by Jimmy O'Connell, but Mick kept running in, and as he turned at the edge of the square, he shouted, 'You're in good form, but you won't smell the next one.'

Mackey could also be a great diplomat and when necessary could switch on the charm to his own advantage. In a Limerick county final, after a 'schemozzle', the referee was about to send Mackey off with his brother John and their immediate opponents. Before the deed could be completed, Mick interjected, 'Why would you do that? What will the crowd think? They came to see a county final, and this is a county final, you know, and not a lawn tennis tournament.' As a result of his comments, no one was sent off.

55

THE LIKEABLE LILYWHITE
PAT MANGAN

Pat Mangan played for Kildare seniors from 1964 to '79, when he retired from inter-county football without ever having been dropped for a match. In 1974, he partnered Bobby Millar of Laois at midfield to win a cherished Railway Cup medal. Although he travelled to San Francisco as a replacement All-Star in 1973, he never actually won one. That a player of his class should be so overlooked is a damning indictment of the selection system: an example of a player who loses out because his county fails to do well in the championship. In 1972, he was Sports Star of the Week in the *Irish Independent* on foot of his commanding display, at centre half-back, against Mattie Kerrigan of Meath in the Leinster semi-final.

In 1964, Mangan made his senior county debut against Wicklow in Aughrim, becoming one of an elite group to play minor and senior county football in the same year. Curiously, he was only a substitute on the under-21 side of that year. The following year though, he announced his arrival on the centre stage with his performances for the Kildare senior team. He starred in the under-21 team's victory over Offaly in a thrilling display of football, easily seeing off a star-studded Down side in their own backyard, before creating history in an epic All-Ireland final against Cork: Kildare's first All-Ireland title since 1928. Senior success was more elusive.

'Even though we had the basis of a very good team and I played in six senior Leinster finals, we never really seemed to get it together. The confidence of the team seemed to wane afterwards. The commitment of the players dipped also. There were certain players – who were exceptionally skilful – who didn't give the commitment that was required at that level, but because they were big-name players they kept getting picked. That in turn had an effect on the morale of some of the other players who may not have been as talented but who were putting in the effort and the training.

'The turnout at sessions then, when you compare it with today's, was pathetic. With our preparations it is no wonder we won nothing. People from other counties can't believe we didn't win an All-Ireland. I remember being on holiday in Kerry and meeting some of their great players, who told me that they couldn't believe we didn't even win a Leinster.'

A spell as player-manager of the county side gave Mangan a greater insight to the shortcomings of the team.

'I did a year as trainer of Kildare in 1972 to '73. Every year we had a different trainer. In fact, we had more trainers than Sheikh Mohammed! It was a difficult task, especially as I found myself doing tasks the county secretary should have been doing: organising matches and pitches et cetera. I put a lot of effort into it and got on well with the players, but it put a big strain on me and my own performance – and I stood down after we lost to Offaly in the Leinster semi-final. It could have been a different story if we had had a good settled team and things had been going well, but we had had difficulties with some players coming to training. Even though I would have come up the ranks with them, I didn't get the response I needed.'

While Mangan feels that Kildare were, in the main, the architects of their own destruction, he also believes there were other contributory factors to explain their failure to make the breakthrough.

'Another reason we didn't win was that we played Offaly a few times in Leinster finals, and although they had great players, it's fair to say they exploited the rules to the fullest – to put it as diplomatically as I can. We were a very skilful team and never resorted to the physical. It's not that we weren't able to, because we had a lot of big fellas, but we weren't that sort of side. Offaly were a very, very tough physical team, but at the time, refereeing wasn't as strict as it is today and usually they didn't take much notice of what was going on off the ball. The umpires were only there to put up the flags. Offaly were a very, very good team and had a lot of skilful players, but I think everybody knows they had a few hatchet men. Some of those guys prided themselves on being hard men. Today, people speak about winning at all cost, but even back then that Offaly team had that attitude.

'Likewise, Dublin had some of that mentality when they came on the scene. They were one of the great teams, and some of the Dublin–Kerry matches of the '70s were some of the classic games of all time. Heffo was very good at sizing up the opposition and pinpointing their weak points. Some of the football they played was very attractive, but they got away – to put it as charitably as I can – with some questionable tactics.'

Fate decreed that Mangan would retire without even a Leinster senior medal.

'I gave up playing for Kildare in 1979, when I was 33, after we lost to Meath following a replay in the second round of the Leinster championship. Probably, if it was now, and I put in the work over the winter, I could continue longer. Having played for 16 years and had all the disappointments in the meantime, it got very difficult to motivate myself again and again. The team at the time didn't look as though we were going to make the breakthrough.

'In the league campaign the previous year, I was moved to full-forward, and when that happens, you know you're getting close to the end. In that campaign, we played Kerry in Killarney when they were at their peak. I played on John O'Keeffe. I got the biggest runaround I ever got on that day. The quality of the ball into me wasn't great, but whatever ball came in to me, O'Keeffe cleaned me out.

'Kerry got seven goals in that game, and the following day a good friend of mine, in the nicest possible way, told me that he thought it was time for me to hang up my boots. I said, "No." I couldn't go out on that performance. I knew I had played dreadfully but equally that I was capable of better. I didn't know whether I'd get picked or not, but I declared myself available for the following match. We played against Cork in Newbridge, and the game went well, and I redeemed myself somewhat. That winter, my head knew where I wanted to be but my legs just couldn't get me there. Your appetite begins to go as well, particularly as your team doesn't show any signs of making the breakthrough. I had family at the time, and you say to yourself, "What's the point?"'

Mangan's dream team, excluding Kildare players, is as follows:

1 BILLY MORGAN (CORK)
2 ENDA COLLERAN (GALWAY)
3 JOHN O'KEEFFE (KERRY)
4 ROBBIE KELLEHER (DUBLIN)
5 PAÍDÍ Ó SÉ (KERRY)
6 KEVIN MORAN (DUBLIN)
7 MARTIN NEWELL (GALWAY)

100 GAA GREATS

8 MICK O'CONNELL (KERRY)
9 BRIAN MULLINS (DUBLIN)
10 MICHEÁL KEARINS (SLIGO)
11 MATT CONNOR (OFFALY)
12 PAT SPILLANE (KERRY)
13 COLM O'ROURKE (MEATH)
14 SEÁN O'NEILL (DOWN)
15 JOHN EGAN (KERRY)

56

DOWN TO BUSINESS
MÁIRÍN McALEENAN

The president of the Camogie Association, Miriam O'Callaghan, described Máirín McAleenan as 'one of the finest ambassadors that the game has ever had'.

In March 1986, Máirín made her senior debut in Portglenone against Antrim as a wing-forward in a game won by Down. She has won a multitude of honours, including Down senior championships; Down senior league; Ulster club championships; Kilmacud Sevens Player of the Tournament; Ulster minor championships; Ulster minor league; Ulster junior championships; All-Ireland junior championships; All-Ireland junior national league; All-Ireland intermediate championships; Ulster GAA Writers' Player of the Year; Ashbourne Cup Player of the Tournament; and All-Star awards. She has many happy memories from her playing days.

'My fondest memories are of Sheila McCartan, a highly rated inter-county player, presenting me with my very own Liatroim Fontenoys senior camogie jersey around 1984; winning Feile na nGael Division Three in Wexford in 1984; and almost bursting with pride at the brilliant Liatroim performance in the Ulster club championship final in 1998.

'My biggest disappointments were losing the Down championship final in 1990; the poor performance of the Down team in the All-Ireland intermediate final against Limerick in 1996; the poor performance of Liatroim Fontenoys in the Ulster club championship final against Loughgeil in 1997; and not being selected on Liatroim Fontenoys's team for the Down final in 1989.'

To what does she attribute her own success as a player?

'Any achievements which I have attained in camogie are as a result of the hard work of all team members, and I think it unfair, in a team game, that scoring forwards always grab the headlines, while tenaciously tackling defenders and midfielders, who always play fairly, are rarely recognised for their contribution. These players I hold in the highest esteem.'

Máirín's career has been enriched by her interaction with a number of characters.

'I have been fortunate enough to play for club, county and province with great players and characters on and off the field. Bonnie McGreevy [Down] talked incessantly throughout a match, frequently using phrases borrowed from other sports, like "Good dee-fence." She instilled great confidence in her teammates with her ability to score or win a free almost every time she got possession and enjoyed celebrating a score. She scored an unforgettable goal against Tipperary in the All-Ireland junior final in 1991.

'My clubmate Donna Greeran's performances are all heart and totally committed. Donna would rather be chased by a Rottweiler than give away a score! She gives lots of encouragement to me during a game.

'Another clubmate, the age-defying Bernie Kelly, played every game with the experience of a veteran and the enthusiasm of an eight year old. At 43 years, Bernie continued to power Liatroim's efforts from midfield, 22 years after helping her club to their first Down senior title. Bernie possesses an indomitable and unquenchable will to win, as well as a Rolls Royce engine! She scored a goal in each of the All-Ireland junior finals of 1976 and 1991. On the way to the Ulster club final in 1998, I was reading a newspaper article on the match. The journalist in question had put Bernie in the "veteran" bracket and questioned the wisdom of playing a 42 year old in midfield at such a high level of camogie. Fully aware of the effect this would have on Bernie should she hear it, I said to her, "Do you hear that, Bernie? They reckon here that you're past it!"

'"Huh! Past it!" said Bernie, "I'll be hurling for Liatroim when I'm f***ing 90!"'

Máirín's career has been punctuated by many light moments.

'A Derry player [Kitty Morgan] was sent off in a championship versus Down in 1987. However, she refused to leave the pitch but sat down on the halfway line. The match continued, and she eventually got up and walked to the line.

'Down trainer Bill Smyth is renowned for his funny statements, and one night at training our efforts at sprinting were less than satisfactory. Bill gave us a bit of a tongue-lashing, finishing up by saying, "My granny could run faster than that!" At this, I turned to Joan Henderson, who had just joined our panel from Tipperary, and said, "Bill's granny ran in the Olympics, you know!" It was amusing to see Joan waiting behind after training to enquire of Bill which event his grandmother took part in and her overall finishing position!'

Asked about her most difficult opponent, Máirín's answer is less than straightforward.

'It's very difficult to say who my toughest opponent was, since it depends on my own form and that of my opponents – which can fluctuate greatly. For example, I can recall scoring two or three goals and four or five points while marking Cork captain Eithne Duggan in a Gael Linn final years ago. However, the next evening I only managed a couple of points while marking a player who wouldn't be considered county material, in a Down league match!

'Some of the toughest opponents would be Deirdre Costello [Galway minor centre half-back in the All-Ireland semi-final in 1985]. I remember wondering how a 16 year old could be so physically strong. Ann Lenihan [Limerick] is a very tight marker and frustrates a forward with her hooking, blocking, hassling and nudging the sliotar just beyond the forwards' reach. Catherine Murphy [Rathnure] inspires confidence with her excellent reading of the game and lengthy clearances and is a very experienced defender.'

Given the difficulties Máirín experienced choosing her most difficult opponent, it is not surprising that choosing her dream team posed great problems.

'The players I have selected are players whom I have played with or against and who in my opinion have extra-special qualities. Many, many excellent players have been left out of my final 15, like Sandie Fitzgibbon and Irene O'Keeffe [Cork]; Tríona Bonnar and Sinéad Nealon [Tipperary]; Denise O'Boyle and Bróna McCorry [Antrim]; Ann Reddy and Ger Codd [Wexford]; and Germaine Noonan [Dublin].'

Her dream team is as follows:

1	LOUISE CURRY (GALWAY)
2	DONNA GREERAN (DOWN)
3	CATHERINE MURPHY (WEXFORD)
4	PAMELA NEVIN (GALWAY)
5	DENISE CRONIN (CORK)
6	SARAH ANN QUINN (DERRY)
7	MAIRA MCMAHON (CLARE)
8	SHARON GLYNN (GALWAY)
9	LINDA MELLERICK (CORK)

100 GAA GREATS

10 SINÉAD MILLEA (KILKENNY)
11 LYNN DUNLEA (CORK)
12 FIONA O'DRISCOLL (CORK)
13 ANGELA DOWNEY (KILKENNY)
14 DEIRDRE HUGHES (TIPPERARY)
15 GRACE MCMULLAN (ANTRIM)

57

PARTING IS SUCH SORROW
CORMAC McANALLEN

Death always sends a chill through the bones. Each death is a painful reminder of the ultimate and unwelcome end for us all. It is all the more harrowing when a young person dies and all the promise of a young life is denied. Cormac McAnallen's funeral was like no other. Never did such a young player in his prime die like that in the GAA. Most funerals are a burial of someone already gone. Cormac's death pointed in exactly the opposite direction and was, therefore, all the more poignant. Normally we bury the past, but in burying him, in some deep and gnawing way, we buried the future.

We live in a strange world that, at times, is very difficult to understand. We have a habit of getting our priorities all wrong. The most famous saying in the sporting vernacular is Bill Shankly's oft-quoted dictum that 'Football is not just a matter of life and death. It is much more important than that.' However, Cormac McAnallen was to prove this wrong. This thought struck me on 2 March 2004, when we heard the shocking news that Cormac had died from Sudden Adult Death Syndrome. It is difficult to comprehend that this young man, who gave new meaning to the phrase 'larger than life', is no longer with us. Cormac was an icon of modern-day Gaelic football. A tremendous athlete, he was blessed with a great engine. He was an outstanding fielder and a versatile performer. But it was another quality that meant he stood out from all his colleagues: he was blessed with a maturity that stretched way beyond his tender years. It was no surprise when Mickey Harte chose him to captain Tyrone in 2004.

In his tragically short time on earth, Cormac achieved more than most will ever manage in a lifetime. He captained Tyrone to victory in the All-Ireland minor and under-21 championships; won an All-Ireland senior medal; was a young player of the year and an All-Star; and represented Ireland with distinction in the 2003 International Rules series. These are just the high points.

Until 2003, Tyrone football had been a story of a nearly team. They really gave Kerry a scare in the All-Ireland final in 1986. With a display of positive football, they had the greatest team of all time on the ropes. Early in the second half, Kerry trailed them by seven points. And it could have been worse had Tyrone right half-back, Kevin McCabe, not blasted a penalty over the bar. But Kerry pulled them back to record a memorable win. In 1995, Dublin beat them by only a point, but, driven on by Cormac McAnallen at full-back, in 2003 Tyrone made no mistake. Their dominance over Kerry in the All-Ireland semi-final – in a classic case of nouveau riche versus old money – will never be forgotten, and the defeat of reigning champions Armagh in the All-Ireland final unleashed a tidal wave of emotion.

The decision by Mickey Harte to switch the star midfielder to the edge of the square after the team leaked four goals in the drawn Ulster final was the final piece of the jigsaw. From that moment on, Tyrone never looked back. To outsiders, these top-level competitors are not of this world, but Cormac lived and breathed the game. He knew why second best was just not good enough. He knew that it is the small things that make the big differences.

A lot of the time, winning is not about being 100 per cent better than your opponents but about doing 100 things 1 per cent better than the other team. In 2003, in the build-up to the All-Ireland final, Cormac was having problems sleeping before the match. His brother doctored a picture of Peter Canavan and produced a computer image of Peter holding the Sam Maguire trophy. Cormac hung it above his bed the week before the final. It was the first thing he noticed every morning when he woke, and that put him in the right frame of mind to win his All-Ireland medal.

Cormac produced his fair share – way more than his fair share – of memorable victories and epic performances that have ignited the imagination of Gaelic football fans. The craft and courage of this young man have added another marvellous chapter to the already richly garlanded history of a sport that demands skill, speed, strength and character. The fervent hope is that others can emulate his lofty standards. If young players in the future can live up to his trademark determination and staggering dignity, it will be a magnificent legacy he has left to us.

Cormac was a hero in the true sense of the term, because, when he performed well, *do lioigh an laoch san uile dhuine* (the hero in all of us was exulted). The truth is, it is more important to be a great man than a great player. Cormac was both, and his presence will linger with us for ever. The grooves in the mind hold traces and vestiges of everything that has ever happened to us. Nothing is ever lost or forgotten: a ruin is never simply empty; it remains a vivid temple of absence. Cormac's absence will always be keenly felt by his parents, Brendan and Bridget, his brothers, Donal and Fergus, his teammates at club and county level and the people of Tyrone.

All football fans were numb when they heard the news of Cormac's death. Nobody did more than him to make Gaelic football the beautiful game. The fact that the trophy for the International Series between Ireland and Australia is named after Cormac is a worthy tribute to a great man.

With apologies to John Donne, the Gaelic games are a family unit. When a great player dies, all the pages are not tossed aside but translated into a new language. In the fullness of time, God's hand will bind our scattered leaves into that library where all books will lie open to one another. All football fans in Tyrone and beyond are the curators of Cormac's memories.

Ar dhéis Dé go raibh a anam.

58

THE WANDERING EVANGELIST
JUSTIN McCARTHY

Rugby is a sport for ruffians played by gentlemen, Gaelic football is a sport for gentlemen played by ruffians but hurling is a sport for gentlemen played by gentlemen. One man who proves the last part of this adage is Justin McCarthy.

Like Liam Griffin, McCarthy is one of the great evangelists of the game.

'Hurling identifies my Irishness. I'm not an Irish speaker, so the game portrays my national spirit. It's so Irish, so unique.'

The year 1966 was McCarthy's finest as a player, when he won both All-Ireland under-21 and senior medals with Cork and was chosen as hurler of the year. Fresh talent is the lifeblood of hurling. New shoots will spring up every season, but it is only occasionally that you realise you are watching the emergence of a full new flower. That was the excitement of September 1966, with the arrival of the three Macs: Charlie, Justin and Gerald McCarthy. The night before the All-Ireland final, they were supposed to be tucked up in their beds. The three young men decided to take a trip into the city centre to sample the atmosphere. The problem was that it was much harder for them to get a taxi back to the team hotel. Two of the team mentors, Jim 'Tough' Barry and Donie Keane, were patrolling the corridor. The three lads knew they would be read the Riot Act, so they hid until the coast was clear and then raced up the stairs and into their beds. Within moments there was a rap on the door. The three amigos pretended they were fast asleep. Then came a louder rap they could not possibly ignore and the question, 'What were ye lads up to?'

'We're in bed.'

'Open the door.'

Charlie McCarthy nonchalantly walked to the door, pretending to rub the sleep from his eyes as he let the two mentors in: 'What's the problem, Jim? We were fast asleep.'

JUSTIN McCARTHY

Jim looked at him with steely eyes: 'Is that so? Jaysus, Charlie, you're the only man I know to wear a collar and tie in bed.'

Although Kilkenny were the favourites, Cork won the All-Ireland by 3–9 to 1–10. McCarthy went on to win Railway Cup medals with Munster in both 1968 and '69, but in the run-up to the 1969 All-Ireland final against Kilkenny he broke his leg in three places in a motorbike accident on his way to training. He worked his way back and won league and Munster titles in 1972 and retired in '74.

Not all counties are a natural hinterland for hurling. The great Paddy Downey, the distinguished former Gaelic games correspondent of *The Irish Times*, described hurling in Kerry as 'a lot like Compulsory Tillage'. After his retirement, McCarthy took up coaching and shocked the hurling world when he took on the job of coaching the Antrim team. As a coach, McCarthy's intelligence came into focus. In west of Ireland parlance, 'He wouldn't take a bite out of a stone.' Stints coaching Clare and Cork soon followed, and then McCarthy succeeded his old teammate Gerald McCarthy as manager of Waterford, where he showed the complex web of talents that are necessary to be a successful manager.

However, no trainer is an island. Ultimately, the boundaries to the success that a trainer can achieve are defined by the players at his disposal. McCarthy had a hugely successful spell with Waterford, winning three Munster titles and a National League, but he was unable to lead them to an All-Ireland final. Hurling managers can be classified into two categories: those who have been sacked and those who will be sacked. In 2008, after the Waterford players made known their dissatisfaction with his regime, Justin stepped down as the county's manager. Later that year, he succeeded Richie Bennis as Limerick manager. However, his tenure as manger was dogged by controversy, with so many senior players for the county refusing to play for him. As a consequence, there was significant unrest over a protracted period about Justin's stewardship of the team.

The late RTÉ Gaelic games correspondent Mick Dunne was an admirer of McCarthy's.

'Justin was a wonderful hurler, and had not injury intervened I am sure we would have heard even more about his talents as a player. Even after the accident, he still had the "know-how", and he called the shots and dictated the flow of the game. It was an education just to see him in action. You sometimes hear a player described as "a class act". If there ever was a class act, it would have to be Justin. I also found him to be one of the great characters in the game, though in a quieter way than a lot of players.

'He was very committed to everything he did and left nothing to chance. It was a very different time during his playing days. In 1966, he deservedly won the Texaco Hurler of the Year award. The morning after the reception when he was presented with his award, Justin celebrated in style – by having a massive fry-up for breakfast. The problem was that in those times Catholics were not allowed to eat meat on Fridays, with the result that fish was on the menu in most Irish homes on Fridays. And when Justin realised the terrible sin he had committed, he went to his priest for absolution!'

59

THE MAN IN THE CAP
PETER McDERMOTT

Down the years, the GAA has produced a number of players who have had bad hair days. A case in point would be the celebrated Rasher Duignan of the great Clann na nGael club in Roscommon. As his career progressed, his hairline receded, necessitating the application of suncream to his bare top during a game one scorching summer's day. As the game unfolded, Rasher was beginning to get very distressed, and his performance fell well below his normal standards. During half-time, in consultation with the physio, it emerged that a tragic mistake had been made. It was not suncream he had applied to his bald patch but Deep Heat! Undaunted, Rasher put his head under the shower and in the second half went out to have the game of his life, scoring a stunning 2–4.

However, the most celebrated headgear in the history of the GAA was unquestionably that of Peter McDermott, famously christened by the voice of Gaelic games Micheál O'Hehir as 'the Man in the Cap'. The cap was to control what Peter modestly described as his 'fabulous head of long hair'. He was the driving force behind a mighty Meath team who won two All-Irelands, two league titles and six Leinster triumphs between 1940 and 1954 and has the unique distinction of being the only man to referee an All-Ireland final both before and after winning one as a player.

Peter also made his mark as an official. He was county secretary when he captained Meath to the All-Ireland in 1954, was a key advisor to Down when they won their first All-Ireland in 1960 and coached his native county when they won the All-Ireland in 1967. The following year, he initiated the link between Ireland and Australia Rules by lining up games for the county's tour of Australia.

The late Mick Dunne was a big admirer of McDermott.

'He continues to occupy a hallowed place in the annals of the GAA as a star of All-Ireland winning teams in 1949 and '54. If I was going into battle, the one player I would choose would probably be Peter.

He had the heart of a lion but was a gentleman to his fingertips. When the chips were down, he would always come through for you. His nickname added to his iconic status, particularly as back then the GAA did not have a tradition of exotic nicknames, other than Roscommon's Bill Carlos, 'the Lion with the Velvet Paw'.

'Peter's childhood and, indeed, his adult life were dominated by football. There were no distractions when he was young, other than the wireless with the wet batteries and dry batteries. And, of course, people listened to Micheál O'Hehir's commentaries religiously.

'He had a great understanding of the place of the GAA in the lives of people. Success at either parish or county level, albeit on a very modest scale, increased people's self-esteem. They talked just a little more boldly, they walked that little bit taller and they waved their flags with pride. It is impossible to explain the intense, almost tribal, loyalty that genuine followers of the GAA give to the team. There was close identification between the fans and the players. The players represented the community. The GAA was part of what and who the community was, and that was why Peter thought it was a national treasure and why he gave so much of his life to it and why he took on so many roles.

'Although he had a great appreciation for the princes of football, like Seán Purcell, he had a keen admiration for those who made a huge contribution to the GAA but whose services were often forgotten. Indeed, given the centrality of the club in the GAA, he was a massive fan of unsung heroes of club football, especially the many who soldier on long after reaching the "veteran stage".

'As a referee, he was probably as good as we've seen. It was much harder in his day to keep control. At that time you couldn't pick a ball off the ground. If you dived on the ball, you had to get up and put your toe under it and lift it. There was little chance of that in a goalmouth. There was way more body contact then, which Peter relished as it made the game very exciting. Mind you, if you lost possession, you couldn't always use it well because the game was so crowded. So you needed eyes in the back of your head. So you couldn't be a shrinking violet if you were a referee.

'As a naive young journalist, I found myself standing alone with him on the sideline at a match when a schemozzle broke out that would leave the toughest contest today looking like a harmless tiff between two little girls in a playground. Think Mayo versus Meath in 1996, and multiply by four, with the combatants bunched so close together on the centre of the pitch that they could hear each other's inner thoughts. The referee was not having a good day, and Peter gently said to me, "The advantage law is the best, because it lets you ignore all the others for the good of the game."

'He also has a good sense of humour. Last time we met, he told me the story of how Dublin have been waiting for the Sam Maguire Cup for a long time. In Meath they tell the story that in the middle of the night the then Dublin county chairman, John Bailey, was woken up by a call from his local Garda station: "I'm afraid the trophy room has been broken into, sir."

'Horrified, Bailey asked, "Did they get the cups?"

'"No, sir," replied the Garda. "They didn't go into the kitchen."

'Rumour had it the Dublin County Board were sued by the burglars for wasting their time.'

60

THE HOMES OF DONEGAL
BRIAN McENIFF

The highlight of Brian McEniff's playing career with Donegal came in 1972, though earlier in the year few could have predicted the end of the county's provincial subjugation.

'We played Leitrim in the league in Carrick-on-Shannon. I think the score was 4–13 to 1–3 to Leitrim. I was player-manager at the time. I got the lads into a room in Bush's Hotel in Carrick-on-Shannon and said, "Right, boys. The only way we can go is up. Today was the lowest we could possibly go. The championship is coming up soon, and are we going to make an effort for it or are we not?" We all made a vow there and then that we would all train hard for the championship, and we did.

'We beat Down after a replay and Tyrone in the Ulster final. It was kind of a fairy tale after so bad a start to the year. As it was Donegal's first ever Ulster title, the whole county went wild. It was like winning the All-Ireland. We had a great week afterwards! The celebrations probably affected us in the All-Ireland semi-final against Offaly, the reigning All-Ireland champions. We were playing very well up to half-time, but we gave away a very bad goal to Kevin Kilmurray. Even though we lost, we were probably happy enough with our performance, because Ulster teams weren't doing well in Croke Park at the time. I'd say Offaly got a bit of a shock that day.'

Donegal were brought down to earth with a bang the following year.

'In 1973, we were beaten in the first round of the championship by Tyrone. Tyrone were a coming team and went on to win the title. Ulster was always a graveyard for reigning provincial champions.'

In 1974, though, Donegal were back on the glory trail.

'In the Ulster championship we beat Armagh and Monaghan in the semi-final. We beat Down in the Ulster final in a replay. At one stage in the second half, we were eight points down with about twenty-two minutes to go.

BRIAN McENIFF

'It is always disappointing to lose when you are one step away from playing in an All-Ireland. In 1972, we didn't really expect to win. We had achieved our main goal to win an Ulster title, and I suppose at the back of our minds we had settled for that. The biggest disappointment was losing to Galway in 1974. We were very unfortunate. At one stage, Donal Maughan and Pauric McShea went up for the one ball and collided with each other. Johnny Tobin stood back, and as they were falling down he was collecting the ball and racing through to score a goal. Galway raced into the lead, but we pulled them back. Seamus Bonner, after about 25 minutes, had a collision with Gay Mitchell and had to be carried off. He was no sooner in the dressing-room than I came in with a split thumb. I always feel that was the semi-final that got away, because Galway only beat us by a few points, and if it wasn't for those injuries, I think we could have won.'

In 1989, Brian McEniff took charge of training Donegal again, and he had his finest hour in 1992 when he masterminded Donegal's All-Ireland 0–18 to 0–14 triumph over hot favourites Dublin to win the county's only All-Ireland.

'We had been so unimpressive in the All-Ireland semi-final against Mayo that nobody gave us a chance against Dublin. I think that gave the Dublin players a false sense of security. The media really built them up, and I think the Dubs started to believe their own publicity. In contrast, there was no hype about us, because we hadn't done anything to deserve it. None of our fellas were going on radio shows blowing our own trumpet.

'You can't win an All-Ireland without leaders on the pitch, and we had four of them in 1992: Anthony Molloy at midfield, Martin McHugh at centre-forward, Tony Boyle at full-forward and Martin Gavigan at centre-back were all leaders in different ways. Molloy was a superb leader. He could catch a ball in the clouds, and that would lift the team. If you could get past Martin Gavigan, you were doing well. Tony and Martin could get you a score from nowhere. Winning the final was like a dream come true. As it was our first ever All-Ireland, it meant so much to the people at home.'

In his time, McEniff has seen some unusual sights.

'In 1979, we qualified for the Ulster final against Monaghan, but they beat us well. The match is best remembered for an infamous incident. The referee threw in the ball, Seamus Bonner won possession, sent in the ball to the forwards and one of our lads popped it over the bar.

The only problem was that the band were still on the far side of the pitch and they were playing the national anthem! The referee had to restart the game, and our point was disallowed.'

Pat Spillane offers an appraisal of McEniff.

'He would rank up there as being as cute as O'Dwyer, and that would be as high a compliment as you could give. He's the same sort of guy as O'Dwyer in the sense that, when you are talking to him, you think you are asking him questions but he's really picking your brain. He was a very intelligent and stylish footballer himself and one of the best defenders in the game in the early 1970s. In 2003, he was the county chairman and the Central Council delegate, as well as team manager. He did everything but drive the bus and wash the jerseys. As a manager, he really shone after their defeat to Fermanagh in 2003. In that match they gave an abysmal performance, but McEniff picked them off the floor to bring them within a whisker of qualifying for an All-Ireland final – which was an absolutely incredible achievement.'

61

LAST NIGHT I HAD A PLEASANT DREAM
PACKY McGARTY

Born in Mohill in 1933, Packy McGarty's senior inter-county career began in 1949 and finished in 1971, when he was 39. He played in six Connacht senior finals without winning one of them and reached the National League semi-final in the spring of 1959. The closest he came to glory was when Galway beat Leitrim by 2–10 to 1–11 in the 1958 Connacht final. Football dominated Packy's life from an early age.

'Football was all you had. Every evening as a boy I'd go with my friends to see the men training. We'd be hoping that the ball would go over the bar, and we'd be fighting just to get a kick of it. As kids, we hadn't footballs, just a sock with grass in it. You'd be listening to a match on a Sunday, which was the highlight of the week because my father had fifteen shillings a week to keep a family of five of us. I remember working for three shillings a week.'

No one was more surprised than McGarty at his astonishingly quick elevation to inter-county status.

'I was selected for my first match for Leitrim when I was 16, against Offaly, and I didn't even know I was picked. A fella came to the door the day of my match and said, "Where's your stuff?"

'"How do you mean?" I answered.

'"You're playing today."

'I didn't believe him, but eventually he persuaded me, and it went OK and I got a couple of scores.'

Who was the biggest influence on his career?

'It was Leo McAlinden from Armagh. He played at midfield for both his native county and Leitrim, and for both Ulster and Connacht. He was a bank clerk and based in Mohill for a while. He was about 6 ft, but he was very light-looking. The first time he came to play for the club, nobody knew much about him apart from one of the mentors, Jim McGann. The manager, as it were, Billy McGowan, said to him, "That young buck. Do you think we could stick him in at corner-forward? Do you think he'd get hurt? Some of those boys are as hard as nails."

'"He doesn't like to play corner-forward," replied Jim.

'"Well, he should be happy to get in there."

'Then Leo, in his strong Armagh accent, said, "If it is all right with you, I'd like to start in the middle of the field, and if I'm not doing well I'll come off."

'Mother of God, once the game started they had never seen anything like him. He was soon the talk of the county. People were asking, "Did you see that fella from Mohill? Where did he come from?" He had a massive impact on attendances in Leitrim because everyone wanted to see him play.

'He could kick accurately with left or right. I imitated his solo run. When he was going to meet his man, he would throw the ball one way and run the other. You don't see that skill so much now. He was a brilliant player. In 1964, I went to America for the Kennedy Games with the president of the GAA, Alf Murray from Armagh, who, I'm told, was a brilliant player, and he was always on about Leo. He had such skill and balance that he could throw a cigarette in the air and catch it with the tip of his toe.

'I idolised him. One evening when I was young he asked me if I would carry his gear back to his digs because he wanted to meet his girlfriend. I had never felt so honoured, because I was carrying Leo McAlinden's stuff!

'I remember him playing in a derby club match when there was a very strong rivalry between the sides. Leo had his penalty saved by the goalie, and he went in and shook his hand and congratulated him. You don't get men like that any more.

'I played on him when he was at the end of his career, and I was only a whippersnapper and I was quicker than him. Some fellas would get mad at you for that, but he didn't. After the match he shook my hand and said, "Well done, young fella." It gave me great confidence.'

Tactics formed an important part of Packy's progression through the occasionally shark-infested waters of junior club football.

'I started playing junior club football at corner-forward. We had a massive full-forward called Billy McGowan. Billy was as strong as a horse and would take half the defence down when he went for the ball. As he knocked it down, I would race in and pop the ball over the bar and get the hell out of there as fast as I could. My father was

Jeepers keepers: Tony Reddan (left; goalkeeper on the hurling Team of the Century) greets Seán Duggan (goalkeeper on the hurling Centenary Team of greatest players never to win an All-Ireland).

A good walk spoiled: Babs Keating (right) with his son-in-law, champion jockey Johnny Murtagh.

An unusual trinity: Mickey Linden (left), Máirín McAleenan and Seán Óg Ó hAilpín.

Goalmouth scramble: From left: Mayo's Tom Acton, and Cavan's Bill Doonan, Brian O'Reilly and Des Benson in the 1948 All-Ireland final. (© Paddy Prendergast)

The Glens of Antrim: Dessie Donnelly showcases his skills.

King size: Stephen King (on the ball) brushes aside Darragh Ó Sé against Kerry in 1997.

Thin blue line: Stephen King leads the Cavan team in Croke Park before the All-Ireland semi-final in 1997.

In full flight: Paddy Quirke (centre) rises to clear the ball. (© Karl McDonough)

In the heat of battle: Paddy Quirke is tackled by Cyril Hughes and watched by referee Gus Hennessy. (© Karl McDonough)

Big Mac: Liam McHale takes on Teddy McCarthy in the 1989 All-Ireland final. (© Henry Wills)

Forever faithful: John O'Mahony puts on a brave face after Mayo's defeat in the 1989 All-Ireland final. (© Henry Wills)

Raise your hands to heaven: Willie Joe Padden soars to win the ball in the All-Ireland semi-final against Dublin in 1985. (© Henry Wills)

The merry ploughboy: Dermot O'Brien leads the Louth team before the 1957 All-Ireland final. Cork players in shot are Paddy Harrington (father of Pádraig) and Seán Moore. (© Liam Horan)

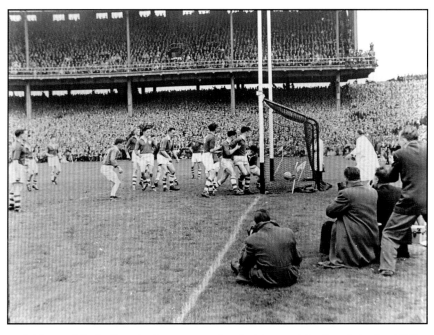

Golden goal: Seán Cunningham scores the decisive goal for Louth in the 1957 All-Ireland final. (© Liam Horan)

Heffo's army: Kevin Heffernan (wearing number 14, second from left) looks on as Dublin take on Louth. (© Liam Horan)

The power and the glory: Richie Power (right), Seán Cavanagh and model Aoife Cogan at the launch of the National Rehab/Powers Whiskey Pub Quiz. (© Robbie Reynolds)

chairman of the club, and he always told me that if I stood around or held onto the ball I would be killed. The opposition would go spare and start screaming, "Who's marking the gasun?" Someone said once, "Well, if he's a gasun, he shouldn't be here." There was one time two fellas came for me, but they collided with each other and fell on the ground, so I had a clear run on the goal. We got to the county final that year, but it was played on a dirty, wet day, which didn't suit me, and we lost.'

It was the Railway Cup with Connacht that brought McGarty his only national honours.

'We won the Railway Cup in 1957 and '58 and were beaten by a point in the final in 1959. I missed it because I was working in England and got a flu because of the smog. I was disgusted missing it, because I loved playing with Seán Purcell and Frank Stockwell.'

McGarty won a third Railway Cup medal as a sub in 1967. He would have needed a trophy cabinet if the plethora of individual awards that we have today had existed in his playing days.

'There was no such thing as All-Stars at the time. The closest thing was to be selected for Ireland to play against the Combined Universities. One year I played for Connacht in the Railway Cup final, my opponent was the Kerry right half-back Seán Murphy, who won five All-Ireland medals and was chosen in that position on the Team of the Century. The next day I played on him for Ireland against the Combined Universities. The following Friday evening, I played on him for my club, Seán McDermotts, against UCD.'

In 1984, McGarty was selected on the Centenary Team of players who had never won an All-Ireland senior medal and 15 years later was the only Leitrim player chosen on the Connacht Team of the Millennium.

Packy's dream team from his own era is:

1   JOHNNY GERAGHTY (GALWAY)
2   JEROME O'SHEA (KERRY)
3   PADDY PRENDERGAST (MAYO)
4   TOM O'HARE (DOWN)
5   SEÁN MURPHY (KERRY)
6   GERRY O'MALLEY (ROSCOMMON)
7   STEPHEN WHITE (LOUTH)
8   PADRAIG CARNEY (MAYO)
9   JIM MCKEEVER (DERRY)

100 GAA GREATS

10 SEÁN O'NEILL (DOWN)

11 SEÁN PURCELL (GALWAY)

12 PADDY DOHERTY (DOWN)

13 DENIS KELLEHER (CORK)

14 TOM LANGAN (MAYO)

15 KEVIN HEFFERNAN (DUBLIN)

62

THE LONGFORD LEADER
EUGENE McGEE

One of Longford's most celebrated sons is Eugene McGee, who famously managed Offaly to the All-Ireland title in 1982. Although not the most distinguished footballer of all time, McGee has a unique distinction as a player: he was once sent off twice in one game. The occasion was a club match for UCD. In the first half, a player on his side was sent off – but gave Eugene's name. In the second half, Eugene himself was sent off – but was too honest to give anyone else's name. When the referee checked his report after the match, he couldn't understand how he had sent Eugene off twice.

McGee first came to prominence in club management in the '70s with UCD. Legendary Roscommon footballer Tony McManus had some of his happiest memories in the game during his time in UCD between 1976 and '80 under McGee's stewardship.

'In 1979, I was captain and Colm O'Rourke was vice captain. We became good friends. He was tremendously witty and sarcastic. Eugene McGee produced a newsletter about the fortunes of the team, and he named the player who never shut up as "the Mouth of the Team", but he added that Colm was a strong contender! O'Rourke is very confident. The only time I ever saw him nervous was when I met him before the All-Ireland semi-final in 2007, when his son Shane was playing. He was never nervous when he played himself, but he was that day.

'From our freshers' year, Eugene had taken Colm and myself under his wing. He was a complex character, but it was very enjoyable working with him. He certainly had a way with him. He commanded respect and had great ideas and was able to communicate them. There were lots of county players around at that time, but he had no qualms about dropping them. Reputations meant nothing to him. You never knew what to expect from him. Days you thought you played well, he might lacerate you. Days you thought you didn't play well, he would encourage you and compliment you.

'My lasting memory of him came the day we had to play Queen's. The night before was the veterinary ball, and I had gone. The next morning, he heard about it and was not happy. He made me travel with him in his car and never said a word to me all the way up to Belfast. In the circumstances, I was really keen to do well, and I scored 2–3. He said nothing to me after the match. Eventually, when all the lads were gone and I was waiting behind for him in the dressing-room to make the journey home, he turned to the caretaker and said in his typically gruff accent, "Would you have a jackhammer to widen the door a bit more? This fella's head is so big he won't be able to get out through it."'

McGee's finest hour came when he guided Offaly to the All-Ireland final in 1982. He identifies the critical part of the game.

'The first half was open, and it was a very good game of football. The second half, it started raining fairly heavily, and the game deteriorated a good bit. Kerry dominated for a long time, and we were lucky enough to stay with them. Martin Furlong's penalty save was very important. If they had scored that, I don't think we would have come back. The rest is history. We were four points down, and we got two frees to put us two points behind. Then a long ball came to Séamus Darby, and he banged it into the net. It was a super shot. All Croke Park went wild, but there was still a minute and a half left in the game, and we had to hold on with all our might.

'The magnificent players on that team personified not only their own accomplishments but the sacrifices of generations of Offaly people who made that moment possible. I was very conscious of all the people who organised games and travelling arrangements down through the years, regardless of personal inconvenience or harsh weather. Without those people, the sequence that led to Offaly's historic success would not have started. The fact that the years of disappointment have been wiped out with that win gave me a certain amount of pleasure. It was a unique occasion.

'Every now and again something happens that brings the memories flooding back: memories of the colour, joy and excitement the supporters brought, especially on the way home after victories in Croke Park, with the flags hanging out the windows.'

Historically, team managers have tended to favour the team who won the All-Ireland the previous year – on the reasonable assumption that if they were good enough to win it once, they would be good enough to win it twice. What that logic fails to consider is the possible diminution of appetite once the cherished All-Ireland medal has been secured for the trophy cabinet. The apparently never-ending round of celebrations that lasts the whole winter also takes its toll, puffing egos and eroding physical condition. This could be the team's real undoing, the possible problem the team might encounter in regenerating the sheer passion and commitment of the previous year. Dublin took Offaly's Leinster crown in 1983, and McGee's team were unable to reach those dizzy heights ever again.

The biggest problem facing a manager can be to get his players to train. McGee, before he resigned as Offaly manager, once threatened his squad that he would write a book of 'Offaly Excuses'. One Saturday afternoon in December, a player with a penchant for such excuses turned up for training just as all the other players were walking off the pitch, as he was wont to do. Eugene asked, 'Well, what happened?'

'Oh, the wheel fell off my mobile home,' replied the player.

Just as he was about to make a sarcastic response, the manager reflected that he had passed a mobile home on the way to training and that the man's story could well be true.

63

THE GEEZER
KIERAN McGEENEY

A loser makes hard things impossible. A winner makes impossible things hard. Kieran McGeeney proved his credentials as a winner when he captained his county to their first All-Ireland in 2002. To complete an unforgettable season for him, he was selected as footballer of the year.

Armagh corner-back that day, Enda McNulty, is keenly aware that McGeeney was crucial to the 'Orange Revolution'.

'Kieran is a leader. When he walks into a dressing-room and talks about dedication, players know that nobody is more dedicated than him. But Kieran would be the first to admit that there were other leaders, like Paul McGrane, Diarmuid Marsden, the McEntees and guys who would have got very little credit, like Andrew McCann, who drove to training every single night from Armagh to Dublin on his own. Andy was a leader in actions rather than words.

'Kieran is a great friend, but more than anything he has a desire for excellence and is unwilling to settle for mediocrity in anything he does – from weight training to nutrition to skills training – and you always know that, even when a game looks as if it's gone, he's not going to throw in the towel.

'We were trailing by seven points to nil in that match against Galway in 2001, and they were on fire. I remember I was out of breath and Kieran was out of breath, as we were both trying to dam the waves of Galway attacks. I can still hear in my ears Kieran saying, as he was out of breath, "Weather the storm. Weather the storm. Weather the storm." I'm sure he said that to the other boys too, and we did and very nearly hauled them back.

'We fancied ourselves, not in a joking way, as a band of brothers. We knew each other better than some of our own brothers; we spent so much time together. One of the things that encapsulates him is that in every one of the big games, when he talked to us in the circle before the game, he'd be nearly crying, and that's how emotional he would be. He was very focused. After we won the Ulster finals, he'd say, "Boys, take a good look at the cup. That's the last time ye're going to look at it. The next cup we want to see is the All-Ireland." He was very good at bringing guys down to earth. He would be very good at calling a spade a spade. If one of the guys was not pulling his weight, he'd say, "What the f*** is going on here? You're dossing, Enda," or "Oisín, you're not up to your own high standards. I'm disappointed in you." Because he was able to walk the walk, you could never argue with that.

'I know people see Kieran as being incredibly serious, but he can have a laugh like everybody else. Like us all on the team, he loved when [in July 2002] the *Sunday World* got Pat Spillane to do player profiles of everyone due to play in the All-Ireland quarter-finals. There are not too many things you can say about a goalie, other than "He is a good shot-stopper", "Great reflexes", and "Has a good kickout". Generally, the only variable is whether you can use "Very agile". By the time he got to the last goalkeeper on the list, our Benny Tierney, Spillane was getting very bored with repeating himself, so he described Benny as "fat and overweight". We were all tickled with Benny's great retort. He said, "Spillane is right. Yes, I am fat and overweight now, but he will always be ugly."'

McGeeney also brought his formidable presence to bear on the international stage, captaining Ireland against Australia in the International Rules series. Former Donegal and Mayo player Martin Carney was a selector on the International Rules team who toured to Australia in 2003. McGeeney made a strong impression on him.

'Kieran was a great leader. I was very taken by him, because he was the guy who would get things to happen and he raised the standard for others.'

Sligo's Eamonn O'Hara was another person inspired by McGeeney on that International Rules series and used his time with him as a personal research project.

'I was mixing and sharing rooms with players, like Kieran, who had won All-Irelands or experienced great success. I saw myself as a messenger who would relay what I learned to the Sligo team. The big players on the Irish team, like Kieran, were all winners. In Sligo we went out to play games in hope. Kieran McGeeney went out in expectation. Kieran would never accept our mentality in Sligo, which was that we were happy with a good performance. He knew that with such an attitude you would never be good enough to win anything. What was different about his attitude was that it was no longer about doing well but about winning and doing whatever it took to get a title at last.'

Given his leadership qualities on the field, there were high hopes that McGeeney would bring the same success he had as a player to management when he was appointed manager of the Kildare team. He got off to a rocky start when Kildare were shocked by Wicklow in the Leinster championship in 2008, but he rallied his troops and brought them to a Leinster final against Dublin the following year. Further chapters in McGeeney's management career are yet to be written, as the circle of victory spins incessantly, beckoning him like an irresistible force. It can be safely predicted that he will replicate the same ethos he displayed as a player: ask not what your teammates can do for you; ask what you can do for your teammates.

64

MIGHTY MAC
PETER McGINNITY

One vignette that illustrates the character of Peter McGinnity – the man and the footballer – comes from a Railway Cup semi-final against Connacht in Ballybay played in the kind of wind that seems to peel the flesh off your bones and come back for the marrow. The gale blew from one goal to the other so that one team had a distinct advantage. Connacht won the toss, elected to play with the wind and led by 2–12 to 0–2 at half-time. In the second half, McGinnity took control of the game, scored two goals and orchestrated a gallant Ulster fightback. Connacht managed only one point in the second half, but that was their winning margin at the end.

In 1988, McGinnity played his last senior game for Fermanagh at the end of a 19-year career with the county that had begun when he was 17. He won four Railway Cup medals. In 1982, he had become the first Fermanagh player to win an All-Star, being selected at right half-forward. He jokes, 'I'm not a great man for individual awards, but I dare anybody try and take it from me!'

Although he was starved of success with Fermanagh, the towering midfielder, at 6 ft 3 in., does not resort to the obvious excuse of the county having a small playing base – which is remarkable, given that it was once said of Fermanagh, 'Half is made up of water, and half of the remaining half are Protestants.'

After his retirement from the playing fields, McGinnity ventured into management.

'When my playing days with Fermanagh were coming to an end, I became player-manager. It was a stopgap measure. I had been captaining the team, and I thought it would be a natural progression for me to become a player-manager – but I was very wrong. I don't think the player-manager system can work. I was too close to the players, and I wasn't prepared for the politics that goes on behind the scenes in terms of clubs wanting their players on the team. I was glad to be finished with it, and I made it clear then that I didn't want to go through the experience again.'

So why, then, was he persuaded to take the Leitrim job?

'*Persuaded* is the key word. The Leitrim county secretary, Tommy Moran, had been very helpful to me down through the years, helping me to organise pitches and so on. He more or less made it clear to me that he was going to keep hounding me until I accepted the job.

'It was a real learning experience from the point of view of observing the changes that have taken place in the game even in the ten years since I started playing. It's become a lot more scientific now and much more time-consuming for both the players and the manager. I also learned that you need great man-management skills to have a successful team. I was always told that if you had organisation and money you were on the road to success, but I was to learn that you need the players as well.'

His reasons for stepping down were complex.

'In the early months of 1999, I was having serious health problems. I was coaching a crowd of young fellas one day, and a ball struck me on the side of my head. It left me with a detached retina, which required major surgery. It got detached again in July 1999. So the fact that my general health was not good was one of a combination of factors.

'Leitrim were in a very difficult section in the league. We were having major problems with illness and injury. I felt if we got just one win we would turn the corner. Before Christmas, we drew with Tyrone in a game we should have won, and I thought that might do it, but after Christmas we slumped again.

'A county with a playing base as small as Leitrim's will only get success in cycles. They'll always have good players, but it's not often they will have enough of them to make a good team. Leitrim were in that situation from 1990 to 1994, but, with all the miles they had to clock up going to train, the end had really come for the 1994 team. Declan D'Arcy's switch to Dublin was a huge loss. I felt in those circumstances that we had to start from scratch and do new things, but there were those living on the memory of 1994 who felt we should continue on with the old ways.

'After Christmas 1999, I no longer seemed to be able to get the players to do what I wanted. What was happening on the pitch bore no relation to what I had planned. Things came to a head when we

PETER McGINNITY

played Offaly in the league. By their own admission, they played very poorly on the day and the game was there for the taking for us, but we didn't take it. After that, my two selectors and I decided we couldn't take the team any further.'

Who was his most difficult opponent?

'I would have to say, though, that the player I found toughest of all was in club football: Paddy Reilly from Teemore Shamrocks. One of the funniest incidents in my career happened when I was marking Paddy. Paddy's brother Barney and I played for Fermanagh under-21s together, and we came up the ranks together, and I always had great time for him. In one club match, the ball went up between Paddy and myself and a kind of ruck developed. I snatched the ball as Barney came charging in to give Paddy some "assistance". Happily for me, but not for Paddy, in the melee and confusion Barney struck his own brother instead of me. It still sticks in my memory. As I was heading up the field with the ball, before Barney started chasing me, he said, "Sorry, Paddy," as his brother lay stretched out on the ground!'

McGinnity prefaces his dream-team selection by referring to the problem of picking players from different eras. He has decided to include one player he never saw playing but whom he has met and heard much about: Seán Purcell.

'One other player in this category who very nearly made my team was Derry's Jim McKeever. When I went to college, he was my coach, but my earliest football memory is listening to commentaries of big games on the radio back in 1958. It almost seemed to be that Jim McKeever was on the ball. So when I started playing imaginary games as a very young boy, I was always, "Jim McKeever on the ball".'

McGinnity's dream team is:

1 BRIAN MCALINDEN (ARMAGH)
2 ROBBIE O'MALLEY (MEATH)
3 JOHN O'KEEFFE (KERRY)
4 PAÍDÍ Ó SÉ (KERRY)
5 PADDY MORIARTY (ARMAGH)
6 KEVIN MORAN (DUBLIN)
7 HENRY DOWNEY (DERRY)
8 JACK O'SHEA (KERRY)
9 BRIAN MULLINS (DUBLIN)

100 GAA GREATS

10 SEÁN O'NEILL (DOWN)
11 SEÁN PURCELL (GALWAY)
12 MATT CONNOR (OFFALY)
13 JIMMY BARRY-MURPHY (CORK)
14 EOIN LISTON (KERRY)
15 NUDIE HUGHES (MONAGHAN)

65

FRANKLY SPEAKING
FRANK McGUIGAN

One of the proudest moments in Frank McGuigan's eventful life came in 1972.

'It was a great honour for me to be captain of the Tyrone minor team and to lead your county out in Croke Park that narrowly lost to Cork in the All-Ireland final. They were powered by the great Jimmy Barry-Murphy. I always believe that sportsmanship is very important. At the end of a match, the winners should always console the losers. Cork were very gracious that day. Our full-forward that day was Mickey Harte. Thankfully, for the sake of the county and my own sons, he has had happier experiences in Croke Park on All-Ireland final day since.'

In 1972, shortly after collecting the Ulster minor trophy, McGuigan played for the senior team in the Ulster final, only to lose to Donegal. Frank McGuigan was only the second player in history to play inter-county football at minor, under-21, junior and senior levels in the one year. The first was Roscommon's Dermot Earley. The following year, McGuigan would captain the senior team to their first Ulster title in 16 years. Assuming the captaincy at such a tender age did not create the fuss that might have been expected.

'Earlier that year, our manager, Jody O'Neill, announced out of the blue, "By the way, Frank McGuigan is captain this year." It happened as simply as that.'

In 1977, McGuigan's status in the game was reflected when he went to New York with the All-Stars. As he recalled to me, it was a tour that brought some shocking news.

'At the time, instead of us staying in hotels, we often stayed with host families. On one of those trips, Tom Prendergast from Laois went to stay in an apartment owned by a Laois man. There was a foreign man staying there, and Tom decided to stay with some friends. The next day when we went to play our match there were police everywhere. The guy staying in Tom's apartment had been shot dead there the night before, and Tom was a suspect. We often wondered what would have happened if Tom had stayed there that night.

'We were managed by Seán Purcell. Seán called out the team before the first game and announced that he was playing centre half-forward. That got a great laugh, but Seán turned on us and said, in all earnestness, "What's so funny, lads?" Because it was Seán Purcell, everybody wanted to play their best.'

One of McGuigan's teammates, Johnny Hughes, saw McGuigan at close quarters on that tour.

'Frank McGuigan was my most difficult opponent. He was both very strong and very skilful and could take you to the cleaners, and he had two great feet and a great head. He was also the best character I ever came across. We went on an All-Stars trip together. I was the captain of the team, and Frank had been out on the town all night. I remember knocking on his door and wondering would he be able to get up – knowing he had had only an hour and a half's sleep. He got up and destroyed Brian Mullins in the Dublin midfield and was head and shoulders above any other player on the day. Frank took it upon himself to organise the social side of things, and he took us to the sorts of places some of us had never been in before!'

Donegal great Seamus Bonner was also on that trip and was another big fan of Frank.

'Frank McGuigan was one of the most stylish, exciting and best players around over my career. He was, without doubt, one of the greatest players never to win an All-Ireland medal. He had a mighty stand and catch. He once scored eleven points in an Ulster final: seven with one foot and four with the other. All I can say about being with Frank McGuigan on the All-Star trip was that it was an education. I can't elaborate further on the grounds that it might incriminate all of us!'

That tour to America gave Roscommon's Pat Lindsay some of his favourite moments.

'Two footballers stood out for me on that trip: Frank McGuigan and Peter McGinnity. They were just incredibly talented. Frank was probably the most gifted player I ever saw, though he would probably be the first to admit he was never a 100 per cent fit. He loved life! I roomed with Frank for a while. It was an education! One time we stayed out all night, and in the morning we went to a diner for breakfast. We had a massive fry-up. A very nice waitress came over and asked if we had enjoyed our meal. Frank was a big man, and he replied, "It was so good I'll have the same again!"'

So enjoyable did McGuigan find the experience that he stayed on in the States for the next six years. On his return home, the Ulster final in Centenary year would see him write his name in the pages of football immortality when he scored a stunning 11 points from play against Armagh. His preparation for the game was less than ideal.

'I did not have any breakfast that morning. All I had was an egg and onion sandwich in a hotel in Clones during the pre-match talk.'

Later that year tragedy would intervene.

'I played a club match for Ardboe and afterwards had a few drinks, and on the way home my van went out of control and hit a wall. My leg felt the full force of the impact and was broken at both knee and hip. I waited a long time before help arrived, and when I finally arrived in Altnagelvin Hospital in Derry I was told I would never play football again, but it was the fear in the eyes of my wife and children that bothered me the most. I spent no less than 20 weeks in bed. A year later, I was out walking again – but with a limp that would endure. I have no memory of what happened on that night because I think that I had a bit too much whiskey in me! I have learned since that my life is better without drink.'

The only bit of good news to emerge in those dark times was that McGuigan won an All-Star on foot of his stunning performances earlier that year. Though he never won the All-Ireland medal his rich talents deserved, he at least has had the pleasure of seeing his sons Tommy and Brian win All-Irelands with Tyrone.

Frank's trips to America with the All-Stars did create some lasting friendships, such as that with star Galway midfielder Brian Talty.

'Frank McGuigan was a great tourist. He'd play games after having had a few pints and still go out and grab great balls out of the air. I always wondered what he'd be like if he had no pints!'

66

BIG MAC
LIAM McHALE

Mayo star Liam McHale first made his mark in another code.

'Basketball was my game when I was young. I had offers of scholarships to go to colleges in America. In 1985, I was brought onto the Mayo bench for the All-Ireland semi-final replay against Dublin. It was only when we got to the All-Ireland final in 1989 that I decided that I was really going to give football a serious go.

'That year holds very strong memories for me. My father died from cancer the day of the Connacht final. I rushed home after the game, and he died ten minutes after I arrived. The next Sunday was the Connacht final replay against Roscommon. I scored four points and had one of my best games – though the All-Ireland semi-final against Tyrone was my best game for Mayo.

'Up to then, people in Mayo thought of me as "the basketballer". In 1989, I won some of them over, but there were always a number of people who saw me as lacking the toughness that was needed for Gaelic football. I found it very strange, but for some of them I "proved" myself in the Connacht final in 1993 when I was sent off for striking against Roscommon. I struck my opponent that day by accident and was horrified when I realised it, but some of the Mayo fans thought I was making my mark at last and showing my steel. I found that attitude very sad.'

The Sam Maguire Cup remained as elusive as ever after 1989.

'I had given some thought to retiring, because I was working my socks off and tired of us always falling short before John Maughan took over the Mayo job in 1995. I played with and against John, and I really admired what he achieved in Clare. I thought he would make things happen, and he was very unlucky not to have won an All-Ireland. At that stage, I had developed into a leader of the team. I did a lot of directing of the team and was used to barking out orders from basketball. It suited John Maughan to have someone like that around.'

LIAM McHALE

It was a case of 'so near and yet so far' for McHale when he was controversially sent off in the All-Ireland final replay.

'Nineteen ninety-six was my greatest year and my worst year. They say you make your own luck, but we were unlucky. I will never get over that. I felt I had no choice but to get involved. Fellas on my team were getting hit with haymakers, and I was their leader and had a big bond with those guys. There was no way I could just stand back and watch and leave them to their own devices. If I had done nothing, I would not have been able to live with myself. If I was presented with those circumstances again, I would still do the same thing. I have a clear conscience, because I didn't shirk my responsibility.'

McHale's regret about the sending-off is tied in with his view of the way that game unfolded.

'Well, I believe the outcome would have been different if Meath had had a midfielder sent off. When I went off we had to get another midfielder on, which meant that we had to take Ray Dempsey off. Ray had scored 1–2 in the All-Ireland semi-final and was in great form, so losing him was a blow. You have to remember we could only use three subs then. If Meath had lost a midfielder too, we wouldn't have had to replace Ray.'

Many people were surprised when McHale stated that getting sent off was akin to hearing that your mother had died.

'Losing an All-Ireland final is far worse than losing any other game. When you get that far and lose, especially to lose by a point in those circumstances was sickening. We put in an astronomical effort, working very hard, but had nothing to show for it.'

After McHale's retirement from football, John Maughan invited him to become a selector when Maughan had his second stint in charge of Mayo.

'In '89, '96 and '97, we were genuine contenders for an All-Ireland. When we got to the final in '04 and '06, we were overachievers. We have seen since how good that Kerry team who beat us both those years was.'

The big midfielder tells a tale of lost opportunities that he thinks symbolises Mayo's fortunes in Croke Park in recent years.

'Before the 2004 All-Ireland final, I saw that there were great odds on Alan Dillon to score the first goal in the match. I called my wife, Sinead, and asked her to place a big bet for me. After five minutes,

Alan, on cue, scored the goal and I did a dance for joy. Afterwards, I learned that Sinead had forgotten to place the bet.'

McHale still has unfinished business with Mayo.

'I'd love to manage Mayo some day. As a player, I dreamed of winning an All-Ireland, but I still have the dream – but now to do so as a coach. I think I am a coach and would do a good job if I got the chance.'

When asked for a funny incident from his career, Liam provides a classic.

'We were staying in Maynooth College for the All-Ireland semi-final the day Princess Diana died. On the Sunday morning, I was walking down into the breakfast room with P.J. Loftus, who is a bit of a character. We were met at the door by the head priest, who is a very holy man.

'He said, "Howya Liam, Howya P.J. Did you hear the awful news?"

'I immediately went into a panic, because I feared that James Nallen or someone might be injured. He told us that Diana had died.

'P.J. Loftus replied, "F*** off."

'I asked, "How did she die?"

'The priest: "She was killed in a car crash."

'P.J.: "F*** off."

'Me: "What kind of crash was it?"

'The priest: "The paparazzi were chasing her."

'P.J.: "What the f*** was Pavarotti chasing her for?"

'At that stage, the priest said nothing and walked away in disgust!'

McHale's dream Connacht team is:

1 EUGENE LAVIN (MAYO)
2 KENNETH MORTIMER (MAYO)
3 KEVIN CAHILL (MAYO)
4 DERMOT FLANAGAN (MAYO)
5 DECLAN MEEHAN (GALWAY)
6 JAMES NALLEN (MAYO)
7 SEÁN OG DE PAOR (GALWAY)
8 KEVIN WALSH (GALWAY)
9 T.J. KILGALLON (MAYO)
10 JA FALLON (GALWAY)
11 KIERAN MCDONALD (MAYO)

LIAM McHALE

12 MICHAEL DONNELLAN (GALWAY)
13 KEVIN MCSTAY (MAYO)
14 PÁDRAIC JOYCE (GALWAY)
15 VAL DALY (GALWAY)

67

THE DOYEN OF DERRY
JIM McKEEVER

In 1958, the GAA world witnessed a shock of seismic proportions when Derry beat Kerry by 2–6 to 2–5 in the All-Ireland semi-final. The Foylesiders were led to the promised land by prince of midfielders Jim McKeever. His ability to jump and catch the ball was the hallmark of his play. He could jump so tidily that he would be almost like a gymnast in the air, toes extended and fingers outstretched as he grabbed the ball way above the heads of anybody else. Then he would hit the ground, turn and play. McKeever's mastery of his position was recognised in 1984, when he was chosen at centre-field on the Centenary Team of greatest players never to have won an All-Ireland, partnering the legendary Tommy 'the Boy Wonder' Murphy of Laois.

Born in Ballymaguigan in 1930, his love of football was nurtured as a boy when his father took him to games on the bar of his bike. The bonus of talking to him is his quiet, self-effacing warmth and the way he speaks matter-of-factly about a glittering career. At the age of 17, McKeever made his senior debut for Derry.

'I remember listening to the famous All-Ireland final in the Polo Grounds in 1947. I didn't think then that a year later I'd be playing in a challenge game for the county against Antrim. It wasn't until the following year, though, that I made my championship debut. When I was in my teens, Derry used to play in the junior championship. We didn't have a senior team then. At that stage, there was a tremendous gap between Cavan and Antrim and the other seven counties in Ulster. We played in the Lagan Cup at the time, which featured the eight counties in Ulster apart from Cavan.'

The high point of McKeever's career came against Kerry in 1958.

'I have no recollection of great excitement when we won the Ulster final. However, when we beat Kerry in the All-Ireland semi-final, the response was sensational. I remember the great John Joe Sheehy saying to me, "That's a rattling good team you have there."'

Dublin beat Derry by 2–12 to 1–9 in the All-Ireland final despite an imperious display from McKeever in midfield.

'I have no great recollection of great disappointment when we lost the final to Dublin. We were happy just to be there. If someone had told us a few years before that we would play in an All-Ireland final, we would have been absolutely delighted.'

McKeever was chosen as footballer of the year that year, much to the chagrin of some Dublin supporters who felt that the honour should have gone to one of their stars, like Kevin Heffernan.

McKeever led Derry to National League finals in 1959 and '61 – both of which they lost to Kerry – before his retirement in 1963. It is fascinating, for a player of his stature, that it is not his own achievements but the juvenile club match in Derry he watched the evening before that really ignites the passion in his voice.

Derry's first All-Ireland win in 1993 was a source of great pride to McKeever.

'It was very emotional when the full-time whistle went. The fact that all the years of disappointment had been wiped out with the 1993 side gave me a certain amount of pleasure. It was a unique occasion.'

Who was the greatest player of them all?

'It's so difficult to judge. The greatest fielder and the most stylish footballer was definitely Mick O'Connell.'

Who was his most difficult opponent?

'One of the toughest guys to play against was Galway's Frank Eivers. He was just massive. You couldn't get near the ball with him standing there beside you.'

After his playing days were over, McKeever went on to become a trainer and a manager with both St Joseph's College and Derry.

'I didn't enjoy it near as much as playing. Most times, it's two nights' training, but you've got to be thinking about games and planning ahead for them. Of course, it's a great buzz when you win, but it can be very, very demoralising when you lose and you know your team has passed its peak. I know there are a lot of people interested in administration, but it was never for me. I don't think people appreciate how much stress is on the manager – especially trying to do the job in bits of free time. Anybody who says it's easy is not talking about the job I recognise.'

McKeever has noticed some major changes in the game since his own playing days.

'I think the players of today are better than the players of my time in terms of fitness but not in terms of the skills. It takes a team five years to develop. Nowadays, a bit of a win-at-all-cost mentality has crept into the game, and only experienced players can handle that.'

Many of his happiest memories are of the club scene.

'Ballymaguigan were playing Coleraine in a club game in Coleraine. The pitch wasn't very well marked. The crossbar was only a rope, and there weren't any nets. The ball was bobbing around, and somebody pulled on it. One umpire gave it a goal, the other a point. Our umpire gave the decision against his own team. Likewise with the other. The referee split the difference and awarded two points. The really comic part of the story was that one of our best players, the late Michael Young, did not want to play as he had hay ready for baling and the weather forecast was not good. However, he was persuaded to play. When the controversy emerged, Young went up to the referee and told him that he should hurry up and make a decision, as he had to go home to bale the hay!

'I remember a seven-a-side match one evening. Before the match finished, darkness was falling quickly. We had a famous character in the side at the time who we suddenly saw tearing up the sideline with the ball. We couldn't believe the speed he was going at. We found out afterwards the secret of this new-found speed. As he was running, he wasn't bothering to solo the ball, but it was so dark that nobody could spot him!'

68

McKNIGHT MOVES
JOHN McKNIGHT

As a player with Armagh, John McKnight had few peers, and this was reflected in his selection at left full-back on the Centenary Team of the greatest players never to have won an All-Ireland medal. His football career began with street and altar-boy leagues in Newry and at the local Christian Brothers' school.

'I played minor for two years with Armagh. We won the All-Ireland in 1949. I was at school in St Pat's, Armagh, and in the previous two years, Tyrone, powered by Eddie Devlin, had won the minor All-Ireland. There were a lot of Tyrone boys in our school, and this gave us a great determination to take their crown off them. It was a very momentous occasion. The turning point of the game was when our captain, Seán Blaney, who was [Down star] Greg's father, got the ball a long way out, soloed through and put the ball into the net. As the years go by, that solo run gets longer and longer!'

McKnight made the breakthrough with the Armagh junior team in 1951 and won an Ulster junior championship medal in the same year. Inevitably, opportunities to play for the senior team quickly followed.

'I started getting games with the senior team after that. I was a permanent fixture by 1953, and in my first year we got to the All-Ireland final! We beat Roscommon in the semi-final.

'I suppose the county went wild. We were the first team from the six counties to get to the final, and that, by our standards, was a great achievement. I think that was probably the wrong attitude in a sense, because we thought, "It's great to be here," and if we won it – even better. We should have gone in there thinking, "This is our title, and let's go out and claim it." Nonetheless, defeat [by four points] was hard to take, especially because we missed a penalty.

'The ball had been kicked in by Brian Seeley, and our fellas maintained that the Kerry goalie, Johnny Foley, carried the ball over the line. The umpires didn't flag it, but Peter "the Man in the Cap"

McDermott gave a penalty. Billy McCorry took it. He was a great man to take a penalty and had never missed one before. I think Billy's attitude was that he was going to put the goalkeeper, ball and all, behind the line.'

McKnight was involved in an amusing postscript to the incident shortly after.

'I was playing for UCD in a club league game in Belfield. It had been alleged that, just as Billy was going to take that penalty, a Kerry player ran across him as he was about to take the kick. It went through my mind in that club match that I would do something similar. After the ball was kicked, I stuck my foot out, and the ball made contact with it and looped up high in the air and landed gently into our goalie's arms afterwards. The penalty didn't have to be retaken, but there was a bit of a rumpus!'

The clash between Roscommon and Armagh in the 1953 All-Ireland semi-final provided McKnight with what he considers to be his finest game.

'It was one of those days when everything went well for me. The match was on the 9th of August. The following day was my 21st birthday. We won by a point. I started off marking Michael Regan, who was drowned shortly after that. In the second half, he was moved out to the half-forward line and John Joe Nerney came into the corner. My clearest memory of the game was of Jack McQuillan coming on as a sub late in the game – because he was marking me and he gave me a clatter!'

Which game does he remember least fondly in terms of his own performance?

'I had a few of them! I remember once marking Mayo's Tom Langan. For the first 20 minutes, everything was going perfect for me. Then he started doing flicks and punching the ball away from me and set up goals and points all over the place. He really ruined that day for me!'

Why did Armagh not build on the success of 1953?

'We lost the Ulster final in 1954 to Cavan. We thought we had a better team in 1954, because we had an experienced team. Meath beat Cavan in the All-Ireland semi-final and walloped Kerry in the final, so maybe if we had beaten Cavan we could have gone all the way. We had much the same team as the previous year, but it's so difficult to come out of Ulster two years in a row. You also have to bear in mind that the GAA population in Armagh is quite restricted. There is not much support for Armagh football in certain parts of Portadown!'

Although only one Ulster medal was to come his way, there were other honours.

'I played with UCD with the likes of Eddie Devlin, Jim McDonnell and James Brady of Cavan, and we won the Sigerson a couple of times. I played for the Combined Universities when we beat the Rest of Ireland. Those were great matches, because the standard was very high. That match started to sink with the Railway Cup.

'I won one Railway Cup. That competition was always taken seriously, and I played for Ulster for about five years. I made the mistake of playing one year and not being fit because I was doing my finals. I was never asked to play for Ulster again.'

McKnight has no difficulty putting this disappointment into its proper perspective.

'Jim Devlin went to school in St Patrick's, Armagh, like me. The last time I played for Ulster, Jim was full-back. He was shot with his wife in Coalisland by Loyalists during the height of the Troubles.'

McKnight's dream team is as follows:

1   JOHN O'LEARY (DUBLIN)
2   WILLIE CASEY (MAYO)
3   PADDY PRENDERGAST (MAYO)
4   TOM O'HARE (DOWN)
5   JIM MCDONNELL (CAVAN)
6   JOHN CRONIN (KERRY)
7   SEÁN QUINN (ARMAGH)
8   JACK O'SHEA (KERRY)
9   MICK O'CONNELL (KERRY)
10 PADRAIG CARNEY (MAYO)
11 SEÁN PURCELL (GALWAY)
12 PADDY DOHERTY (DOWN)
13 KEVIN ARMSTRONG (ANTRIM)
14 SEÁN O'NEILL (DOWN)
15 KEVIN HEFFERNAN (DUBLIN)

69

THE BABYFACE KILLER
SEÁNIE McMAHON

When Clare won their historic All-Ireland in 1995 it was such a big story that *The Irish Times* devoted an editorial to it. There was one moment when Ger Loughnane came to realise that his star of that game, Seánie McMahon, was more than meets the eye.

'Coming up to the championship in 1994, we had a team meeting to discuss our plans in the Clare Inn. Seánie had just come onto the panel that year. At the time, I would have seen him as one of those quiet lads who plays away and never says anything but who wouldn't be half-aggressive enough for inter-county hurling. The meeting was nearly over, and Seánie got up. Well, you could hear a pin drop. Here was a young lad of 20 years of age, and he gave a speech of such viciousness that it left everybody absolutely stunned! The gist of it was, "Look at what those Tipp f***ers have done to Clare, and, by Jesus, this year we're going to put them down." When he was finished, I said, "Stop it now." There was no need to say another word. We beat Tipp.'

As Clare marched on to glory, Seánie – who doubled up as a lethal attacking weapon with the accuracy of his long-distance frees – established himself as one of the finest centre half-backs in modern times. He won three All-Stars, was chosen as hurler of the year and won an All-Ireland club title with St Joseph's Doora-Barefield in 1999. Ger Loughnane tops his list of admirers.

'There are men, and there are men – and then there's Seánie McMahon. You just couldn't have greater regard for a person than you'd have for Seánie. If you had a daughter, and she brought Seánie home, you'd be really, really delighted. You'd think, rightly, that here comes the nicest, most sociable, most humble and intelligent person you could ever meet. Put him on a field and that is his demeanour, but inside is the mind of a killer! He was the Bertie Ahern of hurling: the most cunning and most ruthless of them all.

'He'd do anything to win. That doesn't mean that he'd cut anybody's head off, but he would do what had to be done, coolly and calmly. If

SEÁNIE McMAHON

Seánie was in the mafia, he would be a killer. He'd be a babyface killer. He's a fantastic person above all else, and in spite of what I said he's a very ethical person, a terrific hurler and a real leader. The substance and depth in Seánie is such that you meet in very few people in life. That is the really, really great thing to admire about him. Whenever things were at their worst, Seánie always did something to redress the situation.

'In the All-Ireland final in '95, who got Clare's first two points? Seánie McMahon. When chances were going astray, he showed the way with a sixty-five and one from play. Look at all the vital scores he got from frees in the most pressurised of situations. If you were listing all the best qualities you would want in a person, you'd find them in Seánie, but when you wanted a job done, Seánie was the man. For his skill, his character, the inspiration he gave in the dressing-room, his loyalty and his mental toughness, I admire him as much as I admire any person in the world. He was a leader behind the scenes off the pitch and a colossus on it.

'If there was one example of Seánie's mental toughness, it has to be the Munster semi-final against Cork in '95. He broke his collarbone, and we'd already used three subs. I said, "F*** it, Seánie, you're going to have to come off."

'He replied, "I can't go off. We can't play with 14. I'll go corner-forward."

'All I could say was, "Fine."

'Up he went to corner-forward, holding his shoulder. With a few minutes to go, Timmy Kelleher got the ball in the Cork back line. Seánie went towards him to put him under pressure, and Kelleher sent the ball over the sideline. Fergie Tuohy, who I'd never seen in my life taking a line ball, took the perfect line ball, and Ollie Baker put it into the net. From the puck-out, Alan Browne got the ball out near the sideline and went for a point. His shot hit the post and fell straight into the hands of a Cork forward with a goal at his mercy. As he threw up the ball, out of the corner of my eye I saw Frank Lohan coming out of nowhere, and he flicked the ball away and cleared it out. It came to Fergie Tuohy, and the final whistle blew. Clare had won by a point, and that set us off to win the All-Ireland. Without that win would anyone have ever taken notice of us?'

Given the absolute centrality of McMahon to the Clare team, Loughnane resorted to unusual tactics to conceal his injury.

'In the week leading up to the Munster final in '95, there was a debate about whether Seánie McMahon should play after his shoulder injury. Opinion in our group was divided. Their job was to advise me. My job was to make the decision. I decided that we'd do something I never did, which was to have a match between backs and forwards for five minutes. Nobody was trying too hard, but Seánie seemed fine.

'The problem was we knew the first thing that would happen was that Limerick were going to hit him on the shoulder. We decided to strap him up on the wrong shoulder. Practically, the first thing that happened was that a Limerick forward crashed into Seánie's shoulder. There was a terrific outcry from the crowd, but it was the wrong shoulder! Seánie was outstanding in the Munster final.'

In his distinctive soft-spoken manner, Seánie McMahon plays down all talk of his greatness but, when prompted, reflects on his day of days.

'Personally, the memory that will stand out was when we won the first Munster final in 1995. I never dreamed of All-Irelands, just the Munster final, and I remember when we won I just went down on my knees and said, "Thank you, God." It was such a relief. There were lots of tears shed – but for once Clare people were crying tears of joy. It brought a huge uplifting for Clare people.'

70

'OVER THE BAR,'
SAID LORY MEAGHER
LORY MEAGHER

An unforgettable photograph in *Edge of Madness: Sarajevo, a City and its People Under Siege*, a book of photographs taken during the war in Bosnia, shows a young woman, immaculately attired, walking with immense dignity along a city pavement – against a background of piles of sandbags and a soldier holding a machine gun. The caption reads, 'Looking proud and dignified, Meliha Vareshanovic's dress, demeanour and action are richly symbolic.' The writer of the caption went on to explain what her action meant to him: 'Her message to the surrounding Serbs is simple: "You will never defeat us."'

A regular feature of Kilkenny's matches throughout the 1920s and '30s was Lory Meagher – in a blood-stained jersey or head bandage – making scything tackles, immune to the threat to his own safety. As his only protective gear was a peak cap, he collected many stitches, mostly facial, in his inter-county career – and lost enough blood to keep Dracula going for months. The message to his opponents was loud and clear: 'The black and amber will not be beaten.'

Kilkenny's Lorenzo Ignatius Meagher was perhaps the first true star of hurling. Meagher could not have chosen a better nor more nurturing environment to begin his career. During the 1930s, he would both feed off and fuel the fires of passion in one of hurling's greatest shrines. The obsession created in Kilkenny is the envy of nearly every hurling side in the country, and Lory was always quick to acknowledge the debt of gratitude owed to the most benevolent of patrons. He was to hurling aficionados in the county what Nureyev was to the ballet enthusiast.

Meagher won three All-Irelands in the 1930s. He entered the club of GAA immortals on foot of his towering performance in midfield – and in dreadful weather – when Kilkenny beat hot-favourites and reigning champions Limerick in the 1935 All-Ireland, having previously won All-Irelands in 1932 and '33.

237

Croke Park on a September afternoon separates the strong, the enduring and, above all, the brave from the rest. In full flight in countless training sessions, Meagher had been something to behold, and those demonstrations of his talents implanted the thought that Kilkenny might be just about unbeatable. Many a team had arrived for a final with seemingly unlimited potential only for Croke Park to ruthlessly expose their flaws. Would all the endless training sessions prove justified? Would a momentary lapse of concentration lead to a great team being beaten? Maybe the team were more vulnerable than their most fervent admirers would admit? On that wet September day in 1935, Meagher answered all these questions with an outstanding exhibition from midfield. Nine years earlier, he had lost an All-Ireland final to Cork, when his brothers Willie and Henry were also playing for Kilkenny.

In his later years, Meagher would delight in recalling an amusing anecdote from the 1935 final.

'A few days later, a stranger approached me and said, "Well, Lory boy, you did all right on Sunday."'

Lory was brought up in a very nationalistic family. As a boy, he was exposed to the beliefs of Michael Davitt, the driving force behind the Land League in the latter part of the nineteenth century. One of Meagher's favourite passages was Davitt's comment that '. . . [O]ld men have forgotten the miseries of the Famine and had their youth renewed by the sights and sounds that were invoked by the thrilling music of the camán.' Meagher did indeed make magnificent music with the camán – whenever he lined out in the black and amber.

Lory embodied the incomparable appeal of hurling, the blood-stirring excitement that takes ten of thousands to Croke Park – buoyed by the certainty that they are about to share in not only hurling's greatest event but one of the most enjoyable experiences the entire sporting calendar can offer. Lory was a great reader of the game and one of the few hurlers of his time who could actually sidestep: many of his peers seemed content, when they got the ball, just to drive into their opponent.

In Ireland, we don't like players or personalities who get too big for their boots. This was best illustrated in the 1970s when someone said to Gay Byrne, 'There are no real stars in Ireland. You are the nearest thing we have to it, but you are not there yet.' Lory experienced this uniquely Irish trait when a fan approached him and said, 'You are a great forward. You always get great scores, but you shoot the wides as well.'

Lory had a funeral fit for a prince when he died in 1973, such was his status within the game. For years, young Kilkenny hurlers chanted, 'Over the bar, said Lory Meagher!' when they scored in training sessions. His legacy is commemorated in the Lory Meagher Heritage Centre, which was opened by former president Mary Robinson in 1994.

It is said that when a prominent hurler – who shall remain nameless – dies, the presiding clergyman will have to break with liturgical convention. Such is this hurler's liking for publicity that, instead of saying 'May perpetual light shine upon him,' the priest will probably say, 'May perpetual *limelight* shine upon him.' Aside from his genius on the field, Meagher was renowned for his modesty off it. This character trait was most vividly illustrated when a journalist met him on the roadside one day and asked where he might track down Lory Meagher. The Kilkenny ace's reply was, 'You've just missed him. He passed up this way a few minutes ago. If you hurry, you've a good chance of catching him.'

71

A DUAL STAR

KEVIN MORAN

If GAA fans were to choose a sporting subject for a screenplay, they would surely choose Kevin Moran: a success in the academic world and in business and a man who reached the very top of the ladder in not just one but two sports. Moran was the rock on which so many attackers foundered, and his courage and commitment could earn him a deserved place on any fantasy team of great Gaelic footballers.

Dave Sexton's reign at Manchester United was celebrated in the song 'Onward Sexton's Soldiers'. To no United or Dublin player did the metaphor of a soldier apply more appropriately than Kevin Moran. Moran exploded onto the Irish sporting scene like a hurricane with his spectacular displays for the Dublin Gaelic football team. He almost scored a dazzling goal in the opening minute of the 1976 All-Ireland final against Kerry, following a surging run and a stinging shot that sailed narrowly wide. Moran won All-Ireland medals in both 1976 and '77. This was a time when the Dublin–Kerry rivalry was at its height. In the 1978 All-Ireland final, despite sustaining injuries to both the head and the leg, Moran played through the pain barrier with characteristic bravery, but, this time, his heroics were not enough to stop Kerry from claiming the title. How did he assess the greatest team of all time?

'Kerry were a team with so much talent that if you stopped one of their stars from shining, somebody else would raise their game and grab the match by the scruff of the neck. You couldn't single out any one player on that Kerry side. They were a team of stars. They weren't just a very skilful side; they always played very intelligently. Mike Sheehy was a player I always admired. He was always very cool, never under pressure and was very effective.'

Moran had played a few games for Bohemians in the League of Ireland in the 1974–75 season. As Gaelic football took precedence over soccer, Moran dropped down to play non-league football with the

KEVIN MORAN

UCD team, Pegasus. Ronnie Nolan, a coach at UCD, recommended Moran to Billy Behan. In 1978, having first obtained a degree in business, Moran sensationally became a Manchester United player for a nominal fee. Initially, Dave Sexton deployed him in midfield in United's reserves, but when Ron Atkinson arrived on the scene, he immediately moved him to centre-half. In October 1981, Moran made his debut against Wolves. Injuries to Gordon McQueen and Martin Buchan opened the door for Moran to win a place in the heart of United's defence.

Moran won an FA Cup medal in 1983. In 1985, he became the first player to be sent off in an FA Cup final when Peter Willis gave him a red card for a clumsy – rather than a malicious – tackle on Peter Reid. A major controversy developed when Moran's medal was initially withheld.

Inevitably, given Moran's bravery – he would throw his head and body where no sane person would go – injuries came his way. Ron Atkinson once joked that he was going to give him a part-time contract because he never finished a match.

In 1988, following over 280 appearances and 24 goals for United, Moran left to join Sporting Gijon in Spain on a free transfer. After a short stint in the sun, Kevin returned to England and became a central plank in Blackburn Rovers' resurgence over the next four seasons. Although he was 24 by the time he won his first cap – against Switzerland in 1980 – he went on to win 70 caps. At 38, he was the oldest member of the Irish squad in the 1994 World Cup, but injury robbed him of the chance to play any matches.

It is sometimes forgotten that Kevin was a great goal-scoring power the majority of them coming from set pieces when he attacked the ball powerfully to give the goalkeeper no chance. Although he was not the tallest player in the world, he was very effective in the air because of his combative qualities.

A revealing insight into Moran's character comes from his mentor at UCD, Ronnie Nolan, himself capped ten times for Ireland.

'Kevin used to come to training at 6 p.m. and do a heavy training session with us. After a while, he started to come to me about five or ten minutes before the end of the session and ask if it was OK for him to leave. I discovered later that he was hopping on his little motorbike and going to train with the Gaelic club in Drimnagh for 8 p.m. His commitment was amazing. He would turn out for us in matches and give his all even if he was only half-fit because of injury. His dedication to his sport was awesome, and everything he has achieved in the game and in life he richly deserves.'

Even when Kevin switched codes to soccer, he still retained a special place in the affections of Gaelic football fans. A case in point was Roscommon football's best-known fan, Paddy Joe Burke. One incident epitomises his admiration for Moran.

'I think back to FA Cup final day in 1985, when Man United beat Everton by a magnificent Norman Whiteside goal and myself and a few friends were seeing history in the making. Peter Reid was in possession of the ball as Kevin Moran came in to tackle. It was a red card, despite Reid's plea not to send Kevin off. Kevin was the first winning player to be refused a winner's medal when he went up the steps to collect it. That action prompted the late Val McCrann, George Bannon and myself to send Kevin a medal on behalf of the Church Street Traders Association, Roscommon town. Kevin was delighted with our response and forwarded a letter of thanks back to the Church Street Traders. And when he was next in Ireland, he came to meet us and thank us personally. A great gesture from a great man and one of the greats of Gaelic football.'

72

FINDING NEMO
BILLY MORGAN

Billy Morgan and Offaly's Martin Furlong are the only goalkeepers to have won the prestigious Texaco Footballer of the Year award. The high point of Morgan's illustrious playing career came when he captained Cork to an All-Ireland in 1973.

'It was hugely important for Cork to win that year. It was 28 years since we had last won a senior football All-Ireland, and the longer it was going on the harder it was becoming. We beat Galway easy enough in the end, but what I most recall was the homecoming. When we got into Cork, there were crowds in the station and all the way up MacCurtain Street. The biggest thing is when we turned Barry's Corner; looking down on St Patrick's Street, it was just a sea of people. I never saw anything like it before. You couldn't see the streets; it was just people all the way down to the Savoy.'

The emergence of the greatest team of all time in Kerry deprived Morgan and Cork of many opportunities for further glory. However, after winning their eighth All-Ireland in twelve years in 1986, the great Kerry team started to go into decline. That same year, Billy Morgan was appointed Cork manager. Kerry's difficulty was to be Cork's opportunity, and Morgan would go on to lead the county to four consecutive All-Ireland finals – initially losing to Meath in 1987 and '88 before beating Mayo in '89 and old rivals Meath in 1990.

'In 1988, I had thought we might be getting such a homecoming when we played Meath. They had deservedly beaten us the year before, but we had a year's experience behind us in '88. We drew the game, even though we should have won it. In the drawn game, Dinny Allen had caught Mick Lyons with his elbow and Barry Coffey had tackled Colm O'Rourke and caught him with his shoulder behind the ear. People said Niall Cahalane had "caught" Brian Stafford. All the talk between the drawn game and the replay was that Meath were going to sort us out. My own instructions were that if that was the case – if there was any trouble – stand together and be united.

'It didn't come as a huge surprise when Gerry McEntee hit Niall Cahalane. All our lads got involved in the flare-up. When it was over and McEntee was sent off, I said to our fellas, "OK now, that's it. We'll play football from here on in. No retaliation." I repeated the same message at half-time. It was the biggest mistake I ever made as a manager. What I should have said was, "Meet fire with fire, and, if necessary, we'll finish this game ten-a-side." Fair play to Meath. They beat us with 14 men.

'I suppose it was sweet, then, to beat them in the final in 1990. It was a great feeling to manage my county to an All-Ireland in 1989. It was one of the more open All-Irelands. When Mayo took the lead in the second half, they looked as if they were in the driving seat, but we got the extra couple of points up to have the cushion there at the end of the game. When Mayo put the gun to our head, we rallied and pipped them in the end. It was a very sweet moment, especially after the disappointment of losing the two previous years to Meath. As the '88 final and the replay were such tough and dour games, it was nice that both teams played such pure and positive football. Mind you, of course, I have heard it said that Mayo were "too nice" in that game.'

Roscommon's Dermot Earley got to know Morgan when they studied physical education together at St Mary's University College in Strawberry Hill, London. They won the first All-Ireland Sevens together.

'Billy was as good a goalkeeper as we've ever seen. Actually, he is the best I have ever seen. He had this mighty leap off the ground and was the archetypal safe pair of hands. In those days, you had forwards and backs all coming in on top of him, and Billy would come out on top of everything and soar through the air through the melee and grab the ball – or at least punch it to safety. He had great guts. He was scared of nothing and would go in where no sane person would to protect the goal. The best thing, though, was that he had the sharpest eye I've ever seen, which left him with such great anticipation that he could make a really difficult save look very easy.'

Pat Spillane came up against Billy Morgan as a player and as a manager.

'Any time I have ever been asked to choose my greatest Gaelic football team of all time, Billy Morgan has always been my automatic choice for goalkeeper. He was a great reader of the game, a superb organiser of defenders, an inspirational leader and had excellent reflexes – and he brought all of these qualities to the manager's job. I attribute much of Cork's success in the late '80s and early '90s to Billy Morgan. He brought a very professional approach, which involved drawing on the expertise of other experts.

'After the disappointment of the Larry Tompkins management, Billy Morgan's return was expected to be the second coming of the Messiah, but it did not work out that way. It is a great tribute to Billy Morgan that when Kerry played Cork in the Munster semi-final in 2004, Kerry fans were worried not because of any of the Cork players but because of the admiration they had for Morgan's record against Kerry down the years. Their fears were totally unjustified, as Cork had little to offer.

'His leadership and motivation are second to none. He will probably rank as one of the greatest club managers of all time with Nemo Rangers. I have heard it said that he would die for Nemo but would only get wounded for Cork. He can have a short fuse, and you wouldn't want to be around him then. He is a real gentleman though.'

73

THE STRIFE OF BRIAN
BRIAN MULLINS

In any assessment of the greatest midfielders of all time, Brian Mullins is guaranteed to feature prominently. He bestrode the Dublin team like a colossus when Dublin won All-Irelands in 1974, '76 and '77, doubling up for a time as the team's penalty-taker.

Perhaps the player best equipped to appraise Mullins's career is Brian Talty, whose name has been imprinted on the public consciousness alongside that of Mullins ever since the infamous 1983 All-Ireland final.

'I remember waking up on the morning and being very disappointed that it was such a wet and windy day, because I knew it was going to spoil the match a bit. The game ended with us having fourteen players and Dublin only twelve, but it could have been six versus six – there were so many blows flying in. Despite the extra men, we still lost, because we missed so many easy chances. The Dubs manager, Kevin Heffernan, got his tactics right. He withdrew everyone else from the full-forward line and left Joe McNally up on his own. With the wet and windy conditions, it was the sort of day you could crowd your opponents. We didn't have the tactical variation to respond to the circumstances or even the conditions.'

The boil must be lanced. It is time to hear what really happened with Brian Mullins.

'From a personal point view of view, it was a massive disappointment to become embroiled in the worst controversy of my career. That was the hardest part for me, not that Brian nearly took the top of my head off! If you look back at it on TV, you will see he really made contact with me! Brian was one of my heroes when I went to Thomond College and played with him. When I got married in 1980, Brian was at our wedding. I was on my honeymoon when he had that terrible car accident. As he started to rehab, I played soccer with him, so I knew at first hand how far he had to travel to get back to the level he did. Nobody else would put themselves through what he did to get back to the very top. I'm sorry that his achievement in getting back was tainted a bit by him being sent off in an All-Ireland final – and especially because it was for striking me. I think what Dublin did that day was incredible, but it is such a pity for their own sake that the controversy took away from what they did. It was heroic stuff.'

Talty found himself in the wars again when he received a punch in the tunnel at half-time from a Dublin player.

'There was a bit of pushing and shoving, and I was struck. The real damage to me was not that one, nor Brian's one, but after the Mullins sending-off I was charging through to the Dublin goal when P.J. Buckley caught me in the head. Having said that, after Brian and P.J. I could have done without the one in the tunnel!'

There was unfinished business to be resolved afterwards.

'There was a lot of tension the next day when the two teams met up for the meal, which was the tradition at the time. A few words were exchanged! Joe McNally got up to sing "The Fields of Athenry". I remember thinking, "Jesus Christ, wouldn't I love to kill you!"

'Brian and I went outside to the car park to have a conversation. What sticks in my memory is what – when Brian was coming towards to me – I was thinking: "I hope he's not going to strike me again!" He told me – and he was probably right – that I was pulling and dragging out of him and that is why he reacted. To be honest, I'm not sure if the talk accomplished anything. My other vivid memory is seeing the way Galway's Stephen Kinneavy and Dublin's Mick Holden, Lord have mercy on him, blocked off the car park, and nobody was going to disturb us.'

Talty is thankful for small mercies.

'Brian was teaching in Kilbarrack at the time. Before I got my teaching job in St David's, Artane, I had done an interview in Brian's school – but didn't get it. Imagine if I had had to work with him as well while the controversy was raging!'

A complication for Talty was that he was playing his club football in Dublin.

'The Parnell's fellas thought I was there just to take the clatters! A lot of club players decided to take out their frustration on me after that All-Ireland. As long as we won championships, I didn't care. It was my first year with Parnell's. At the end of the year, the club gives an award to anyone who has played in the All-Ireland during the year. There was no one from Dublin that year, so I was the only one to receive one. I think I pulled a hood over my head to collect mine! With the passing of time though, when I think of Brian now I just remember him as one of the all-time greats.'

Pat Spillane was a big admirer of Brian Mullins as a player.

'I believe the central components of success are commitment and belief, but they are no good in football if you can't kick a ball. Success as a player is due to a combination of factors: inner drive, belief, hard work and commitment. Brian Mullins made sacrifices, worked hard and was also focused and single-minded. You have to be to make it to the top. He was very keen to improve himself. We take for granted many skills we have without realising they can be developed further. Brian was motivated to become the best he could be. Of course, he was only one of fifteen, but when it came to commitment and a willingness to die for the cause, nobody surpassed Brian Mullins.'

74

CAPTAIN SENSIBLE
JIMMY MURRAY

Kevin McStay describes the late Jimmy Murray as 'the father of Roscommon football'. Jimmy had the distinction of leading his team on five occasions on All-Ireland final day: twice in 1943, once in '44 and twice in '46. When he got his first football though, the omens did not suggest that such a glittering career lay ahead of him.

'Santa brought it to me. I spent all of Christmas Day and St Stephen's Day kicking it with my neighbours. To preserve its grandeur I thought I should grease it with neat's-foot oil, which farmers used to soften leather boots. When I had it greased, I left it, in my innocence, in front of a big open fire to dry. After a few minutes, there was a loud explosion and the ball was in bits. Happily, Santa came back again two nights later with a new and better ball.'

Religion was invoked to help Roscommon win their first All-Ireland.

'Our county chairman, Dan O'Rourke, and our county secretary, John Joe Fahy – just as we were about to go to bed the night before the 1943 All-Ireland – led us in a recitation of the rosary. I don't think that would happen now.'

For Jimmy Murray, the experience was the culmination of a dream.

'I had always looked at the newspapers on a Monday morning after a final and stared in wonder at the photograph of the teams marching behind the band. Now here I was not only in the parade but also, as captain of my beloved Roscommon, about to lead it. In addition, my brother Phelim was in the parade, as he was a member of the team. When the actual parade began, I momentarily became very afraid and wished that I was away from the pitch and sitting up in the stands. I then looked up at Micheál O'Hehir in the commentary box. I imagined he was probably saying, ". . . and here comes Roscommon, led by the fair-haired Jimmy Murray from Knockcroghery . . ." My spine started to tremble, and I immediately thought of my home village and my mother saying the rosary for us, and my father and all our neighbours would be huddled together, listening intently to the radio.'

Although Jimmy tasted glory in 1943 and '44, the year 1946 brought a tale of disappointment. With just minutes to go in the All-Ireland final against Kerry, Roscommon were leading by six points, but with Murray forced to leave the pitch with a broken nose, Kerry forced a replay with two late goals.

'That was our greatest-ever display as a team, yet I do not know how we managed to lose such a commanding lead. One of my most vivid memories of my playing career is my brother Phelim telling me that the prince of midfielders, Paddy Kennedy, came over to him in the 1946 All-Ireland final and said, "Phelim, I think it's your All-Ireland." Phelim replied, "You never know. Anything can happen; there's still over five minutes to go." Phelim's words were prophetic, because Kerry drew the game and they went on to win the replay. It will always rate as my greatest regret.'

Murray's pub-cum-grocery in Knockcroghery, now run by Jimmy's son John, is arguably the spiritual home of Roscommon football – with all its memorabilia from the county's only All-Ireland successes in 1943 and '44, including the football from the 1944 final. The football survived a close shave some years ago when Jimmy's premises were burned down, as he recalled to me with mixed feelings.

'The ball was hanging from the ceiling, and, of course, the fire burned the strings and the ball fell down and rolled safely under the counter. The fire happened on a Saturday night, and when the fire brigade came, one of the firemen jumped off [the fire engine] and asked me, "Is the ball safe?" As I was watching my business go up in smoke, the ball wasn't my main priority! But the fireman came out later with the ball intact. The next day, I got calls from all over the country asking if the ball was safe. I was a bit annoyed at the time that all people seemed to be concerned with was the safety of the ball and that nobody seemed to be too bothered about what happened to the shop!'

Why was his Roscommon team so successful?

'We had great players. Donal Keenan was one of the best men I ever saw to take a free. I saw him play one of his last matches of his career in Carrick-on-Shannon. Roscommon got a free along the sideline, but it was an awful wet day. There was a long delay before the free was taken because of an injury to one of the players, and they were throwing a coat on Donal to keep the rain off him, and then he stepped up and slotted the ball between the posts. I said to myself, "That's some free."

'We also had some powerful men. Bill Carlos had legs like tree trunks. Brendan Lynch was like a tank. I remember reading an article by one of the greats of Mayo, Eamonn Mongey, which asked the question, "Who is the toughest player in Ireland?" His answer was Brendan Lynch. I mean hard but not dirty. You'd prefer not to be playing on him.'

Behind the scenes, Jimmy played a significant role in one of Roscommon's most glorious triumphs. His message to the Roscommon minor team before the 2006 All-Ireland final was taken to heart: 'The will to win is the most important thing of all. There must be nothing else on your mind – only winning. Never think of getting beaten out there.'

Jimmy's son John describes his father as 'a GAA Catholic': 'He went to one Mass on a Sunday and two matches!'

Jimmy selected his dream team for me:

1 DAN O'KEEFFE (KERRY)
2 ENDA COLLERAN (GALWAY)
3 PADDY PRENDERGAST (MAYO)
4 SEÁN FLANAGAN (MAYO)
5 BRENDAN LYNCH (ROSCOMMON)
6 BILL CARLOS (ROSCOMMON)
7 JOHN JOE O'REILLY (CAVAN)
8 MICK O'CONNELL (KERRY)
9 PADDY KENNEDY (KERRY)
10 MICK HIGGINS (CAVAN)
11 SEÁN PURCELL (GALWAY)
12 PADRAIG CARNEY (MAYO)
13 SEÁN O'NEILL (DOWN)
14 TOM LANGAN (MAYO)
15 KEVIN HEFFERNAN (DUBLIN)

75

THE OFFALY ROVER
WILLIE NOLAN

Willie Nolan captained Offaly to a place in the 1961 All-Ireland final. In front of a record crowd, which exceeded 90,000, his team lost by a solitary point to the reigning champions Down. Nolan is keen to give much of the credit for Offaly's emergence to an outsider.

'There was no such thing as a manager then, but Peter O'Reilly had trained the Dublin team to win the All-Ireland in 1958 – but he fell out with Dublin. Some of our boys knew him from playing club football in Dublin and knew he was at a loose end and asked him to take us on. He loved the idea of the chance to get back at Dublin.

'In 1960, Carlow were leading us by six points at half-time in our first match in the championship, but we beat them by three points at the finish. That meant we would be playing in the Leinster semi-final against Dublin. I had seen them play in the previous round against Longford, and they beat them by seven goals. I thought to myself, "We're rightly bunched." We beat them by 3–9 to 0–9. It was one of the biggest thrills of my life. Peter [who died in 1998] was the figurehead and was a lovely man, so we were really fired up to win the match for him.'

In the Leinster final, Offaly were unable to raise their game to the same standard but scraped a one-point victory over Laois. It was a historic occasion, as it was the county's first Leinster senior title in either football or hurling. Their opponents in the All-Ireland semi-final were Down – who had the advantage in terms of experience, having contested the All-Ireland semi-final the previous year – and, after a replay, the northerners came out narrowly on top. In 1961, Carlow were knocked out again in the Leinster championship, which paved the way for a Leinster semi-final clash between Offaly and Kildare, which Offaly won. Having accounted for Dublin in the Leinster final, Offaly then brushed aside the challenge of Roscommon in the All-Ireland semi-final. It was a victory that left Nolan with a tinge of regret.

WILLIE NOLAN

'I was sorry that Gerry O'Malley had to lose that semi-final. He was a great player and had fierce dedication. He was based in Ferbane at the time, and the lads there were always trying to get him to play for Ferbane, but he was always loyal to his home club in Roscommon, St Brigid's. He was one of the greatest players. Although he wasn't a stylish player, he was very dedicated and had a great heart and gave great service to Roscommon.'

Was Nolan nervous captaining the team in an All-Ireland final?

'If you are not nervous before an All-Ireland, there is something wrong with you. It was the thrill of my life, but I was as nervous as a kitten. Basically, all I had to do was keep the backs from roaming up the field.'

Nolan has many memories of playing with 'the Iron Man from Rhode', Paddy McCormack. The Offaly full-back has gone into folklore because of his interaction with Micheál Kearins as the Sligo forward made his Railway Cup debut against Leinster in Ballinasloe. As Kearins was moving into position before the ball was thrown in at the start of the match, he noticed his immediate opponent, Paddy McCormack, marking a line along the ground with his boot. He said, 'You're young Kearins from Sligo. I presume you expect to go back to Sligo this evening?'

'Hopefully,' Kearins replied.

'If you don't pass this mark, you have a fair chance of getting back!'

At twenty-one, Willie did not foresee then that his one chance of winning an All-Ireland had passed him by in 1961. Although in 1962 Nolan had the consolation of winning his second consecutive Railway Cup medal, Offaly surrendered their Leinster title to Dublin in the Leinster final. It was to be Nolan's last game with the county.

'Losing that match was effectively the end for that Offaly team. My great hero Mick Casey had been playing for years, and Seán Foran likewise, and we didn't have replacements for them. Offaly won the minor All-Ireland in 1964, and it wasn't until some of those lads came through that Offaly achieved success.

'We were invited to America a while after losing the 1962 Leinster final. We played New York twice. My brother Peter was playing for them. I stayed on for a few weeks after the tour was over because I had two brothers over there. I came back in November. Offaly had played two matches in the league by that stage. Tommy Furlong, an older brother of Martin, was in goal. The reverend chairman of Offaly at the time was very annoyed with me for staying on in America. Although Peter O'Reilly was supposed to be in charge, the reverend chairman had the final say – and there was no way he was going to let me play again. My heart was broken because I wasn't playing football, so I went back to America to stay. I started playing with New York.

'At the time, every county who won the league came out to play New York. In 1963, Dublin came over and we beat them. That was one of the biggest thrills of my life. Four years later, we beat the great Galway three-in-a-row side, which was another great thrill.'

Although he has many happy memories from his playing days, strangely, Nolan has none of the medals he won as a player.

'I don't have any of my medals because I gave them all away to various people over the years. When you're playing, it's the winning that matters not the medals, but as you get older the medals start to become important.'

76

A CLASS ACT
JAMESIE O'CONNOR

Jamesie O'Connor was poetry in motion. He was almost a professional player in terms of his diet, training and attention to detail, which helped him to become one of the greatest hurling forwards in the modern era – and helped Clare to win two All-Irelands. His speed – of foot, of thought and of wrist – was his hallmark, and his never-to-be-forgotten winning point in the 1997 All-Ireland final epitomised this. His abiding memories of the 1995 Munster final remain very vivid.

'People were in euphoria after we won the Munster final. Sixty-three years was a long wait. People couldn't believe it was actually happening. I remember – towards the end of the game, and as people started climbing in towards the pitch – thinking, "Jesus, get off the pitch or he'll abandon it." I thought some catastrophe was in store for us.

'With that win a massive weight was lifted off the county. Clare people had travelled to so many Munster finals – minor, under-21 and senior – and always come home with their tail between their legs. I had the cup the next week, and I brought it to Don Ryan – who lived just around the corner from my parents' shop in Ennis – who was a diehard Clare fan who had been the first fan to every match for years and years. I said that he might like to take a look at it. He just broke down in tears, and I said, "I will call back later." That's what it meant to the guy.

'There was no discernible air of tension before the 1995 All-Ireland final. We had been through the semi-final against Galway, which, in a way, is a more difficult occasion to cope with. There were very few words spoken. When the game started, everything was going grand. Seánie [McMahon] scored two great points to set us off. We were doing everything we planned. It was a war of attrition. We were blocking them and hooking them. Then, just before half-time, disaster struck. Michael Duignan came along under the Cusack Stand, and he seemed to try and lob the ball over the bar, but it fell short. Fitzy [Clare goalie David Fitzgerald] tried to control the ball with his hurley, which was unusual for him, but the sliotar skidded off his hurley into the net. It looked like the classic sucker-punch that could destroy us. If there was any fragile area in our make-up, that would undo us. Then "the Sparrow" [Ger O'Loughlin] scored a brilliant point from the sideline, and instead of going in on a downer, everyone was in a different frame of mind.

'The second half was tense. We were going well, and then Johnny Pilkington scored a second Offaly goal. With the clock ticking, Anthony Daly and Eamonn Taaffe combined to get us the goal we needed. Offaly came down the field again. They hit the post, but the ever-reliable Frank Lohan was there to relieve the danger. The ball was cleared, and we got a 21-yard free, which I pointed. Then the crowds descended on us. Every inch of Croke Park was covered with Clare people. Winning that All-Ireland was great, and it meant so much to the county, but in many ways for the team the second All-Ireland was more important, because it showed that we were no flash in the pan and that Clare were a force to be reckoned with.'

Ger Loughnane's relationship with Jamesie was a microcosm of his curious relationship with the team: a fascinating combination of closeness and distance. Yet few people are better placed to furnish a glimpse of what stirred silently in Jamesie's cool, dark waters.

'Jamesie always said to me that he never knew who the real me was. Once, he was asked, "What's Loughnane really like?" Jamesie's reply was, "Sure, I don't know!" There was always a bit of distance, that bit of a gap.

'Jamesie was often shocked by things I'd say to him or other players, and they never knew when I was going to rear up on them, but when they went out on the field there was an incredible bond between us. You'd need a great psychologist to explain the links between us. In the Munster final in '95, with four or five minutes to go, we scored a point. I was walking up the sideline, and he put up his fist to me. No word was said, but yet the message was clear.

'Jamesie is a most unusual man! After the '95 All-Ireland was over, to escape the crowd on the pitch we went up into the VIP section in the Hogan Stand and had a cup of tea. Albert Reynolds and all the VIPs were there. Neither Albert nor any of the others were interested in us. We were just a sideshow.

'Jamesie came over to me and said, "Jesus, I'm sorry I let you down today."

'I replied, "What?"

'"I was sh*t. I let you down."

'"But, Jamesie, we wouldn't be here with the McCarthy Cup if it wasn't for you."

'"I know, but I was useless today."

'He was so self-critical. That he came along at that time was such a dream. Without him we would have won nothing. He was a pleasure to have in training. What he would do with the ball was spellbinding. He was always a huge test for the player he was marking in training, even though they often did very well on him. He had this great self-belief, as had the other Doora-Barefield lads, Seánie [McMahon] and [Ollie] Baker, that no matter how badly he was doing in training he would always do it on the big day. He's a brilliant, brilliant man. The best thing I'd say about Jamesie is that if you ever heard anybody saying anything bad about him, you should be really suspicious of that person. He was always extremely popular and well liked by fellow players. At his best, he sent a kind of current inside everybody watching.'

77

THE MEN BEHIND DWYER
MICK O'DWYER

Mick O'Dwyer is widely recognised as the all-time greatest Gaelic football manager because of his achievements: eight All-Irelands with Kerry, two Leinster finals with Kildare and a Leinster final with Laois. In 2007, he marked the occasion of his 70th birthday by becoming manager of Wicklow, where, yet again, he sprinkled his magic dust and transported them from the rank of second worst team in the country to the dizzy heights of a place in the top 12 in 2009. Despite a rare health setback during the summer of 2007, O'Dwyer continued to coach the squad.

O'Dwyer's catalogue of victories with Wicklow was to swell the army of astute judges who put him at the top of the list of the greatest managers in history. For the multitude who are acquainted with him only at a distance, his reputation is based on an astonishing mountain of achievements. His place in the lore of the sport was made additionally secure by the award of Manager of the Millennium. No one doubts that O'Dwyer was born with deep reserves of obsessive will, but the most vital elements of his character seem too enigmatic to be satisfactorily excavated.

Many managers' career statistics have been grossly distorted by an addiction to the game that causes them to go on managing far past their prime. O'Dwyer, though, maintains an unashamedly romantic vision of what his team can accomplish on the pitch, insisting that they should not settle for simply winning matches but must try to fill every performance with flair, verve and originality.

Even without his successes as a manager, O'Dwyer would have been guaranteed a place among the GAA immortals because of his glittering playing career – having won four senior All-Ireland medals and eight league medals and having been voted footballer of the year in 1969.

His early days in the green-and-gold jersey were not without disappointment. O'Dwyer played minor football for Kerry against Waterford in the Munster championship and was replaced in the next match, to his great surprise, by one of Ireland's favourite poets, Brendan Kennelly, who recalls the incident with amusement.

'O'Dwyer told me that I would never amount to anything because my togs were too long! I heard, though, he told someone else that I would never make it because my arse was too close to the ground.'

Shortly after he retired, Mick O'Dwyer took over a young squad and quickly turned them into the greatest football team we have ever seen. Surprisingly, he had a major impact on the philosophy of Ger Loughnane.

'After we won the All-Ireland in 1995, we lost to Limerick in '96. That autumn, I went to Ballincollig. It was a question-and-answer type of thing. Billy George was the chairman, and the panel included Mick O'Dwyer, Jason Sherlock and myself. At one stage, Mick was asked, "What does it take to be a great team?"

'His reply really spoke to me: "Any team can win an All-Ireland, but it takes a great team to win the second one." It rang a bell in my mind immediately.

'We had been beaten by Limerick in '96, but once we started training for the '97 championship, I drove home the message that no one would ever remember us unless we won the second All-Ireland.'

Tony O'Reilly tells a great story about Brendan Behan. Behan turned up on a chat show on Canadian television totally drunk. The presenter was very unimpressed and asked him why he was so drunk. Behan replied, 'Well, a few weeks ago, I was sitting in a pub in Dublin and I saw a sign on a beer mat that said, "Drink Canada Dry". So, when I came over here, I said I'd give it a go!' O'Dwyer deftly uses that story to illustrate the need for a positive attitude that says, 'I'll give it a go.' That is the kind of upbeat mentality he brought to his teams coming into Croke Park.

In 2002, when he was Kildare manager, Micko attended a social function and met the then Dublin manager Tommy Lyons. Tommy said to O'Dwyer at one stage, 'Micko, you and I will fill Croke Park this year.'

Micko replied, 'Tommy, you and I wouldn't fill a toilet!'

O'Dwyer is amused at the kind of highbrow analysis his former protégés Páidí Ó Sé and Pat Spillane sometimes produce in their high-profile roles as pundits. Hence his love of the story of the two former Kerry players attending a Mensa convention, which, naturally, took place in Tralee. Spillane and Ó Sé were the star guests at the official dinner. While dining, they discovered that their salt shaker contained pepper and their pepper pot was full of salt. How could they swap the contents of the bottles without spilling, using only the implements at hand?

The two Kerry immortals debated and finally came up with an ingenious solution involving a napkin, a straw and an empty saucer. They called the waitress over to dazzle her with their brilliant plan. 'Miss,' they said. 'We couldn't help but notice that the pepper pot contains salt and the salt shaker– '

'Oh,' the waitress interrupted. 'Sorry about that.' She unscrewed the caps of the bottles and switched them.

78

CAPTAIN FANTASTIC
SEÁN ÓG Ó HAILPÍN

The most famous quote in the hurling vernacular is Micheál O'Muircheartaigh's observation: 'A mighty poc from the hurl of Seán Óg Ó hAilpín . . . His father was from Fermanagh, his mother from Fiji – neither a hurling stronghold.'

Because of the demands on the modern player, the dual star is an increasingly endangered species. There have been 18 players who have won All-Ireland senior medals on the field in both hurling and football. Eleven of these are from Cork, including such luminaries as Jack Lynch, Jimmy Barry-Murphy, Brian Murphy, Ray Cummins, Denis Coughlan and, famously, in 1990, Teddy McCarthy.

Folklore abounds about Billy Mackessy, the first Cork player to become a dual All-Ireland medal winner, who was also a renowned publican. An enterprising Leesider who was short of a few bob had a penchant for poaching free drink in the hostelries of the city. One day, he sauntered into Billy's pub with another chancer and, in a near whisper, asked Billy how many All-Ireland medals he had, to which the reply was 'Two.' The quick-witted duo then went to the other end of the bar and told the bartender that they were due two drinks 'on the house'. The barman gave them a puzzled look. The resourceful drinkers then confirmed their entitlement by shouting down the pub to the owner, 'Wasn't it two you said, Mr Mackessy?'

Seán Óg Ó hAilpín was one of the last great dual stars. He played at left half-back to win an All-Ireland hurling medal with Cork in a one-point victory over Kilkenny in 1999 and in the full-back line for the footballers when they lost by three points to Meath a few weeks later in the All-Ireland football final.

In the 2003 Munster championship – after getting over grievances with the county board, and with a new management team – Cork were all out to prove that they were right to strike. The only way to do that was to win something. They won the Munster title. During the course of Cork's triumphant march to the All-Ireland final that year, a new sporting icon was launched on Leeside. Seán Óg's younger brother Setanta thrilled the Cork public in the same way that Jimmy Barry-Murphy had inspired Cork to All-Ireland final glory at 19 years of age in 1973. Cork fans were bitterly disappointed when they lost the final to Kilkenny. Their sense of misery was compounded when they heard that Setanta had gone Down Under to carve out a new career for himself as an Aussie Rules player. Yet, the following year, Cork were able to reverse their form when they beat Kilkenny by 0–17 to 0–9 to win another All-Ireland.

The hand of fate is especially fickle when it comes to sport. After a single victory or defeat, the hurlers on the ditch can change their colours faster than Manchester United release new shirts. For all the benefits of leading a confident and unchanged side, Cork really struggled in the 2005 All-Ireland semi-final against Clare. With the minutes slipping away, it seemed that Cork were on their way out of the championship. The Cork fans in the stands were all resigned to a loss, even if none of them had a language that could express it.

As Seán Óg recalled, it was a real test both on and off the field.

'Even the Cork fans felt sorry for Clare. They were arguably the better team. They just didn't take their chances. With twenty minutes to go, we were six points behind and hadn't raised a single flag in the second half. Clare had scored points and were rampant. Brian Lohan was giving one of his greatest-ever displays at full-back and was "cleaning" the great Brian Corcoran. Clare's Tony Carmody was on fire and causing us untold damage in the centre half-forward position. Something had to be done. John Allen courageously took off Corcoran and Ronan Curran, two All-Stars the previous year, and sent on Wayne Sherlock and Neil Ronan. Wayne went to wing-back, and John Gardiner moved to the centre. Neither Carmody nor Lohan exercised the same dominance again. Neil scored a crucial point.

'John Allen rightly said afterwards, "We had to make the call. We would have been lacerated if we didn't. We were five points down, and the game was slipping from us. We have 29 people on our panel. I mean, it was a case of 'What do we do here?' Do we throw in the towel, or do we try and stem the tide?"'

Cork scored seven of the game's closing nine points to sneak a one-point win and then won the All-Ireland against Galway with more comfort by 1–21 to 1–16. To add to the occasion, Seán

Óg captained the team, in the process giving one of the greatest acceptance speeches in the Irish language.

Few hurlers enjoy a higher profile than Seán Óg. However, his Cork teammates have also become the most famous mutineers since Fletcher Christian – thanks to a series of strikes and disputes with the county board. The serpentine manoeuvrings of both parties down the years have been the stuff of a mystery novel, whereby every incident and comment seems to blow up into an entity of near biblical importance. The Cork hurling public have, in the main, been solid in their support for their hurlers. However, the team's player power, which brought about the end of Gerald McCarthy's managerial reign after he received death threats from a fan, has not endeared them to everybody. Babs Keating has been one of the most vocal critics of the Cork squad.

'In '08, we saw that Justin McCarthy wasn't the problem in Waterford; nor was John Meyler the problem in Wexford. Likewise, Gerald McCarthy was not the problem in Cork. The problems are more with the present generation, who have an exaggerated opinion of their own importance. I think it would have been better if the likes of Donal Óg Cusack, Seán Óg Ó hAilpín, Ronan Curran or Eoin Kelly had the approach of J.J. Delaney, Tommy Walsh and Henry Shefflin or Mickey Harte's Tyrone – because they are focused. I think it's time many of our players stopped looking for what others can do for them and started asking what they could do for the game.'

79

THE WEST'S AWAKE
JOHN O'MAHONY

Demoralising defeats. A procession of 'what might have beens'. For 32 years that was too often the story of Connacht football. Galway in 1974: what would have happened if Liam Sammon had scored that penalty against Dublin? Roscommon losing narrowly to the great Kerry team in 1980: if only they could have scored from their frees. Galway versus Dublin in 1983: 14 men against 12 and still a defeat. A match that, almost 30 years later, can only be whispered about. The video is hidden away for ever: the definitive video nasty. A sucker goal given away to Barney Rock and a series of spectacular wides, when it always seemed much, much easier to score than to miss. A story polished with repetition, no longer remembered as much as incanted like a prayer learned by heart. John O'Mahony's Mayo versus Cork in 1989: if only Anthony Finnerty hadn't missed the second goal chance.

Connacht's reign of error reached its nadir in the 1993 All-Ireland semi-final as Mayo capitulated completely to Cork. We couldn't bear to watch. Yet, like a bad traffic accident, we couldn't take our eyes from it, torn as we were between passionate partisanship and the knowledge that here was a lost cause. For fans of Connacht football, this terrible moment is fixed, immovable and incapable of being blotted out, however fervently or passionately they might later have wished for its erasure.

The appointment of John O'Mahony as Galway manager in October 1997 would change all that. Within 12 months he had taken his side to an All-Ireland final. In that patchwork quilt of a game, things did not look promising for most of the first half. When Dermot Earley scored a goal for Kildare, the Galway fans felt sick with contradictory, unarticulated emotion. They were beginning to feel an almost superstitious foreboding. Was it to be just another chapter in the volume of defeat? This was a Connacht team who could win things, but would they let the title slip through their fingers yet again? Was it really true that you had to lose an

JOHN O'MAHONY

All-Ireland before you could win one? One of John O'Mahony's favourite maxims was now to come into play: 'A winner never quits. A quitter never wins.'

In the second half, the westerners produced a display of dazzling virtuosity, with Ja Fallon masterfully orchestrating events. Heroes emerged all over the field: Tomás Mannion, Seán Og de Paor, Kevin Walsh and Seán O'Domhnaill were particularly prominent. Thanks to a stunning performance from Michael Donnellan, a bright new star was confirmed in the football constellation. The boy genius evolved into a fully developed legend thanks to his magnificent searing runs. Prisoners of hope at first, the fans from the west were both beguiled and sceptical, talking to each other to persuade themselves that what lay before them was indeed exhilarating.

The real moment of catharsis came when Pádraic Joyce smashed the ball into the net. The roar that followed was almost orchestral in its sound and feeling. After the goal, Galway supporters inhaled the air, their thoughts sharpening with each breath as though they had been drugged for years and were only now, with a jolt, emerging from the torpor. It wasn't just that Galway were winning. They were playing the kind of slick, sweet, high-speed football that would win them new fans. A wave of euphoria washed over all the pilgrims from Connacht and settled like a sea mist. To fans west of the Shannon, reared on a diet of disappointment, it seemed that everything around them was heightened, emboldened, made larger than in their dreams. Lives that had seemed complete enough only the night before now appeared to have gained an essential missing piece. For the previous 32 years, Connacht teams had known fleeting interludes of brilliance and gaiety but had had reason to fear the collapse that followed, which seemed in keeping with the proper order of the universe. Every fan from Connacht shared a common currency of bad memories.

This day was destined to be different – and glorious. Banners patterned in swirls of maroon and white were proudly displayed. All fans from the west of Ireland will now luxuriate in the memory of that day in September, and though these memories are but echoes of the actual, they are treasures never to be parted with. The image of that magic moment when the final whistle sounded is imprinted upon them – as is light upon photographic paper. This victory was all the sweeter and more magical because of all the disappointments that had preceded it. No other sporting triumph shall ever be so dear.

In an instant, all the hard-luck stories were washed away in the tides of history.

Every team, to a greater or lesser extent, reflects the personality of its manager. It is no coincidence that O'Mahony's Galway represented a fascinating combination of wit and grit, of steel and style. The victory on 27 September 1998 was not just a victory for John O'Mahony and Galway. It was a victory for players like Mickey Kearins, Packy McGarty, Dermot Earley, Tony McManus, Harry Keegan, Johnny Hughes, Willie Joe Padden and T.J. Kilgallon, who had soldiered so gallantly for so long but had missed out on the ultimate prize – and a victory for a generation of Connacht football fans who had suffered and mourned in this valley of tears.

Three years later, O'Mahony would guide Galway to a second All-Ireland. The fact that his two All-Irelands came at the expense of two of the most successful managers in the history of the game – Mick O'Dwyer and Seán Boylan respectively – adds lustre to O'Mahony's achievement.

O'Mahony played with Mayo in the 1970s and has had two incarnations with the county team as manager, the first controversially ending in 1991 when the Mayo County Board refused to allow him to pick his own selectors. Then followed a spell with Leitrim, which saw him in one of the great fairy-tale stories of football history, piloting them to only their second Connacht title in 1994. In the last generation, nobody has done more to show that the west's awake than John O'Mahony.

Despite the setback of losing the 2010 league final to Cork, O'Mahony remains hopeful.

'People often ask me, "Will Mayo ever win an All-Ireland?" Of course Mayo will win an All-Ireland. The question is when, not if.'

80

THE STAR OF THE COUNTY DOWN
SEÁN O'NEILL

Off the field, Seán O'Neill moved with unaffected grace. On the field, he was as incisive and as deadly as a meat cleaver. His absolute awareness of where danger and opportunity lay enabled him to materialise in front of goal with interventions that were as final as death.

The explosion of O'Neill's Down team onto the national stage had a unique appeal in the 1960s, when they won three All-Irelands – in 1960, '61 and '68. Armagh's John McKnight is well placed to identify the secret of that team.

'My family all seem to have married into the great Down team of the early 1960s. My sister Mary is married to Kevin O'Neill, who would be a first cousin of James McCartan. My other sister is married to P.J. McElroy of the Down team. My brother Felix is married to Delia McCartan. Down always had a few good players. They were fortunate in that they had three or four excellent players and the rest were very good.'

That team were great innovators of Gaelic football. They were one of the first inter-county teams to wear tracksuits, which aroused great curiosity at the time. One young boy captured the bewilderment of the fans when he turned to his father and asked, 'Why did they not take off their pyjamas?'

There was controversy in Down's 1960 All-Ireland semi-final against Offaly, as Willie Nolan, Offaly goalkeeper at the time, recalls wistfully.

'We were leading by two points with a couple of minutes to go. Jim McCartan got the ball and charged with it towards the goal, and some of our fellas went towards him and the referee gave them a penalty, which Paddy Doherty scored. We got a point to equalise. Mick Dunne was writing for *The Irish Press* at the time, and in his report the next day he wrote that it shouldn't have been a penalty. It should have been a free out for charging. The final score was Down 1–10, Offaly

2–7. Down won the replay by two points and comfortably beat Kerry in the All-Ireland final.'

Offaly made a tactical blunder in those games that is still a source of regret to Willie Nolan.

'We also had great players up the field. Phil Reilly was a great right half-back. Our centre-back was Mick Brady, father of Offaly star in the 1990s Peter. He was too classy for that position. He was a much better natural footballer than Jim McCartan, but McCartan was a tough man who could push him out of the way. Having said that, the Down team were superb, with some extraordinary players. There may have been forwards as good as Seán O'Neill, but if there were, there were only a handful of them, like Matt Connor. I'm pretty sure, though, there was none better than O'Neill.'

Evidence to substantiate that analysis would be O'Neill's selection as footballer of the year in 1968 (when he scored 12 goals and 65 points for the county); his selection on the inaugural All-Star team in 1971 and the following year; and, above all, his inclusion at right half-forward on both the Team of the Century and the Team of the Millennium. He was the first Down man to captain Ulster to Railway Cup victory, in 1960.

Although he did not play on Seán O'Neill, Pat Mangan is a huge admirer of the Down star.

'We played Down in the league final in 1968, and I was centre half-back on that team, and I played on Paddy Doherty, who was a great footballer. Seán O'Neill, though, was one of the greatest players I ever saw playing, and I had the pleasure of playing with him on the All-Star trip to San Francisco. He was a tremendous two-footed player with a great kick of the ball, a very intelligent competitor. His running off the ball was second to none; his vision and his accuracy were outstanding.'

Mayo's Willie McGee admired O'Neill for his genius on the field and his generosity as a man off it.

'Seán O'Neill was sheer class. I would say he was a pedigree forward if there is such a term. His Down team had great individuals and a great team. I remember watching him when I was young because he was a great goal poacher. I recall one match when the ball was going over the bar but he ran in after it and it hit the post and fell down in front of him and he buried it in the net. It was always something I had in my mind when I was playing, and people might have thought

SEÁN O'NEILL

I was a bit mad to follow in every ball that was going over the bar, but that incident spurred me on.

'I remember playing against Down in Crossmolina in a league match and scoring two goals and a point. If you asked me how I scored them I couldn't tell you, but Seán O'Neill made it his business to see me, and he was able to tell me precisely how I scored them. And the reason he admired me was that I scored one with the right foot and one with the left.'

Enda Colleran was widely recognised as one of the most astute judges of football. His opinion of a player like O'Neill carries a lot of weight.

'Seán O'Neill was the best player I ever came up against. I played on him often, but each time was different because he seldom did the same thing twice. He could feint and dummy with the ball, take a hard shoulder charge and go on to score a goal or a point. He had no weakness in his game. He had exceptional fielding ability and wonderful control. Off the hands, he was deadly accurate with two great feet. He was also deceptively strong. It took exceptional concentration and a high level of fitness to stay with him. He was never beaten until the final whistle. He took football very seriously. I always thought he was the ultimate purist. He was a complete footballer in that he had all the skills – had a great catch, was a great athlete and could kick with both feet. Above all I would regard him as a match-winner, and that is what singled him out.'

81

ACE OF FIVES
GERRY O'REILLY

Mindful of the fact that I was not around to see some of the greatest players of all time, while compiling this book I sought the assistance of one of the most authoritative voices on Irish sport, Jimmy Magee.

'Very close to the top of any list of great players was Gerry O'Reilly. He was a sensational wing-back, but the only time you'd see him play was on Saint Patrick's Day in Croke Park, playing for Leinster. That evening, people would be saying what a marvellous player Gerry O'Reilly was and how they'd have to wait for another year to see him perform again. He was tenacious, a good kicker, worked hard and never seemed to play badly. The closest player I've seen to him in modern times was Kerry's Páidí Ó Sé. They even looked a bit like each other. They both knew that the first job of a back is to stop a forward from scoring. If I was going to war in a big match, Gerry is the type of player I would most have liked to have in my corner. He was tough as teak and played as if his life depended on it. You'd always know he would never let you down, and when the going got tough he'd come up trumps for the team.'

Long before Mick O'Dwyer arrived to manage the county, Wicklow was producing great footballers such as Moses Coffey and Jim Rogers – though never enough at the one time. Among their greatest in the 1940s and '50s was Gerry O'Reilly. On a visit to Ireland from his home in Wales, O'Reilly recalled his memories of his playing career for me.

'Wicklow had a very poor team in the 1940s. Times were pretty hard then, and we had to walk to Donard to get a lift before travelling with the county team. I remember walking one day with Tony Rogers, Jim's brother, when it poured out of the heavens. My feet were so soaked that I had to wear my football boots in the car!

'I was a total unknown in the west of Ireland when I made my debut for Leinster in the Railway Cup against Connacht in 1952. The only

GERRY O'REILLY

Connacht player who had heard of me was Galway's Tom McHugh, who played his club football in Wicklow and had played on me a number of times. Of course, who did I end up marking that day? Only Tom McHugh. The game went really well for me, so after a while they switched the great Seán Purcell onto me. Seán did not last very long, because we had a clash of heads, and then they switched Roscommon's Eamon Boland onto me. He was a very big man, but the first thing he said to me was, "You're playing havoc today."'

Gerry also told me about the many characters he lined out with.

'My favourite was Kit Carroll, who played with me on the Wicklow minor team. Like myself, he was fond of a pint after a game. What was unusual about Kit, though, was that after a match he would always have an auction at the bar for his socks and jersey – and he would always get a pound or two!'

O'Reilly believes passionately that the 1940s and '50s were a vintage era for Gaelic football and is not too impressed by the changes that have taken place in the game.

'The standard is nowhere near as high now as it was in our time. In fact, it's a different game now, with so much hand-passing. The other huge change is that positional play means nothing. Players now can turn up anywhere. A right half-back can pop up to score a goal. Players are much fitter and more mobile now but in my view not as skilful. You could never imagine a player like Pat Spillane staying in the one position in his glory days. In our day, most people were firm believers in all players keeping their positions. It's now a running and supporting game, as they say.'

Gerry attributes the failure of the Wicklow team in the 1950s to the inadequacies of the county board.

'We had a great team from 1953 to 1955, with players like Andy Phillips, a great goalkeeper who played soccer for Shelbourne and could have made it cross-channel if he had gone for it. While we had players to match anybody, our problem was that we had the worst county board in Ireland. The training was terrible. They had the slowest player on the team out in front when we were running laps. I would always have the fastest guy out in front. Is it any wonder we never won anything? Those men on the county board were so incompetent they couldn't even pick their own noses!'

In terms of great players, Gerry O'Reilly ranks Mick O'Connell at the top of the footballing hierarchy.

'He was an exceptional player and a fascinating character. There was a bit of a mystique to him, especially after he left the dressing-room immediately after captaining Kerry to win the All-Ireland in 1959 and headed straight home for Kerry.'

Gerry was right half-back on the Centenary Team of players who never won All-Ireland medals, and he was one of the nominees for the Team of the Millennium. That team was:

1   AIDAN BRADY (ROSCOMMON)
2   WILLIE CASEY (MAYO)
3   EDDIE BOYLE (LOUTH)
4   JOHN MCKNIGHT (ARMAGH)
5   GERRY O'REILLY (WICKLOW)
6   GERRY O'MALLEY (ROSCOMMON)
7   SEÁN QUINN (ARMAGH)
8   JIM MCKEEVER (DERRY)
9   TOMMY MURPHY (LAOIS)
10 SEÁN O'CONNELL (DERRY)
11 PACKY MCGARTY (LEITRIM)
12 MICHEÁL KEARINS (SLIGO)
13 CHARLIE GALLAGHER (CAVAN)
14 WILLIE MCGEE (MAYO)
15 DINNY ALLEN (CORK)

82

THE GALLANT JOHN JOE
JOHN JOE O'REILLY

When listening to sport on the radio, one is essentially blind. The match's images are a private treaty between commentator and listener. The audience must fill out the game with description and information. The commentator dabs words onto an aural canvas. Through the commentaries of Micheál O'Hehir, Cornafean's John Joe O'Reilly became one of the most famous names in Ireland in the 1940s.

O'Reilly won back-to-back All-Irelands in 1947 and '48, National Leagues in 1948 and '50 and four Railway Cup medals in 1942, '43, '47 and '50. Born on a farm near Killashandra in 1918, after receiving a scholarship to St Patrick's College in Cavan he went on to the army cadet school at The Curragh, where he showed promise as a sprinter and a basketball player.

O'Reilly's career coincided with the most glorious era in Cavan football. In 1933, Cavan became the first Ulster team to win the All-Ireland. Further titles followed in 1935, '47, '48 and '52. However, John Joe would taste the bitter pill of defeat in three All-Ireland finals before getting his hands on the ultimate prize: Cavan lost to Kerry in 1937, to Roscommon in '43 (after a replay) and to Cork in '45. The replay against Roscommon was mired in controversy, as Roscommon's wing-back Brendan Lynch recalls.

'We beat Cavan in the All-Ireland final after a replay. I marked Mick Higgins, who was very quiet and a very clean and good footballer. What I remember most was the mayhem at the end. First, Cavan's Joe Stafford was sent off after having a go at Owensie Hoare. We got a point, but Barney Culley didn't agree and put the umpire into the net with a box. Big Tom O'Reilly, the captain of Cavan, came in to remonstrate, and T.P. O'Reilly threw the referee in the air.'

At first, John Joe played at wing-back, but then he switched to the pivotal role of centre half-back and made the position his own. The most famous of his matches was the 'Polo Grounds Final' against Kerry in 1947, when he captained the side, having taken over the captaincy from his brother, 'Big Tom'. Right half-back on that team was the late John Wilson, who went on to become Tánaiste.

'The final was held in New York as a gesture by the GAA of goodwill to the Irish people in America. Once it was announced, it aroused great interest in every county. To get there was a great prize in itself. The teams left Cobh together for a six-day trip on the SS *Mauretania* to New York after getting our vaccinations against smallpox, which were compulsory at the time. The fact that we were playing the aristocrats of football, Kerry, added to the occasion for us, but the fact that it was the first final played abroad gave it a much more exotic quality, so it really grabbed the public imagination.

'The pitch was used for baseball and was much smaller than the usual Gaelic pitch. The grass was scorched and even bald in a few places, and there was a mound in the playing area. The ground was rock hard, and the weather was scorching hot. Kerry got off to a great start, but Peter Donohoe was on fire for us that day. The American press described him as the "Babe Ruth" of Gaelic football – after the greatest star in baseball of the era. We had a great leader and one of the all-time greats in Gaelic football in John Joe O'Reilly, the young army officer who died so tragically after a short illness in 1952 at the tender age of thirty-four. We won by 2–11 to 2–7. By coincidence, one of the biggest stars of our team, Mick Higgins [who sadly died as this book was being finished in January 2010], who scored a goal and two points in that match, was born in New York.

'In 1950, P.J. Duke died suddenly from pleurisy in St Vincent's Hospital. Two years later, on 21 November 1952, thirty-four-year-old commandant John Joe O'Reilly – after being diagnosed with a kidney complaint – died unexpectedly in the Curragh Military Hospital. It was very difficult for all of us to believe that those two great servants of Cavan football, who had played in the county's glory days, had gone to their eternal reward so prematurely. Whenever I talk to GAA fans, there are always great arguments about who had the best half-back line of all time: the Roscommon half-back line of 1943 to '44, with Brendan Lynch, Bill Carlos and Phelim Murray; or the Cavan back line of 1947 to '48. I can still hear Micheál O'Hehir calling them out: "On the right is P.J. Duke, in the centre Commandant John Joe O'Reilly and on the left Lieutenant Simon Deignan."'

JOHN JOE O'REILLY

John Joe's son Brian recalls the trauma for the family.

'My mother was left with four young kids. I was just five when Dad died. It was very tough times. My mother was told she was not entitled to a widow's pension. Years later, I investigated on her behalf and discovered that she had been. I played minor football for Cavan, but it was hard to escape from my father's shadow. I retired from the game at a very young age.'

John Joe's status in the game was confirmed by his selection at centre half-back on both the Team of the Century and the Team of the Millennium. His hold on the popular consciousness is reflected in the fact that, along with Willie Joe Padden, he is one of the elite group of footballers who have been immortalised in a popular song: 'The Gallant John Joe'.

83

MIGHTY MEATH
COLM O'ROURKE

It was at a time when Meath and Dublin were drawing more often than Rolf Harris that Colm O'Rourke was voted footballer of the year. O'Rourke won two All-Ireland medals, three league titles and three All-Stars. However, the games he will probably be best remembered for are those that made up the four-game saga that enthralled the nation in the first round of the Leinster championship in 1991. At a time when Ireland was going through soccer mania – after Italia '90 – and when the nation was under the spell of Jack Charlton, the series of games showed that reports of the GAA's demise had been premature. Territorially, Dublin were dominant in all the matches but still ended up as the losing side. Colm O'Rourke was at the heart of Meath's triumph.

'What I remember most is the intensity of the games. Kevin Foley's goal would have been the most dramatic in anybody's sporting life. There were stages in all the games, particularly in the last one, when I thought it was gone, but we were mentally strong, having been together so long. We didn't play well in some of the games but did just enough to hang on. Morale was very good in the camp. We did very little training between the matches. It was mainly rest and recuperation. There was a very simple explanation why we emerged victorious in 1991: we were the best team.'

Despite their intensity, the four games did produce one moment of light relief. Paul Curran was dropped for the third game but came on in the second half and scored the equalising point. A few nights later, Dublin manager Paddy Cullen had a team meeting with the players and did some video analysis with them. Cullen was severely critical of the forwards' first-half performance and turned to Curran to ask him, 'Where were you in the first half?'

To the hilarity of his teammates, Curran replied, 'Sitting beside you as a sub on the bench, Paddy!'

The 1991 victory did not mean as much to Colm O'Rourke as the victories over Dublin in the mid 1980s.

'For a long time in the '70s and '80s, Dublin had a hold over us. There was a feeling of the inevitable in our camp about Dublin's victory. Nineteen eighty-six changed all that when we reversed that pattern, and that paved the way for our All-Ireland titles in 1987 and '88. We had a settled team at the time, and they hadn't, which gave us a significant advantage.

'Winning the first All-Ireland was obviously a very sweet one for me, but '88 was even better when we won the league and championship. I felt that what made my greatest triumphs all the sweeter was that they came towards the end of my career, particularly as I had so many disappointments and injuries early in my career.'

The importance of O'Rourke to the Meath side was never more clearly demonstrated than when he came on as a sub in the second half of the 1991 All-Ireland final – having gone down with viral pneumonia in the week leading up to the final.

'The year ended a real downer – no pun intended! – for me when we lost the final to Down, particularly as I missed most of the match.'

Paradoxically, O'Rourke feels Meath's place in the affections of the Irish people was greatly boosted by the defeat. The ill-tempered clashes with Cork in the 1987 and '88 finals had left Meath with a reputation, at least in certain quarters, of being a dirty side.

'It would be fair to say I noticed a big change in the attitude of people outside the county to Meath after the game. I think we won a lot of friends because we didn't crow about it or rub it in when we beat the Dubs and accepted our victory graciously and our defeat to Down equally graciously.'

Sligo's greatest footballer, Mickey Kearins, became a referee after he retired from football. He reminded me that his career with the whistle is probably best remembered for the time he sent off Colm O'Rourke.

'It was an incident after half-time, and he got a heavy enough shoulder while in possession. It knocked the ball out of his hands, and he didn't try to retrieve it but came after me. The play moved down the field, and he followed me the whole way down sharing "pleasantries" with me! I had no option but to send him off.'

The two giants of the game subsequently had another heated exchange, in the 1988 All-Ireland semi-final when Kearins was a linesman.

'There was a line-ball incident, and he felt I gave the wrong decision. I know myself now that I was wrong and he was right, having seen the replay on telly. I would have to say, though, he was a great player and actually made the Meath forward line while he was in his prime. He was their playmaker.'

Colm O'Rourke has been an analyst of the game since 1991, when he was still the best player in the country. Liam Hayes, in his autobiography, deals with the ripples of discord that were created on the Meath panel back in 1991, but O'Rourke has been an inspired choice and to this day is one of the best pundits you will find anywhere. His mind is as agile as an Olympic gymnast. When he talks about football, he nearly always seems, quite simply, to hit the right note. You cannot ask any more of an analyst than that.

O'Rourke's biggest challenge now is to match Pat Spillane's quips on *The Sunday Game*, a task he manages with consummate ease. A case in point came in June 2009 when they were both commenting on an abysmal match between Westmeath and Wicklow in the Leinster championship. Spillane was first into the fray with, 'I don't know whether the Americans are looking for any new forms of punishment for Guantánamo Bay, but I have one for them: a video of the first 35 minutes of that game, because that was a horror show.'

O'Rourke showed his knowledge of pop culture in response: 'There was more passion in Croke Park last night [when Take That had been in concert] when "Mná na h-Éireann" took over.'

Another memorable O'Rourke quote was, 'Tyrone are the Taliban of Gaelic football.'

84

THE MAGNIFICENT FIVE
PÁIDÍ Ó SÉ

Páidí Ó Sé is, along with Ger Power, Mike Sheehy, Pat Spillane and Ogie Moran, part of an illustrious quintet – 'the Magnificent Five' – who have each won eight All-Ireland medals with Kerry, and he captained the team to All-Ireland glory in 1985. In his fourteen years on the Kerry team, he won five consecutive All-Stars between 1981 and '85. However, his most impressive statistic is that in the ten All-Irelands he played in he conceded just one point to his immediate opponent – to David Hickey of Dublin in 1976.

Ó Sé's passion for football was evident at an early stage after Kerry beat Meath in the 1970 All-Ireland final. Páidí was a boarder at school, so it was not possible for him to legitimately attend the homecoming celebrations. He arranged to borrow a bike from one of the day students, pinched a brush, dressed it up as a decoy in his bed and set out for Rathmore. When he returned, the college dean, Dermot Clifford, now Archbishop of Cashel, was waiting for him at the entrance: 'Ó Sé, there are more brains in that brush above than in your head.'

Páidí is a first-class storyteller and is well able to poke fun at himself. Many of his stories go back to his time as a Garda. In 1979, after a league match against Cork, he went on the tear. The next morning, when he went in to report for duty in Limerick, he was feeling a bit off colour. He decided that the best way of concealing his discomfort was to take out the squad car and pretend to go on patrol, but, instead, he pulled into a quiet field for a nap. A few hours later, he was awoken by a great commotion and suddenly there were squad cars all over the field. Páidí stumbled out of the car to find himself face to face with the assistant commissioner, who said, 'Páidí, did you nod off for a little while?'

'I'm sorry. I'd an auld game yesterday, and I just pulled in for a few minutes. What are all of ye doing here?'

'We're checking out the venue for the Pope's visit to Limerick next September. The Holy Father'll be saying a Mass out here. We're sussin' out the place for the security plan. Sorry to have disturbed you.'

After a shift ended, it was customary for a Garda to go out for a drink. Sometimes, though, this posed problems when the session carried on after closing time. Early in his career, Páidí was dispatched one night to inspect a pub that was reportedly selling after hours. When he arrived at the premises, he was told to check it out before entering.

'I'm here now. Over,' he radioed back to the station.

'Is there any activity there?' questioned the officer.

'Yes,' he replied. 'I can hear people shouting, I can hear laughter and I can hear glasses clinking.'

'And can you hear a cash register going?' asked the officer.

'No,' Páidí replied.

'Ah, you better leave it, Garda Ó Sé, it could be our own crowd.'

In 1985, everyone on the Kerry team had their hearts set on winning the All-Ireland. None more so than Páidí, as he was captain. As Páidí was trying to gee up the troops before the game, he said, 'We really need to win this one.'

Mick O'Dwyer asked, 'For who?'

'For me.'

'Not for Kerry?'

'Well, for Kerry as well.'

In an effort to add impact to his words, Páidí smashed the ball as hard as he could onto the ground. It bounced so high that it shattered the lights overhead. Glass flew all over the dressing-room. Yet so absorbed were the team in the team-talk that not a single player noticed the incident.

Páidí always enjoyed the social side of the game. In the 1970s and '80s, winning All-Irelands had become such a routine that, as Páidí ran onto Croke Park before an All-Ireland final, John Egan pulled him by the togs and asked him, 'Where are ye going after the game, Páidí?'

Páidí went on to manage Kerry to All-Ireland success in both 1997 and 2000. His style of management was very direct. Once, his half-time talk to his team finished with the immortal words, 'Get the lead out of your arses, and shake your heads up and get out there now.'

Not everyone welcomes having a microphone stuck under his face. Ger Power, Páidí's teammate on the great Kerry team, was once asked a question in the build-up to a big match. He replied, 'Whatever I said last year, put me down for the same again this time.' Páidí has never been afraid to give his often controversial views.

The year 2010 began with Páidí starting a new controversy by claiming that if he was manager of either Dublin or Mayo he would guide them to All-Ireland titles. When pressed on Páidí's claims by the media, John O'Mahony retorted that, if he had been manager of Kerry in the eight years Páidí had been in charge, he would have expected to win more than Páidí's two All-Irelands – given the pool of talent at his disposal. O'Mahony also drew attention to the fact that, in the six years since Páidí's departure, Kerry had won four All-Irelands.

Páidí loves the characters of sport, such as former Irish rugby international Moss Keane and noted footballer Dick Spring. The pair were driving up to Dublin for an Irish training session in 1979. The two boys always shortened the journey by doing the crossword from *The Irish Times*. Moss proudly held the record for getting the crossword done before they reached Kildare. On this day, though, Spring was on fire and answering every question. Spring was driving that day, and as they approached Kildare, Moss noticed that Spring was not pressing the pedal as hard. He had a new record in his sights. Moss called out a clue: 'Postman loses mail.'

Spring scratched his head and observed, 'That should be easy to do.' He repeated the clue aloud a number of times. Finally, he asked, 'How many letters?'

Moss gleefully replied, 'Every f***ing one of them!'

85

MIDFIELD MAESTRO
JACK O'SHEA

Jack O'Shea is one of the giants of Gaelic football, with seven All-Ireland medals, six All-Star awards and an incredible four footballer of the year awards. In 2009, he was chosen by the *Irish Independent* as the greatest footballer of all time. Why was the Kerry team he played on the greatest?

'I always think of the great Kerry team as the prototype of the successful team. We had the four obvious things: we were fit, we trained hard, were talented and gave 100 per cent. We had six other ingredients, though, that made us so successful. Firstly, we never depended on one or two individuals to produce the goods. If Sheehy and the Bomber were having an off-day, the likes of John Egan and Ger Power produced big performances.

'Secondly, we were very much a team. O'Dwyer did not want to see anyone come off the field happy after a defeat. There was no point in saying, "I played well, but the others let me down." O'Dwyer always drilled into us that we won as a team and we lost as a team.

'Thirdly, we were able to handle success, and we used this capacity to motivate us to achieve even more success. We enjoyed it when it came.

'Fourthly, we had a positive attitude. Each of us always believed that we would beat our man even when we were marking a more skilful player, and collectively, as soon as we put on the Kerry jersey, we believed no team would beat us. That is not arrogance but positive thinking.

'Fifthly, all the Kerry players were very intelligent. It is vital to a team to have fellas who think about the game, especially about improving their own game, but in particular lads who can read a game and, when things are going badly, never lose their composure and who can turn things around.

'Sixthly, we had inspired leadership from Mick O'Dwyer. His man-management skills were excellent. He instilled belief and got us right physically and mentally for the big day. He also knew how to motivate us. When it comes to motivation, it is different strokes for different folks. O'Dwyer knew what buttons to push to motivate us individually and collectively. He always provided us with good feedback. It was always positive feedback, which is more effective than negative. Above all, he was a winner. Winners have critical skills, don't leave winning to chance, leave no stone unturned and make things happen.'

After his retirement from playing, Jacko managed Mayo to a Connacht title in 1993 but now does some work in the media as a pundit, while his son Aidan has gone on to play for Kerry. How does he feel the great Kerry team he played on would fare today in the era of packed defences?

'When it comes to comparing standards from one generation to another, the pundit who is an ex-player is always on difficult ground. It is easy to lose track of the boundary between proud self-belief and triumphalism. Training methods, tactics, diet and general preparation for the game have altered dramatically from when Mick O'Connell stopped playing in 1974. It makes it almost impossible to make judgements on how players from the distant past would have performed had they played in a different time. There are players, though, who would have survived in any era. They had that X-factor that set them apart in their own dreams. They had the vision, determination, imagination and, above all, the sheer skill to rise above the players around them, and great players like Mike Sheehy would do just the same if they were playing today.'

In conversation with this writer, Jacko described more in sadness than in anger an incident that nearly ended his career before it had begun.

'We played Roscommon in the under-21 All-Ireland final in Roscommon in 1978. The Roscommon fans gave us a hard time that day. We were motivated, but Roscommon were really hyped up and a Roscommon player "did" me. I ended up in a bad way, but I was lucky that there was no permanent damage. Others haven't been so lucky. It will spoil the game if the thugs are ever allowed to take control.'

Despite his glittering career, Jacko had a few disappointments on the way. When Cork regained the All-Ireland in 1989, one of their stars was John Cleary, a very accurate forward, though not the biggest man in the world. Before Cork's clash with Kerry that year, Jack O'Shea went up to Cleary and, in an effort to psyche him out, said, 'You're too small and too young for a game like this.'

Cleary said nothing until after the game, when Cork emerged triumphant, and as he walked off the pitch past Jacko, he softly said, 'You're too old for a game like this.'

Despite his prominence in the game, Jacko has been humbled a few times. A proud father introduced his young son to O'Shea in the 1980s. The son was very shy, and refused to answer when the father asked, 'Who is he?' The father then prompted him by saying, 'He's the guy you always are when you are playing in the garden.'

The boy thought deeply and finally said, 'Pat Spillane!'

Micheál O'Muircheartaigh has a special memory of Jack O'Shea.

'When you think of the Kerry team, they had great characters like Eoin Liston, Páidí Ó Sé and Jack O'Shea. I remember the Munster final of 1983 for a particular reason. Jack O'Shea was the captain, and I was training Jacko and the Kerry lads in Dublin. Kerry had won the Munster final from 1975, and in '83 most people expected them to win again. I travelled to the match with Jacko, and we had worked on his victory speech, and we were very happy with it. The only problem was Kerry lost the match because of a late Tadhg Murphy goal. Jacko's great speech was never made!

'But there was another twist to the story. Kerry forgot to bring the Munster Cup with them, and it was only quick thinking by Frank Murphy, the Cork secretary, that saved the day. He went into some press in the back and found some cup. I think it was the Cork junior championship trophy. That's the cup that was presented to the Cork captain, Christy Ryan, but I don't think anyone noticed!'

86

WILL GALWAY BATE MAYO?
WILLIE JOE PADDEN

John O'Mahony provides a revealing insight as to why Willie Joe Padden is the most iconic figure in Mayo football.

'In 1989, we were four points down in the All-Ireland final and needed a score badly. Then Willie Joe got the ball and got an inspirational score. I met a fella from Belmullet afterwards, and he said when Willie Joe scored not only did Croke Park rock but the whole of Mayo rocked.'

Having made his debut with Mayo in 1977, and still in his teens, Padden found himself playing in the National League final against All-Ireland champions Dublin in 1978.

'I was 19 and started at full-forward marking Seán Doherty and then was switched to midfield on Brian Mullins. It was a bit intimidating, but I had to get on with it. It was a very good game. I think it ended up 2–18 to 2–13, but we lost. That was a major step up for the county, as we hadn't been in a senior final for years, despite an under-21 All-Ireland in '74 and a minor All-Ireland in 1978.

'We didn't win the Connacht championship in the 1970s, but we were affected by what was going on all round us. Kerry and Dublin had raised the bar. If you were really serious about playing football, and if you wanted to be in the All-Ireland series, you went from basically two nights' training a week to four nights a week. We hadn't been doing the training that was required to make a breakthrough at national level.'

Mayo's philosophy of the game is a source of pride for Padden.

'Down through the years we have provided some very good entertainment. Unfortunately, that's no good to you when you want results. But there would be a great flair in Mayo football. I sometimes think you might be able to compare us to the French rugby team. When we play football to our maximum we are very attractive. We've always had very talented players.'

Some players' careers are defined in moments. Willie Joe Padden was such a player. In the 1989 All-Ireland semi-final against Tyrone, he was forced to the sideline with a dangerous cut to his head. In one of the most iconic images in the history of the GAA, he later returned to the fray covered in blood, his head wrapped in a bandage and his shirt splattered with blood.

'Everybody had written us off before the match. I got an injury. I'm not too sure which Tyrone player it was. He was going for a ball, and he hit his knee off my head, and I got a few stitches in it. You don't mind getting a few things like that as long as you win the game. It was our first experience of getting to a final after all our endeavours from the previous years. From our point of view, and from a spectator's point of view, it was a great period, because we were basking in the build-up to the final – especially being in our first All-Ireland for so long.

'It was one of the more open All-Irelands. Unfortunately, Jimmy Burke, our full-forward, got injured and he had to go off. That really took the wind out of our sails a bit, because he was in there as a target-man and did that job very well. We were forced to rejig the team. Having said that, when we took the lead in the second half we looked as if we were in the driving seat, but we got another injury and had to rejig the team again. I think it was that that cost us the game, rather than a lack of concentration. We were just as well prepared as Cork, so it certainly wasn't a lack of fitness. We didn't press home our initiative. When they were there for the taking we did not put them away.'

There is an undercurrent of sadness in Padden's voice as he recalls the way his Mayo career ended in 1992.

'Jack O'Shea had taken over as manager, and I suppose his reading of it was that some of the older lads had enough mileage on the clock. He decided to bring in some new blood. I felt that I still had a contribution to make to the team for another year or two, maybe as a fringe player. When the panel was picked and I wasn't included maybe it did hurt me a bit. I certainly found it a shock to the system, having been involved with the county for so long, because your life is built around training and playing. You do miss it. But the time comes for everyone to move on.'

In recent years, Padden has had the privilege of seeing his son Billy Joe line out for Mayo.

'It is nice, first of all, to see young lads interested in football, and to see him playing for Mayo is something I'm proud of. The great thing is that they are still, in the main, a young team, and the experience of

WILLIE JOE PADDEN

having played in two All-Irelands will stand to them if they ever get back to another final.'

With five Connacht medals and two All-Star awards to his name, Padden can look back at the disappointments of the past with a wry smile.

'When we played Kerry in the All-Ireland semi-final in 1981, we did well in the first half, but they gave us such a hammering in the second half that our goalkeeper, Michael Webb, said to me, "Every time I kicked out the ball I wondered would I have time to get back into the goal before the ball landed back in!"'

Willie Joe excluded Mayo players from his dream team but claims he could easily pick 15 Mayo fellas who would beat any dream team. His team is:

1   JOHN O'LEARY (DUBLIN)
2   PÁIDÍ Ó SÉ (KERRY)
3   DARREN FAY (MEATH)
4   MARTIN O'CONNELL (MEATH)
5   SÉAMUS MOYNIHAN (KERRY)
6   KIERAN MCGEENEY (ARMAGH)
7   SEÁN OG DE PAOR (GALWAY)
8   JACK O'SHEA (KERRY)
9   DARRAGH Ó SÉ (DUBLIN)
10 MAURICE FITZGERALD (KERRY)
11 LARRY TOMPKINS (CORK)
12 PAT SPILLANE (KERRY)
13 MICKEY LINDEN (DOWN)
14 PETER CANAVAN (TYRONE)
15 COLM COOPER (KERRY)

87

DAYS OF GRACE
PADDY PRENDERGAST

Although he is one of the greatest full-backs in the history of football, Paddy Prendergast had an inauspicious start to his career.

'In 1947, I made my debut for Mayo. I was stationed in Dungloe with the guards at the time and had played with Donegal for a year or so at that stage when the invitation came to play for Mayo. I had a severe dilemma, because I was very happy where I was and I knew very few fellas on the Mayo team. On the day of the game, I travelled down to Ballina for a challenge match against Galway, via bus and taxi, but, typical of the county board, they didn't think of getting me a few shillings to cover my travel expenses. I was brought around and introduced to the players before the game.

'I was selected at full-back, but at that stage I was a midfielder. On my right was John Forde; on my left was Seán Flanagan. I was marking Ned Keogh. The first ball that came in, Ned sold me a dummy and scored a goal with his right. The next ball, he sidestepped me and scored a goal with his left. Seán Flanagan shouted at me, "What in the name of Christ are you doing there?" With the small bit of dignity I could muster, I replied, "To be frank, I have no idea."

'Nobody expected us to go anywhere. Quite frankly, neither did I. We got together for collective training in Mrs Gaughan's guesthouse in Ballina before the 1948 championship. We were under the watchful eyes of Gerald Courell and Jackie Carney, who welded us into a team. They were very disciplined, and there was no drinking nor womanising tolerated. It was the making of us as a team. Living together and sharing breakfast every morning bonded us together. At night, a blackboard was produced and every aspect of the game – offensively as well as defensively – was gone into, as well as the strengths and weaknesses of the opposition. We were not the typical team for the time. We only had one farmer, but he was a big farmer, Henry Dixon. We had four or five lawyers, about as many doctors, an engineer and a priest. Peter Quinn was newly ordained at the time, and the lads exaggerated their atheistic elements just to wind him up. They were intelligent fellas who believed in themselves.

'While we won two All-Irelands, I believe we should have won a four-in-a row from 1948 to '51. We tailed Cavan by a point but were playing with a gale behind us in the 1948 All-Ireland final with three and a half minutes to go when the referee blew for full-time. I am certain we would have beaten them if we had played the full match. There was no objection, but it was savage really that this should have happened.

'In 1949, the belief was that we would win the All-Ireland semi-final by ten points. After 24 minutes, Seán Flanagan and I had a chat about how much we were going to win by. Then, inexplicably, the county selectors took off two of our half-backs and replaced them with two forwards. The Meath half-forwards started to waltz through them. The incompetence of the county board knew no bounds. Their madness cost us an All-Ireland that year. If it was today, we wouldn't have accepted it.'

The ineptitude of the selectors almost cost Mayo the All-Ireland in 1950.

'We had probably the best goalkeeper in the country at the time in Seán Wynne, and he was in excellent form for us all year. Then, for some crazy reason, he was dropped for the All-Ireland final against Louth, and Billy Durkin was brought in for him. Understandably, Billy was very nervous, and the first ball he handled, he dropped it. Seán Flanagan knew we were in trouble and pulled Billy aside. He signalled to the sideline that Billy was injured, and Wynne came in for him. Only for Seán doing that we would have probably lost that All-Ireland.

'I remember the joy was unconfined after the game. People don't realise how different Ireland was back then. We were on our knees in economic terms. The GAA made an awful difference to people at such a black time. The bonfires that blazed after we won were a sign that people could still have hope.'

Another All-Ireland came in 1951, but legend has it that it was then that the seeds of Mayo's woes were sown for the decades to come.

'People tell it slightly differently, but the core story is that when we returned with the Sam Maguire Cup in 1951, we interrupted either a Mass or a funeral and the priest was so enraged that he put a curse on the team that we would never win the All-Ireland again while any of that team were on earth.'

Prendergast was to have one more opportunity for glory in 1955.

'We had a great chance of beating Dublin and qualifying for another All-Ireland final. We were lodged in their half throughout the second half, but still we couldn't put them away. It was to become an all too familiar story for Mayo for decades to come.

'We had great characters in the team. John Forde was very serious. When we stayed in Mrs Gaughan's guesthouse, our routine was to go for a ten-mile walk after breakfast. Before a big game against Kerry, Tom Langan said he was going to skip the walk that day because his stomach wasn't too good. Then Mick Flanagan said he would not go either because his leg wasn't too good. John jumped up and said, "For Jaysus's sake, wire Kerry and award them the game!"

'Since I retired, I look at the failures of Mayo as my personal *Via Dolorosa*. At the moment, I hardly want to see them play. It pains me to see them lose games they should have won, like the All-Ireland against Meath in '96. I am tired of looking at their failures and their lack of determination. You won't win All-Irelands unless you have courage and determination.'

One aspect of modern football really bugs him.

'I hate the cult of the manager. A good manager will bring organisation, but it is 15 good players that win All-Irelands. The financial end troubles me also. Two questions I want to ask about these managers: How much are these managers getting paid? Are they worth it?'

One of Prendergast's big admirers was the late Mick Dunne. This was reflected when I invited Dunne to select his dream team:

1   JOHNNY GERAGHTY (GALWAY)
2   ENDA COLLERAN (GALWAY)
3   PADDY PRENDERGAST (MAYO)
4   SEÁN FLANAGAN (MAYO)
5   JEROME O'SHEA (KERRY)
6   KEVIN MORAN (DUBLIN)
7   MARTIN O'CONNELL (MEATH)
8   MICK O'CONNELL (KERRY)
9   JACK O'SHEA (KERRY)
10 SEÁN O'NEILL (DOWN)
11 SEÁN PURCELL (GALWAY)
12 MICHEÁL KEARINS (SLIGO)
13 PACKY MCGARTY (LEITRIM)
14 KEVIN HEFFERNAN (DUBLIN)
15 JOHN EGAN (KERRY)

88

THE MASTER
SEÁN PURCELL

The illustrious GAA writer Pádraig Puirseál described the late Seán Purcell as 'the most complete Gaelic footballer of all time'. My only meeting with Seán Purcell is a memory that will stay with me for ever. He transmitted vitality and enthusiasm like electricity. In his early days in the maroon of Galway, he was in the right place at the wrong time.

'I came on the inter-county scene in the late '40s. Mayo had a wonderful team and overshadowed us for years. I will never forget one day they beat us very badly in Tuam. I happened to be in Galway that night, and I met a great old friend of mine, Mayo's greatest-ever forward, Tom Langan. Tom was a very quiet man who didn't have much to say. But he had a few pints that night, and he came over to me, and he said, "Don't let that worry you. I played in six Connacht finals before I won one." I think that gave me heart. Before we played Mayo in the Connacht championship in '54, we decided we had to give it everything, that we had a chance. We beat them against all the odds, and after that we took off. From there on, things fell into position easily enough.'

The 1956 All-Ireland final was the apex of the team's achievement when they beat Cork by 2–13 to 3–7.

'We had a great lead at half-time, and Cork came back to us in a big way. They really put it up to us, and they got back within a point or so. We were lucky enough to get back one or two points at the end.

'We got a wonderful reception at home. I remember that quite well, coming from Dublin into Tuam. By present-day standards the crowd was not huge, but it was a great night. The match was broadcast around the town that day, and there would have been a great spirit of victory around the place. When we arrived in Tuam, I think the crowd met us and we were carried shoulder-high or on the lorry down to the town.'

Another national honour came the following year, when Galway beat Kerry by 1–8 to 0–7 in the league final. Kerry, captained by Mick O'Connell, got their revenge in the All-Ireland final in 1959, when they beat the westerners by 3–7 to 1–4.

'I made a stupid mistake early on. I was playing full-forward. My opponent, Niall Sheehy, was a big, strong man, and the ball was going wide. I could have let it go, but I saw Niall coming towards me. I said I'd get my retaliation in first, and I did. I hit him an almighty crack with my forearm across the head, and he got in under me, and he put me up in the air. I really thought I had killed him, but when I looked up all he did was shake his head a few times and trot away. It was a bad start, a foolish mistake, and after that we were well beaten. We didn't really make much of a show. The lads did their best, all right, but we just weren't good enough that day.'

Purcell's final championship game in the Galway shirt witnessed an incident that has become part of GAA folklore. In the 1962 Connacht final, Roscommon trailed Galway by five points with less than ten minutes to go – and looked like a beaten side. A Galway forward took a shot and put his team six points up. As the ball was cutting like a bullet over the crossbar, the Roscommon goalie, the late Aidan Brady, a big man, jumped up and hung on the crossbar – and it broke.

'There was a lengthy delay until a new crossbar was found. The delay disrupted our rhythm and allowed Roscommon to snatch victory from the jaws of defeat, thanks to a vintage display from Gerry O'Malley. I remember talking to Gerry while we were waiting for them to fix the crossbar. He said to me, "It's probably gone from us. We can't turn it around now." Then he went to midfield, and they got two goals to tie things up. When they equalised, Gerry ran over to the Roscommon fans who were on the sideline and asked them how much time was left. They said that time was up. He won the ball and put Des Feeley through for the winning point.'

Seán Purcell's name, good nature and face live on in his son John, who himself played championship football for Galway in 1985. With a twinkle in his eye, John recalls his father's mischievous nature.

'Daddy had a great capacity to become friends with a large section of people. Seán Óg Ó hAilpín was just one of the people who visited him in hospital. He became very friendly with the Dublin team of the 1970s through his role in managing the All-Stars, especially with Tony Hanahoe. They have a charity function every year and present hall of

SEÁN PURCELL

fame-style awards. The night before Dad died, they were presenting
Martin O'Neill and himself with an award and I was accepting it on
his behalf. I asked him, had he any message for them? He replied,
"Tell them, before I got to know them I thought they were a crowd
of f***ers, but once I got to know them I didn't think they were too
bad!" I said a softer version of that on the night!

'One time, he was collecting an award himself up north and the
MC was going on and on about how great a player Daddy had been.
Daddy grabbed the microphone off him in mid-flow and said, "Don't
think I'm that famous. I ran for election once. Both John Donnellan and
I were running for Fine Gael for the one seat in 1965. I barely got my
deposit back – and was lucky to get even that – and John was easily
elected. As I was leaving the count centre, crestfallen, a woman called
me over and said, 'Don't worry, Seánin, there'll be another day. Isn't
it a pity you didn't play a bit of football?'"'

I asked Seán to select the greatest team of players he had seen since
he retired from the game. It was:

1   JOHNNY GERAGHTY (GALWAY)
2   ENDA COLLERAN (GALWAY)
3   NOEL TIERNEY (GALWAY)
4   TOM O'HARE (DOWN)
5   JOHN DONNELLAN (GALWAY)
6   GERRY O'MALLEY (ROSCOMMON)
7   MARTIN NEWELL (GALWAY)
8   MICK O'CONNELL (KERRY)
9   JACK O'SHEA (KERRY)
10 DERMOT EARLEY (ROSCOMMON)
11 MICHEÁL KEARINS (SLIGO)
12 PAT SPILLANE (KERRY)
13 TONY MCTAGUE (OFFALY)
14 SEÁN O'NEILL (DOWN)
15 MIKE SHEEHY (KERRY)

89

THE YELLOW BELLIES
MARTIN QUIGLEY

Martin Quigley was born into a hurling mixed marriage. His mother had virtually no interest in the game while his father was fanatical in his devotion.

'I remember as a kid going to a lot of matches with him. That's where we got our enthusiasm from. Once, he invited a referee to the line to have a fight with him. In his later years, he had to give up going to matches. He used to get totally worked up, which wasn't very good for him.

'My earliest hurling memory goes back to 1960, when I was nine years of age, listening to the great Micheál O'Hehir commentating on the All-Ireland hurling final when Wexford beat Tipperary – although Tipp had been strong favourites. I think he had an unmerciful bearing on my development as a player through his commentaries.'

In the course of Quigley's career, he won four consecutive All-Stars – between 1973 and '76 – and was chosen at centre half-forward on the Centenary Team of greatest players never to have won an All-Ireland. In 1970, during the first 80-minute All-Ireland final, he was part of a unique piece of family history when he and his brothers Pat and John formed an all-Quigley half-forward line as Wexford lost to Cork. To add to the family connection, another brother, 'Big Dan', was selected at centre-back. For Quigley, the downside to a career of longevity has been that he literally wears the scars of his escapades.

'In a league match against Offaly, I was hit on the back of my head as I went for a dropping ball. At half-time, our mentors examined it and I had nine stitches inserted without any anaesthetic. I just clinched my teeth and braced myself. When the question was raised if I was fit to continue, it was said, "He's a hardy young fellow, and he'll be all right." Out I went for the second half, when it was the last place I should have gone.'

MARTIN QUIGLEY

After he retired, he immediately took charge of piloting Wexford's fortunes. His new role was no bed of roses.

'Managing is not nearly as enjoyable as playing. When you are playing you only have to worry about your own job, but when you're the manager you have to worry about everybody else. There are so many things outside your control as a manager – from players getting injured to a bad referee's decisions, which can cost you a game – that you can feel powerless. Once I retired as a player, I missed the buzz of it, and I got involved in managing Wexford almost immediately. With the benefit of hindsight, I should have taken a break from the game and turned to management later, but while hindsight is great, it's not any good when you have to make a decision. I should have given myself a bit of distance from the switch from playing to managing. It's hard to have a clear perspective when emotionally you're too close to the centre of things.'

How would he assess his own term in charge of Wexford?

'I'm not the best person to judge. Ultimately, a manager is judged by results. In my three years in charge, we got to two league finals, but we won nothing. I suppose, though, any manager is only as good as the players he has at his disposal.'

There was media speculation that Quigley might be tempted back to the role of Wexford manager in 1999.

'No way. I don't think people appreciate the sacrifices that are involved or the time commitment that is required. I don't want to offend teachers, but maybe if I had a lot of free time like them I might be interested – but not when I am self-employed [in his accountancy practice]. The pressures are getting stronger all the time, partly because of the media. Even since I stepped down in 1991 as county trainer with Wexford, the pressure has increased enormously.

'One dimension of it is that the level of fitness required now is awesome. In the 1970s, fitness levels in football were stepped up dramatically by Dublin and Kerry. Sooner or later, all the other counties and clubs followed suit. When Clare came on the scene in 1995, they raised fitness levels in hurling to a new high. Very quickly, other counties and clubs responded in the same way, with heavy training programmes over the winter and so on. The demands on players now and on their social lives are incredible. I can't see how players can get any more fit, and I shudder to think that any more can be asked of them or their trainers.'

Kilkenny players are selected as his most difficult opponents.

'Frank Cummins and Ger Henderson stand out. Frank was Mr Consistency. I'd say the amount of bad games he had in his long career could be counted on one hand. He was not the most skilful player in the world. You couldn't have stuck him in at corner-forward or at wing-back the way you could with a lot of stylish midfielders. He was very strong and competitive and always gave 110 per cent. He really dictated things from the centre of the field. The only player I've seen like him in recent years was Clare's Ollie Baker.

'Ger had a lot of the same qualities as Frank did. He was very tenacious and wholehearted and gave everything he had for the black and amber. Fan Larkin is another I must mention. We had many a tough battle against one another, but he's a great character.'

Asked whom he considers to be the greatest hurler never to win an All-Ireland final, Quigley was reluctant to narrow it down to just one.

'To come at it from a different angle, I would say that my sympathy is not so much for players who never won an All-Ireland medal as those who never got the recognition they deserved. I think especially of Paddy Quirke of Carlow. He played with me on the Leinster team, but because he was with a weaker county he never got another stage to show off his talents. If he had been with one of the big powers in hurling, he would have been a household name. You need to play at the highest level all the time to develop your talents to the fullest, and that's another way players from the weaker counties lose out.'

Quigley prefaced his dream team selection by saying that he chose one player even though he never saw him playing.

'I heard so much about Mick Mackey that he must have been a giant among men. That's why I feel I must select him at centre-forward.'

His team is:

1 NOEL SKEHAN (KILKENNY)
2 FAN LARKIN (KILKENNY)
3 PAT HARTIGAN (LIMERICK)
4 EUGENE COUGHLAN (OFFALY)
5 GER HENDERSON (KILKENNY)
6 SEÁN SILKE (GALWAY)
7 IGGY CLARKE (GALWAY)
8 FRANK CUMMINS (KILKENNY)

MARTIN QUIGLEY

9   JOHN CONNOLLY (GALWAY)
10 FRANCIS LOUGHNANE (TIPPERARY)
11 MICK MACKEY (LIMERICK)
12 EDDIE KEHER (KILKENNY)
13 KIERAN PURCELL (KILKENNY)
14 RAY CUMMINS (CORK)
15 SEÁNIE O'LEARY (CORK)

90

THE MIGHTY QUINN
BILLY QUINN

Tipperary came to Croke Park that day armed with a secret weapon in the form of a young full-forward named Billy Quinn. This young hurler's three brilliant goals have literally made him the talk of Ireland's hurling circles. His two goals scored in the first half, mark you he was marked by that prince of hurling full-backs 'Diamond' Hayden who was in sparkling form, were masterpieces of anticipation and execution. They made Kilkenny's task in the second half a well nigh impossible one. His goal after the interval put Kilkenny down for the final count. Undoubtedly this was Billy Quinn's day, and this League final will always be associated with his name. There is every reason that this young star will go from strength to strength.

The *Irish Press* match report after the National League final in 1954. The May sky was bursting with dark, sultry clouds, and the green sod was slippery after a morning of heavy rain as raging-hot favourites Kilkenny took on Tipperary in the final. A star was born that day, as Billy Quinn's performance was the key factor in Tipp's 3–10 to 1–4 victory. A member of the Rahealty club but a native of Rossestown, a couple of miles east of Thurles, Quinn was a prodigious talent as a youngster. He attributes much of his success to his coach at Thurles CBS, a Limerick man, Brother Doody. Genetics also played its part.

'An uncle of mine, Jack, captained the first Harty Cup-winning team, and there was a lot of hurling in the family.'

Billy Quinn had the rare distinction of making his inter-county debut in an All-Ireland final.

'I played for four years on the Tipperary minors. When I was 14, I was brought on as a sub in the All-Ireland final against Kilkenny in 1950. Tipperary had won all their matches up to then by a cricket score. So I never had got a chance to come on and get used to the thing. It was crazy to bring me on for my first match in an All-Ireland final, because I had no idea where I was or what I was doing.'

He won his second minor All-Ireland medal in 1953, when he captained the team and one of his teammates was his brother Dick. Billy was a bit blasé about it all.

'There was no real pressure on me as captain. All I had to do was to call the toss and collect the cup! The only work I had to do was before the All-Ireland final, when our goalie got a panic attack on the way out. The lads called me back, and I got him back up against the wall of Hill 16. He was more afraid of me than of the opposition, and he went out and played a blinder.

'We were so used to winning that I got the cup and threw it somewhere else and we went home. There was no celebration as such. The big thing was to win the Munster final. There was a massive crowd at the Munster final then. When you came out of the ground, your feet would hardly touch the road because there'd be so many people.

'The big thrill was to be hanging around with the senior team. The Munster final in Killarney was a classic match, though I'd an awful experience when a Cork man dropped dead beside me with the excitement of the match. The crowd invaded the pitch a few times, and Christy Ring had to escort the referee off the pitch.'

A decade previously, such had been the intensity of one Tipperary–Cork match that a man had had to be anointed on the ground. The entire crowd knelt down as a mark of respect.

Within months of captaining Tipperary to the All-Ireland minor title, Billy was making his senior debut.

'My first senior match was against Laois. It was in the middle of winter and not a suitable day for hurling. All I remember from the match is that we got a 21-yard free. It was blocked down, but I ran in and put the sliotar in the net. The referee disallowed it. To this day I don't know why. I was disgusted.'

Unfortunately, Billy's inter-county career coincided with a barren spell in Tipperary's fortunes in the championship.

'We played Cork in 1956, and Seamus Bannon got the best goal I ever saw. He ran down the wing and lashed the ball in the net, but one of our lads threw his hurley twenty yards in celebration and the referee disallowed the goal – and Cork beat us. It was the greatest injustice I ever saw in hurling. We got dog's abuse listening in to the All-Ireland in Thurles that year because everyone was saying, "Ye should be there if you were any good."'

The year 1956 would be Billy's last in the Tipperary colours. A taxing job in Boland's bakery in Dublin, where he worked six days a week from 7 a.m. to 10 p.m., restricted the commitment he could give to hurling. Although he played club hurling for Faugh's, it was not conducive to keeping the attention of the Tipperary selectors. While he played a few games for Dublin, his commitment to their cause was not total, because there was always talk that he was on the verge of a recall to the Tipp side. This indecision cost him the opportunity to play in an All-Ireland senior final.

'Dublin had a great team then, with exceptional players like Lar Foley, Des Foley and Des Ferguson. I thought I was going to go back playing for Tipperary, but I'm half sorry I didn't pursue the opportunity to play for Dublin more. They only lost the All-Ireland to Tipperary by a point in 1961.'

Ireland's World Cup clash with Holland in 1990 marked a restoration of the fortunes of Billy's son Niall, as he scored the crucial equaliser in response to Ruud Gullit's goal and secured Ireland's passage into the knockout phases of the competition. The gloss was taken off the occasion somewhat when a burglar raided their house as the family went out to celebrate – in the process stealing Niall's mother's bracelet, the most prominent feature of which were Billy's two All-Ireland minor medals. Like his father before him, Niall played in an All-Ireland minor hurling final – for Dublin against Galway in 1983. Despite his pride at Niall's great success in soccer, Billy still feels the game is no match for hurling.

'I put my foot in it in 1990 when a journalist came to interview me about Niall after he scored the goal against Holland. When he asked me if I was proud of him, I said, without thinking, "To tell you the truth, I'd rather he had won a Munster medal!"'

The family, though, would suffer from young Niall's early interest in Ireland's national game.

'Niall always had a hurley in his hand when he was young. One famous day in Killarney, Babs [Keating] scored a last-minute goal from a free. That was the day when Donie Nealon came on with a towel and was supposed to have switched the ball and swapped a wet one for a dry one to make it easier for Babs to score. Niall was about five at the time, so he was practising frees in the back garden after the match, and my wife, Mary, was doing the ironing when the window was shattered to smithereens by Niall's sliotar. Mary nearly dropped dead with the shock of the shattering glass. All Niall said afterwards was, "I was only doing Babs Keating!"'

91

QUIRKE OF FATE
PADDY QUIRKE

Paddy Quirke hurled for Carlow at senior level from 1974 to '90, and – disproving former Tipperary great Tony Wall's adage that 'Football is a game for those not good enough to play hurling' – he played senior football with the county from 1974 to '87. Quirke played in 31 senior county finals: hurling, football and replays. He played 106 times for the Carlow hurling team.

One of Quirke's clubmates, Tom Foley, was the trainer of the famous racehorse Danoli.

'Tom Foley played wing-back and centre-field. He was a very good character and is a very determined man. Now when you meet him he is much more likely to talk about hurling rather than horses.'

Quirke played for the Leinster football team in both 1979 and '81 and for the Leinster hurling side in four consecutive years between 1978 and '81. Which experience did he enjoy the most?

'I preferred playing most for the hurlers, because I felt more like I was on a par with them than with the footballers. I think I was just one of the lads with them, but it was a bit more difficult with the footballers. In 1979, I played in the Railway Cup final in Thurles against Connacht. I was playing in my favourite position, midfield, along with Ger Henderson. Fan Larkin was the captain. I was marking John Connolly. At that stage, I feared no one, and I could mix it with the best. I was playing with the best in Leinster – Tony Doran, Frank Cummins, Noel Skehan, Martin Quigley, Pat Carroll, Mark Corrigan, Peadar Carton – and enjoying it.'

Hurling was Quirke's passport to San Francisco.

'I played a few games out there, and it was really tough and physical. At one stage, I put in my hurley – angled with the bos to the ground – to block an opponent, got a severe belt across the face, was taken off course and rushed to hospital. I had no social-security cover, but my friends who were with me decided I was Patrick Foley [a genuine holder of social security]. So, all of a sudden, I was somebody else. The only problem was, when I heard the name Patrick Foley being called out in the hospital I forgot that was supposed to be me and had to be reminded who I then was!

'At that stage, I was not in very good shape and was expecting some sympathy from the doctor. Instead, all he said was, "Were you playing that crazy Irish game?"'

The highlight of Quirke's career came in 1990 when he was chosen as the dual All-Star replacement. He played for most of the football game against Kerry after injury to Roscommon's Dermot Earley and marked Eoin Liston. At the banquet after the game, he was shocked to discover that he had been chosen as man of the match.

As Paddy takes a nostalgic trip down sport's memory lane, one football game lives vividly in his consciousness.

'In 1985, we qualified for the National League quarter-final and lost to Armagh in Croke Park, but the game that stands out for me for Carlow was playing against Kerry in the Centenary tournament in 1984. The county grounds were packed. I remember Lar Molloy holding Pat Spillane scoreless and taking a fine point himself. We ran them very close, and I was marking Jack O'Shea. Mike Sheehy got the vital scores for Kerry in the end. It was obvious that Carlow had lots of potential. Vincent Harvey was training us at the time, and one of his favourite chants was, "Get the ball in around the blue grass area." Kevin Madden was on the team then but is now living in New York. He sent me a Christmas card a couple of years ago, and the PS was, "Quirke, I'm still looking for the blue grass area."'

Paddy experienced some major frustrations during his career.

'Winning our only football title in 1986 and achieving a rare Double was a career highlight for me. In '87, we were going for the Double again. Éire Óg were the opposition. We were playing great football halfway through the second half when a bizarre thing happened. Seán Kelly, the referee, gave Éire Óg a free. Just after he blew the whistle, I could see an Éire Óg supporter running towards him. She had a flagpole in her hand. I tried to bring it to the ref's attention. He thought I was complaining about the free, so he ushered me away. The next second, he was floored by a blow from the flagpole. The game was held up for five minutes. We lost the game by the minimum 2–9 to 2–8.'

Who was the greatest character he ever played with or against?

'There were a lot of them. I played a shinty match for Ireland against Scotland on the Isle of Man in 1979, and one of my teammates was Limerick's Pat Hartigan. He was really a great character and mighty craic.

'The late James Doyle, "the Jigger", from my own club was a great character. In 1985, we played the Westmeath champions Brownstown away in the first round of the Leinster club hurling championship. This was a hard-fought game and a great victory for Naomh Eoin. The Jigger was asked a few days later how bad the pitch was. He replied, "Well, the grass was so long a hare rose at half-time!"'

Quirke's dream football team is:

1   MARTIN FURLONG (OFFALY)
2   ROBBIE O'MALLEY (MEATH)
3   JOHN O'KEEFFE (KERRY)
4   NIALL CAHALANE (CORK)
5   PAÍDÍ Ó SÉ (KERRY)
6   KEVIN MORAN (DUBLIN)
7   MARTIN O'CONNELL (MEATH)
8   BRIAN MULLINS (DUBLIN)
9   JACK O'SHEA (KERRY)
10 MATT CONNOR (OFFALY)
11 LARRY TOMPKINS (CORK)
12 PAT SPILLANE (KERRY)
13 COLM O'ROURKE (MEATH)
14 PETER CANAVAN (TYRONE)
15 MIKE SHEEHY (KERRY)

He also picked the hurling team he would have liked to have played on:

1   NOEL SKEHAN (KILKENNY)
2   AIDAN FOGARTY (OFFALY)
3   PAT HARTIGAN (LIMERICK)
4   JOHN HORGAN (CORK)
5   MICK JACOB (WEXFORD)
6   GER HENDERSON (KILKENNY)
7   IGGY CLARKE (GALWAY)
8   FRANK CUMMINS (KILKENNY)
9   PADDY QUIRKE (CARLOW)
10 JOHNNY CALLINAN (CLARE)

PADDY QUIRKE

11 MARTIN QUIGLEY (WEXFORD)
12 JOHN FENTON (CORK)
13 ÉAMONN CREGAN (LIMERICK)
14 TONY DORAN (WEXFORD)
15 EDDIE KEHER (KILKENNY)

92

THE PURPLE AND GOLD
NICKY RACKARD

From the dawn of time, identification with heroes has been an integral part of the human condition. Great sporting performances have always grabbed the imagination of the young as they fantasise about emulating the glorious feats of their idols. Thanks in no small part to television, sports stars occupy an even larger part of the imagination today than in earlier generations.

Even the most casual of hurling fans took vicarious pride in the style, craft, courage and character shown in the performances of Nicky Rackard, which were among the finest creative manifestations of our popular culture. As Liam Griffin put it so memorably, 'In a land without royalty, the Rackards were kings.'

Few families have had as big an impact on hurling as the Rackards. Nicky's status as one of the greatest full-forwards in the history of the game was reflected in his selection in that position on the Team of the Century, while his brother Bobby was picked at right corner-back on both the Team of the Century and Team of the Millennium. Meanwhile, their younger brother Billy won three All-Ireland medals. Traditionally, only Christy Ring and Mick Mackey have been placed ahead of Nicky Rackard in hurling's hierarchy of greats.

Rackard was one of the most colourful characters hurling has ever known and changed the whole sporting – and, to some extent, even the social – structure of Wexford. He went to St Kieran's College in Kilkenny and there developed a love for hurling that he brought home to his brothers and to his club, Rathnure. Wexford had traditionally been a football power – going back to their famous four-in-a-row side of 1915 to '18 – but Nicky Rackard turned Wexford into a recognised hurling bastion almost overnight. He was crucial to Wexford's two All-Irelands in 1955 and '56. In the 1954 All-Ireland semi-final against Antrim, he scored an incredible seven goals and seven points.

The 1956 All-Ireland final between Cork and Wexford was one of Rackard's happiest memories and is acknowledged as one of the greatest hurling finals of them all. In the build-up, the media had been fixated by the possibility of a historic occasion, as Christy Ring was seeking a record ninth All-Ireland medal. The game will always be remembered above all for Art Foley's save from Ring. It was a match that captured the imagination like few others. Tradition favoured Cork: going into the game, they had won twenty-two titles against Wexford's two. Such was the interest in Wexford that two funerals scheduled for the day of the final had to be postponed until the following day because the hearses were needed to transport people to the match! Over 83,000 people attended. The final had to be delayed until 23 September because of a polio scare in Cork: the authorities did not want a huge crowd assembling in one place.

The crucial contest was that between Christy Ring, playing at left corner-forward, and Bobby Rackard. It was the Wexford man who would win out – in every sense. Wexford had the advantage of a whirlwind start with a goal from Padge Keogh after only three minutes. Two minutes later, Ring registered Cork's first score with a point from a twenty-one-yard free. Wexford went on to win by 2–14 to 2–8.

Significantly, that Wexford team had a special place in Christy Ring's affections.

'I always loved our clashes with Wexford in Croke Park. It's a different climate in Croke Park, because you didn't have the pressure of the Munster championship on your back. It was the same for Wexford: they didn't have the pressure of beating Kilkenny on them. Both of us could relax a bit.'

Rackard's success bred jealousy and the full glare of media intrusion. Mercifully, he was no paragon. There were times when he sought solace in the bottom of a bottle. After his playing days had ended, Nicky went through a turbulent time with alcoholism, but, true to form, he rallied and drew on his own darkness to bring light to others with the same condition when he became a counsellor with Alcoholics Anonymous. He died in 1975 at the age of 53. The knowledge that we had lost him too early generated a sense of sadness that far exceeded anything that would have been felt for any politician or media personality.

Nicky Rackard was more than a hurler; he added the intangible qualities of magic and mystique, which preserved the sense of continuity with the glories of the game's hallowed past. The most moving tribute to this extraordinary man, though, were the tears at his funeral from those who had never met him but felt they knew him as a friend: a poignant, and appropriate, homage to a man who embodied the virtue of total commitment. It has been said, 'Be ashamed to die until you have won some victory for humanity.' When Nicky meets his maker on the ship of eternal life, bound for the shores of promise, he need not have any worries on that score.

Nicky Rackard revealed a few flaws during his life. But perhaps these add to rather than detract from his popularity. George Michael, in a moment of exceptional, perhaps surprising, psychological insight, said that a star is not a person who has a little bit extra but someone who has a little bit missing. Evidence to support this analysis can be found in the icons of the twentieth century, the ones who keep you staring into the television screen or the newspaper image long after it is necessary to look, who dazzle you with the life and radiance in their faces even though you know they are dead – such as Evita, Elvis Presley, Marilyn Monroe and James Dean. It is perhaps significant that Ireland's favourite sporting hero over the last generation has been Paul McGrath, a footballer of sublime skill and a wonderful human being with a few blemishes.

Nicky was a very resourceful man. During the 'Ban', he joined what was, in effect, a vigilante committee of the GAA – to protect its 'cultural purity'. In his official capacity, he went to rugby and soccer matches to check if any GAA players were in attendance, which enabled him to break the Ban with the official sanction of the GAA!

Nicky Rackard's story would have made Aristotle leap about in his sandals, it is such a brilliant illustration of the classic precepts of tragedy: the hero with a flaw and the audience torn between awe and pity. He became one of Ireland's favourite sporting heroes because, in some way, he was a mirror of our inner selves. Hurling owes a deep debt to Nicky Rackard and his brothers, who injected an exhilarating new dimension into the sport.

93

RUNAROUND SUE
SUE RAMSBOTTOM

Laois has produced many football greats, like Tommy 'the Boy Wonder' Murphy, Tom Kelly, Ross Munnelly and Sue Ramsbottom. Along with Mayo's Cora Staunton, Sue is recognised as one of the greats of the modern game. She has boldly gone where no female has gone before. What made her Laois under-12 county championship medal unique was that she won it playing with the parish boys' team.

'I played in my first senior inter-county All-Ireland against Kerry when I was 14. It was the first ladies' football final played in Croke Park, and partly because of that it got great coverage in the local papers. I scored, so that was a big thrill, even though we lost. It's a great stage, and to be playing in an All-Ireland final at 14 is fabulous. I got my first All-Star that year – so that was great.'

The teenage years are notorious for their fads, prompting many a frustrated parent to say, usually more in hope than in confidence, 'It's just a phase they're going through.' When most of her contemporaries were besotted with the fresh faces of Jason Donovan and Bros – there were many who said the band should have been called Dross – Sue's two heroes were less likely pin-up material: Barney Rock and Colm O'Rourke.

'I went through a huge phase of being Barney Rock! I used to think I was him taking frees. I had him off to a T with the "seven steps back" routine. When Barney retired and Charlie Redmond took his place, I experimented with his technique at frees for a while. When I was playing, though, I was always Colm O'Rourke. He was the ultimate footballer. In 1996, I was chosen as *The Sunday Game*'s player of the match for the All-Ireland final. It would have been a great honour for me in any circumstances, but what made it one of the highlights of my career was that the selection was made by Colm O'Rourke.'

In fact, Sue found herself in the exalted company of such players as O'Rourke and Mickey Linden when, in an imaginative effort to increase the profile of Gaelic games among children, the GAA introduced a collection of cards featuring the photos of top players. Sue became part of many a family's breakfast throughout the country when she was one of the few ladies to feature in multiple boxes of Kellogg's. Despite her admiration for O'Rourke though, he has to take second place in Sue's hierarchy of GAA greats.

'One of the most special moments in my life came after one of the All-Irelands when I was approached by Micheál O'Muircheartaigh and he drove me out to RTÉ for an interview. Just to be in his company meant an awful lot, but the fact that they went to such trouble for me really made my day.'

Sue is a natural athlete. Apart from winning All-Ireland medals in basketball and volleyball, she is also an international rugby player. She has seen some of the prejudices that exist towards ladies' football, like the controversy in Roscommon over Malachy Byrne's opposition to a £900 grant from Roscommon Vocational Education Committee for the promotion of ladies' football. The controversy was fuelled further as he sought to explain himself on Shannonside radio, saying, 'I reckon that a lady or a girl's body is too precious to be abused, bumped and humped playing football. Their bodies are not made for humps and bumps. They have their own natural humps and bumps.'

Given this type of attitude, is it not surprising that the overwhelming majority of coaches in ladies' football are men?

'You need a strong character to manage a team, and most men learn to adapt. Our club coach, for example, was Pat Critchley, who trained the Carlow men's team, and he knows that you have to modify your style a bit when coaching ladies, but many of the principles are the same, like knowing how to coach different players in different ways. Some need to have the pressure put on them; others need lots of encouragement. Some things, though, that might work well with men don't work as well with women.

'I think back to one of our All-Ireland finals. We were losing at half-time, and when we got back to the dressing-room, one of our mentors, who is a lovely, considerate woman, said, "I've put the kettle on, and we'll have a cup of tea." Our manager immediately thumped the table ferociously, and everything on it went flying all over the place. Then he yelled, in less polite language, "How the hell could you think of tea at a time like this?" To be honest, I find that kind of thumping on the desk approach to motivation more funny than inspirational. I think, though, it's time now for us to have more female coaches.'

SUE RAMSBOTTOM

Would Sue consider a coaching career herself?

'Give me some men's county team and I'd get them into shape. There'd be some shock wouldn't there? Pat Spillane would have something to say then!'

How would Sue like to see the game marketed?

'People like Helen O'Rourke are doing a great job on that front. We have so many great players in the game, and I think they are the best promotion for it.'

The long-awaited All-Ireland senior medal finally came Sue's way in 2001 when Laois beat Mayo in the All-Ireland final. However, her memories of that famous win are tinged with sadness because of the premature death of her teammate, the great Lulu Carroll, on that day.

Selecting the dream team she would like to play on produced many agonising choices for Sue, but eventually she settled on the following from her era:

1. THERESA SWAYNE (LAOIS)
2. MAIRÉAD KELLY (MONAGHAN)
3. MARTINA O'RYAN (WATERFORD)
4. NOREEN WALSH (WATERFORD)
5. KATIE LISTON (KERRY)
6. JENNY GREENAN (MONAGHAN)
7. MARGARET PHELAN (LAOIS)
8. MARY JO CURRAN (KERRY)
9. KATHLEEN MURPHY (LAOIS)
10. ANGELA LARKIN (MONAGHAN)
11. SUE RAMSBOTTOM (LAOIS)
12. CATRIONA CASEY (WATERFORD)
13. GERALDINE O'RYAN (WATERFORD)
14. ÁINE WALL (WATERFORD)
15. EDEL BYRNE (MONAGHAN)

94

THE CHESS PLAYER
MIKE SHEEHY

For many of us, sport rekindles memories of triumphs and tragedies in childhood, adolescence and adulthood; it evokes a field of dreams. There is an exquisite self-contained quality, though, about memories of an All-Ireland final. All the build-up matches, whatever their own resplendent excitements, can only nourish the expectations of that ultimate collision in the final. All irrelevance is cast aside. The semi-finals offer sudden death, but the final tantalisingly offers instant immortality. No matter how many teams start out, regardless of back doors or side doors, in the final only two can play – and only one can win.

Those who were thrilled during their childhoods and adolescences by Micheál O'Hehir's commentary have been captivated by the mythology of Gaelic games ever since. The All-Ireland final is more than a mere sporting contest; it is, inevitably, a spiritual and identity-forming occasion. With that heightened sense of anticipation before a match, even the most trivial preliminary is invested with a tremor of pleasure. Bad jokes seem funny. Complete strangers take on friendly faces. Supporters are even more raucously lively and colourful than usual. Opposing fans, with sometimes gigantic flags streaming behind poles thrust from their car windows, weave hazardously to Drumcondra, seeking victims for their banter. Predictions and extravagant statements abound, and there is little place for objectivity.

The All-Ireland final is part of the heartbeat of the Irish nation. It is the ultimate fix for the sports junkie. Few people have experienced the joy of playing and winning an All-Ireland final as often as Mike Sheehy. Winner of eight All-Ireland medals and seven All-Stars, Sheehy was 1979 footballer of the year and chosen on both the Team of the Century and the Team of the Millennium.

Sheehy was a ruthlessly efficient scoring machine, as Roscommon great Dermot Earley observed at first hand.

MIKE SHEEHY

'A penalty was awarded to Kerry against us in the 1979 league quarter-final. I felt it was a harsh decision against us, and I said to Mike as he placed the ball for the kick, "Mike, that penalty should not have been awarded to Kerry. In fair play, now, you should send it wide." He looked at me and smiled, and then he thundered the ball into the back of the net. That was his answer.'

When I spoke to Mikey Sheehy in the Berkeley Court Hotel, it emerged, as our conversation unfolded, that we had a mutual admiration for Dermot Earley.

'Dermot was a wonderful player. He had so many facets to his game. He was an exceptional fielder, always controlled things very well in the middle of the field, always scored a lot and was deadly from frees. He was a very powerful man on a pitch. He had a perfectionist streak to him; he trained very hard and he looked after himself really well. I doubt if he ever smoked or drank, and he was always very fit. He must rank as the greatest player never to win an All-Ireland medal.'

Sheehy's ability to take defences apart clinically was the product of a footballing brain that overflowed with ideas. His approach to the sport seemed to borrow heavily from chess, insofar as he always seemed to be thinking three moves ahead of his opponent. Dublin corner-back Gay O'Driscoll witnessed this aspect of Sheehy's personality.

'I marked Mike in his first match for Kerry in Killarney, when he was picked at top of the left. He never played on me again. Before we played Kerry in a league final, Kevin Heffernan came to me and reminded me about that and encouraged me to renew my acquaintance with Mike. I went in on him early in the game with a hard shoulder and knocked him over, and a free was given against me. As he pulled himself up, he said, "Ah sh*t, Gay, that's not your game." It completely took the wind out of my sails and was a brilliant piece of psychology on his part.'

Mike Sheehy's best moments are legendary, especially the famously cheeky free kick when he chipped Paddy Cullen during the 1978 All-Ireland final. Con Houlihan memorably described Cullen's frantic efforts to keep the ball out: 'He was like a woman who smells a cake burning.' In his commentary, Micheál O'Hehir described it as 'the greatest freak of all time'. Unusually, O'Hehir got it wrong. It was a moment of pure genius. The speed of thought and the execution of a very difficult skill showed Sheehy's footballing genius.

Sheehy has a strong desire to sing the praises of Kerry's then manager, Mick O'Dwyer.

'It is difficult to keep a positive attitude in the face of criticism or negative feedback. Negative sometimes seems more powerful than positive feedback. O'Dwyer always told you that you were the best. Before big games, we never concentrated on the opposition. We just focused on our own game. The great leader is the one who enthuses others to rally to the cause. O'Dwyer had that gift. We would have won All-Irelands without O'Dwyer because we had so many talented players, but we would not have won eight. He kept us wanting to come back for more.'

The passage of time has allowed Sheehy to look back on the biggest disappointment of his career – the defeat to Offaly in 1982 as Kerry sought a historic five-in-a row, only to sensationally lose to a late Séamus Darby goal – with wry amusement.

'In 1982, we planned a holiday to Bali in the Far East to celebrate what we had expected to be our five-in-a-row. After sensationally losing the final to Offaly, one of the lads said that the only Bali we would be going to was Ballybunion!'

95

KING HENRY
HENRY SHEFFLIN

'Big, lanky and not much pace,' was one description of Henry Shefflin as a teenager. As a 17 year old, he played as a forward in the Leinster minor final, then was relegated to sub goalie for the rest of the campaign. In the modern era, Shefflin has taken over from D.J. Carey as the undisputed king of hurling. Even in his most sublime moments, he plays with a competitiveness that is as essential to him as breathing.

Shefflin's performances were central to Kilkenny winning the league, Leinster and All-Ireland titles in 2006; and scoring 1–13 in the 2006 All-Ireland final, with 1–6 from play. As early in his career as 2002, he was the unanimous choice as hurler of the year. After Kilkenny won the 2002 All-Ireland, Shefflin took the cup to St Columba's Hospital in Thomastown and had his most embarrassing moment when he was asked to mind a child who was wearing a Wexford jersey.

Yet, for all his successes, to speak to him is to appreciate that even the greatest and most successful players are still haunted by memories of past disappointments. In 1997, he tasted defeat in a minor All-Ireland final against Clare.

'A few of us didn't perform that day. I hit a few frees and missed a good few of them. There was a breeze blowing in the second half, and I went out to hit a few 65s – right into the Clare crowd. All I could see was these lads waving behind the goal – the Clare hurlers as well as umpires. It was a tough and lonely place. When you're a minor, you'll always remember those kinds of days; you'll take it to heart. You heap some of the blame on yourself when you're hitting the frees. It was a day I wouldn't like to go back to again.'

Shefflin studied at Waterford IT and emerged with an honours degree in business studies and financial services. As a student, he lived in a house designed for four – with six others. First to bed got the bed. Shefflin lost his first senior All-Ireland title in 1999, when favourites Kilkenny were defeated by Cork.

'We were kind of in shock. I remember walking out of Croke Park and there were still Kilkenny people around coming over congratulating us, saying "Well done" and all this. It just rubbed it in more. To think you have to go home and face these people the following night! They come out clapping you, and you're after losing an All-Ireland. It's gut-wrenching. I took it badly. It upset me a lot.'

In 2000, he won his first senior All-Ireland, against Offaly. The next year, though, Shefflin was to experience the bitter taste of defeat again when Kilkenny were sensationally beaten by Galway in the All-Ireland semi-final.

'After winning the All-Ireland in 2000, there was great hype about us. We thought we were great lads, and a small bit of that seeped through to our hurling. We probably didn't think we'd have to put in the hard work, and we definitely didn't put in the hard work. Training was very poor, and you could feel in training that it wasn't going well.

'It was a turning point for some of us, that we had to cop on. It was a wake-up call. I didn't hurl well all year. I think I was a small bit gone away from the game, concentrating on maybe other things – certainly not focused on the game and the things you have to do. And doing the simple things instead of doing the great things.

'Against Galway we were horsed out of it, simple as that. We weren't hungry enough. We weren't able for the physical battle. Hopefully it was a turning point for myself. I went looking for protection that day. I went on to the referee and the umpire and the linesman. You don't do that. Hurling is a man's game. Rather than look for protection, you have to drive out and try to win the next ball and horse on.'

Later that summer, Henry and two friends went to New York. Shefflin played a match on the Sunday. Two days later, the twin towers of the World Trade Center were attacked.

'I don't know how many blocks we were from it, but it was a crazy feeling. Unbelievable. Unbelievable. We didn't know what hit us: three Irish lads over in the fastest city in the world. We didn't even have any experience of going to New York. We ended up staying for about a week. Couldn't get out of there. We walked down Times Square, and we were looking at the big screen.

'We rang home, and our parents were there: "Are ye all right? Are ye all right?"

'"Ah, we're grand."'

HENRY SHEFFLIN

Shefflin gave an intriguing insight into the intensity of Kilkenny's preparations in his description of the pre-match routine for the All-Ireland final of 2002.

'John Hoyne was warming up in the dressing-room, and he got a slap of a hurl in the head from someone. He got four staples before he went out. That was just the warm-up.'

Despite his status within the game, Henry has not had his head turned by success. He refuses to take the credit for Kilkenny's great performances in recent years.

'Brian Cody believes there is no me in team. All of us have the reponsibility to win together rather than to focus on our individual performances. On any given day any of our lads can be a match-winner.'

Shefflin was central to Kilkenny's historic four All-Irelands in a row. In 2009, after Kilkenny's thrilling victory over Tipperary, a new joke was born: What does NAMA stand for in Tipperary? No All-Ireland medal again.

To cap a year to remember, Shefflin – with Pat Spillane and D.J. Carey – became the third player to win nine All-Star awards and was chosen by the *Irish Independent* as the greatest hurler of all time.

With characteristic panache, John Allen summed up Shefflin's place in the pantheon of current hurlers.

'Joe Canning might be the prince in waiting, but . . . Henry Shefflin is definitely the king in situ.'

96

RAISING THE BANNER
JIMMY SMYTH

One of the oddities of the 1984 Team of the Century was that it did not include a single player who had not won a senior All-Ireland medal. Had one such hurler been included on the team, the odds are pretty high that it would have been Clare's Jimmy Smyth – although he was chosen at top of the right on the Centenary Team of greatest players never to have won an All-Ireland medal. Born in Ruan on New Year's Day 1931, he first made his mark at St Flannan's College in Ennis, winning three Harty Cups and an equal number of All-Ireland colleges medals. For twenty years he was never off the Clare team, and during that period he was selected for twelve years on the Munster team, winning eight Railway Cup medals. He was also honoured with a coveted Ireland jersey six times.

Smyth's home bears ample testimony to his days acquiring a philosophy degree from Trinity College, with a multitude of books from the pens of the giants of philosophy – from Thomas Aquinas to Bertrand Russell. There is little visible evidence of his hurling glory days. It is the achievements of his children that are celebrated in the photographs on the wall. Which was his greatest game?

'It was against Limerick in the first round of the championship in 1953. I scored six goals and four points.'

Two years later, his biggest disappointment came against the same opposition.

'We lost the Munster final to them by 2–16 to 2–6. Not only had we defeated Tipperary and Cork in qualifying, but we also beat Wexford in the Oireachtas final the previous October, in front of 30,000 in Croke Park. Losing to Limerick was a massive blow to Clare, and it took us a long time to recover. If Clare had won in 1955, I believe we would have won several All-Irelands.'

In 1999, Smyth was presented with the award of Clare Person of the Year.

'It was a great honour because it never crossed my mind that I would even be considered for such a prestigious distinction. I was reminded of a story my uncle used to relate regarding a fellow who couldn't get out of bed in the morning and who made a firm resolution that this would be rectified. He employed the services of a landlady in this regard, and she assured him that in the future he would be called at 8 a.m. sharp in the mornings. The prime boys, as my uncle called them, heard of this resolve and blackened his face with shoe polish when he was asleep. The landlady was true to her word and called him promptly at 8 a.m. He got up immediately, looked at his face in the mirror and said, "Good God, 'twas the wrong man she called," jumping back into bed again. The polish was used so liberally the night I got my award I didn't recognise myself either!'

Throughout his career, Smyth came across many characters.

'Nicky Rackard was a great personality and was, in my opinion, the third best hurler of all time, behind Christy Ring and Mick Mackey. Although he became addicted to alcohol, he had the courage to tell the whole country about it and tried to get people to stop abusing drink.

'There were a lot of great characters in Clare hurling. In 1949, on the way up to the north, one of our lads stole a key from a lock from the customs post, and on the way back they read him the Riot Act.

'Our goalie at home, Christy, had a great puck-out. Back then, the sliotar was much heavier than it is today. We grew up in Ruan, which is about six miles from Ennis and eight miles from Doora. Doora might as well have been South Africa, because it was too long a distance for us to travel at a time when no one had a car. I asked Christy once what was the greatest puck-out he had ever struck. He answered, "If I had the ball they had today, I'd drive it to f***ing Doora."

'There was a man in Ruan who was a great admirer of mine. One day, I was bearing down on goal in a very tense match and the harder I ran the more the Ruan crowd was getting excited. Everyone was giving me advice, and I could hear all kinds of suggestions about what I should do. Then, just as I was trying to concentrate, I heard my number-one fan roaring out over the din, "Take no notice of them, Jimmy. Make your own arrangements."'

Jimmy has no time for dream teams or for man of the match awards.

'Jack Lynch told me once those sorts of awards are a lottery. There were too many great players to pick a dream team. Des Foley, for instance, was a great midfielder because he was never beaten.'

Since his retirement, Smyth has seen many changes in the game.

'Forward play has deteriorated since my time, but back play has come on a lot. They mark forwards so tightly now you can hardly do anything. I just wonder how Ring would cope now. He would still get a lot of scores, but I think he wouldn't have got quite so many.

'Ring was like Muhammad Ali. He once said, "Modesty is knowing where you stand." He always knew. If he thought he had played below his own high standards, he would be the first to say so. He was well aware of his own ability and didn't believe in concealing the fact that he knew. I remember we were playing in a Railway Cup match once, and he said to me, "When I get the ball, you run in for the pass. And remember, I don't miss."

'He once talked to my mother for a half an hour about this and that and when he was leaving he just said, "Your young lad is a great hurler."'

At an early age, Smyth was given a lesson in the value of a positive attitude.

'I was 13 when I played my first senior game for St Flannan's in the Harty Cup. I was left half-back and marking a guy who had been an inter-provincial player the year before. In the first three or four minutes, he had two points scored. Then I saw a black form approaching me, and it was Monsignor Dr Maxwell, and he said to me, "Jimmy, you're beating the Dickens out of him." He said nothing else. I thought to myself, "God, I must be really holding him." So for the rest of the match I never gave him a puck of the ball.'

However, Smyth had not always such a happy relationship with priests on the hurling field.

'I was playing a club match one day when a fracas developed and most of the crowd invaded the pitch. A priest came and abused me, but I simply said, "Father, you should be on the sideline giving a good example to the young." The next day, his mother came to visit me and thanked me for the good advice I'd given her son!'

Smyth's prodigious talents were recognised when he was chosen on the Centenary Team of greatest players never to have won an All-Ireland medal. That team was:

JIMMY SMYTH

1 SEÁN DUGGAN (GALWAY)
2 JIM FIVES (GALWAY)
3 NOEL DRUMGOOLE (DUBLIN)
4 J.J. DOYLE (CLARE)
5 SEÁN HERBERT (LIMERICK)
6 SEÁN STACK (CLARE)
7 COLM DORAN (WEXFORD)
8 JOE SALMON (GALWAY)
9 JOBBER MCGRATH (WESTMEATH)
10 JOSIE GALLAGHER (GALWAY)
11 MARTIN QUIGLEY (WEXFORD)
12 KEVIN ARMSTRONG (ANTRIM)
13 JIMMY SMYTH (CLARE)
14 CHRISTY O'BRIEN (LAOIS)
15 MICK BERMINGHAM (DUBLIN)

97

SPAT SPILLANE
PAT SPILLANE

Given Pat Spillane's penchant for controversy, an RTÉ announcer made an interesting slip of the tongue when she introduced 'Spat Spillane' in 2009. True to form, Pat Spillane took it in his stride and said, 'I've been called worse.'

Aside from his genius on the field, Spillane also changed the face of punditry in the GAA with his straight-talking style. A small illustration of this came after his beloved Kerry team lost to Cork in the Munster semi-final replay in 2009.

'You know that great piece of Irish literature we were all subjected to when we went to school? *Peig*. Her opening line about herself was that she was an old woman now, with one leg on the bank and the other in the grave – and in a way it could sum up this Kerry football team.'

Spillane is phlegmatic about his reputation as a pundit.

'When I retired from playing, I never expected a new career to open up for me as a pundit with the *Sunday World* and on *The Sunday Game* – but it did. To me, the media is a home from home. Mind you, it can get hot in the kitchen at times! The ultimate job in life is to get paid for doing your hobby. The next best thing is to get paid for talking and writing about your hobby, and I'm lucky in that respect.

'I know I should be thankful for this second career, and I really am. I know for a lot of people that is not the case. At various times, I have annoyed every county in the country. Football fans in Kildare, Mayo, Roscommon and every county in Ulster would be at the top of a very long list [of people] who have let me know of their unhappiness with my analysis. Former Liverpool manager Bill Shankly said of his full-back, Tommy Smith, that he would raise an argument in a graveyard. The same comment could be made about me! I'm sure that there are many people who would compare me to Tony Soprano, because they would say my mouth is a weapon of mass destruction!

PAT SPILLANE

'No matter where I go, I get people slagging me for things I said about their team and especially about things I'm supposed to have said. The best of all came a few years ago when I met the Kilkenny county chairman in Nowlan Park and he said, in all earnestness, "What have you got against us? You're always slagging off the Kilkenny football team." That was a new one on me! I've never even seen the Kilkenny football team playing so I don't know how I could be criticising them all the time. People's memories often play tricks on them. They remember what they think you said rather than what you actually said.

'Thankfully, I grew up in the family bar, and the interaction with customers, from a young age, sharpened my wits and prepared me for my subsequent career in the media, when I have to think quickly.

'I absolutely cringe, though, when I look back at some of my early appearances on television. I was invited by RTÉ to compete in their inaugural sports superstars championship to be recorded early in 1979. I joined Limerick hurler Pat Hartigan, Dave O'Leary, swimmer David Cummins, Formula One driver Derek Daly, athlete Noel Carroll, Dublin footballer Jimmy Keaveney, boxer Mick Dowling and Cork's Jimmy Barry-Murphy. To give a light touch to the proceedings, the sports personalities were divided into teams, each made up of two "superathletes", one female athlete, one personality and one politician. Personalities who agreed to take part included Father Michael Cleary, Frank Kelly and Dickie Rock. After I won the competition, I took part in the world superstars competition in the Bahamas. I did not know much about protecting myself from the sun, and as a result of my pink visage and body a new phrase entered popular currency: "Pat Spillane tan"! When I think of how I looked, and the things I said back then, I am mortified.'

In any discussion about the greatest players of all time, Spillane's name is sure to figure prominently. He won eight All-Ireland medals, nine All-Stars, was one of the biggest stars of the legendary Kerry team of the 1970s and '80s and was chosen on both the Team of the Century and the Team of the Millennium. In rural Ireland parlance, he didn't pick his talent 'off the trees'. His late father, Tom, was himself a Kerry footballer, and his uncles the Lynes, Jackie and Dinny, won All-Ireland medals for Kerry.

To add to his treasure trove of golden memories, Pat was joined on the great Kerry team by his brothers Mick and Tom. The Spillanes were not just part of Irish sporting history; they were also centre stage at one of Ireland's greatest religious occasions. Early in 1979, news broke that the Pope would visit Ireland that September. During the Papal Mass for the youth of Ireland, Mick Spillane made a presentation as part of the giving of gifts.

In a career that had so many highs, Spillane can see the silver lining in his biggest disappointment.

'In 1982, Kerry were going for a five-in-a-row. As everybody knows, we famously lost to Offaly. Yet, if we had won, I would have retired and missed out on winning three All-Irelands in '84, '85 and '86. In fact, winning the All-Ireland in 1986 is probably the happiest memory of my career, because it was my best performance in a final.'

Spillane was one of the many players who made trips to America to play in the New York championship. It was an ideal opportunity to make a few dollars and have a holiday. Big-name stars over from Ireland were always subject to 'robust' play on the field. On one occasion, this necessitated Spillane visiting the medical room with blood pouring from his nose. An Italian doctor was on duty and was more interested in reading *The New York Times* than attending to Spillane. Without looking up from his paper, he asked Spillane what was wrong. The Kerry star said, 'I think I've broken my nose.' With no concern in his voice, the doctor told him to go over to the mirror and clean off the blood.

When this task was completed, the doctor enquired, 'Does it look different from how it looked this morning?'

Spillane replied, 'Yes, it's crooked.'

The doctor calmly replied, 'You probably broke your nose then.' So ended the medical consultation.

98

THE TERRIBLE TWIN
FRANK STOCKWELL

The 1956 All-Ireland final turned the late Frank Stockwell into one of the GAA immortals. The late RTÉ Gaelic games correspondent Mick Dunne coined the phrase 'the Terrible Twins' to describe Seán Purcell's unique partnership with Frank Stockwell. Dunne explained the origin of the phrase to me.

'Galway's Seán Purcell was the best player I ever saw. It could be said that there were better players in different positions, but, as far as I'm concerned, he was the best all-round footballer. I remember him at full-back in the Connacht semi-final in 1954 against Mayo. It was one of the finest individual displays I've ever seen. He played on the great Tom Langan, then Danny O'Neill, and then John Nallen, but it was all the same: Purcell was superb. He was also a magnificent midfielder, and he was the brains of the Galway team that won the All-Ireland in 1956, at centre-forward. He had such a wonderful combination with the other Galway maestro, Frankie Stockwell, and they performed such a lethal duo that I described them in that way, and, to my pleasant surprise, the phrase entered the GAA vernacular about them.'

In conversation with me, Seán Purcell reserved a special place for Stockwell.

'We were known as "the Terrible Twins" because we had such a great understanding and because we did a lot of damage to opposing defences. Frank was a fabulous footballer. The fact that he scored 2–5 in the 1956 All-Ireland final speaks for itself. They were all off his foot – no frees. He destroyed the Cork defence on his own. It was just a matter of getting the ball in to him the best way we could. We tried the old tricks we had worked on over the years. Things were much less scientific, I suppose, than they are now. We all contributed to each other, but we all knew Frank was the man to give the ball to and he'd do the rest. You have to remember that was a 60-minute final. I'm great friends with Jimmy Keaveney, but when he broke Frank's record by scoring 2–6 in the 1977 All-Ireland final, he had a 70-minute game to do it in.

'It's a simple game really. If you give the ball to somebody, the best way that he can get it is if you don't pass when he has two or three men marking him. You give it to him so that he can run and move to get it himself. Frank would know that you were going to put the ball in a particular place. He would sense that. There was nothing made up about it. It was natural skill on Frank's part. We'd a natural sort of empathy with each other, and it worked out well. We managed to click together. There was nothing too organised about it. We just took it naturally.

'I always tried to get the ball and part with it to the best of my ability, whether to score or to give it to somebody in a better position. I suppose I was lucky to have a good sense of anticipation. I remember when I was a young lad in the college we used to have a couple of hours free after school and we'd be kicking the ball around. There would be a great crowd out on the field, and you had to be very lucky or very good to get a kick at the ball. It would certainly improve your anticipation. You'd nearly know where everybody was going to kick it. You had to if you were going to get a kick at it yourself.

'Frank would have been a brilliant soccer player. He knew the simple things of the game, especially to pass. I'd give it to him, and he'd give it back to me or vice versa. We knew how to pass the ball to one another and give each other the old one-twos. I'd give it to him, so that he could move to get it, and sometimes he would give me the ball back. We knew each other's play, and wherever we might be we could find each other easy enough. 'Twas a natural knowledge of each other's strengths and weaknesses. In that way, we managed to put up the scores.'

Enda Colleran also had great affection for Stockwell.

'Football left him with a wealth of happy memories. He once told me about one of his first club games as a minor. At that stage it was hard to field a team. There was one guy roped in to play for them, and he was provided with boots, socks, a jersey and the lot. They were thrashed, and, of course, when that happens everybody blames everybody else. When unflattering comments were put to the new recruit, his riposte was, "Well, you can't blame me. I never got near the ball!"'

FRANK STOCKWELL

Frank, though, was sometimes frustrated by the GAA.

'When Roscommon played in the 1980 All-Ireland final, there had been controversy in the build-up because Dermot Earley had led his four-year-old son, David, with him during the pre-match parade in the All-Ireland semi-final against Armagh. Few players have made a greater contribution to the game than Dermot Earley in a career that spanned 20 years in the Roscommon colours. Yet, instead of honouring him, the GAA went into a tizzy because he had committed that most heinous of crimes. He had broken a rule. Talk about warped priorities.'

On a wet November evening, Frank Stockwell picked his dream team together with Seán Purcell. That team was:

1 DAN O'KEEFFE (KERRY)
2 ENDA COLLERAN (GALWAY)
3 PADDY PRENDERGAST (MAYO)
4 SEÁN FLANAGAN (MAYO)
5 SEÁN MURPHY (KERRY)
6 JOHN JOE O'REILLY (CAVAN)
7 STEPHEN WHITE (LOUTH)
8 MICK O'CONNELL (KERRY)
9 JACK O'SHEA (KERRY)
10 SEÁN O'NEILL (DOWN)
11 SEÁN PURCELL (GALWAY)
12 PADRAIG CARNEY (MAYO)
13 MATT CONNOR (OFFALY)
14 TOM LANGAN (MAYO)
15 KEVIN HEFFERNAN (DUBLIN)

99

THE FIRST PROFESSIONAL FOOTBALLER

LARRY TOMPKINS

Fitness gurus are all the rage in the GAA. When 'the Iron Man from Rhode', Paddy McCormack, was training Offaly for a year, his style of training was laps, laps and more laps. Eventually, the players said to him, 'We're sick to death of all these laps. Tonight, we're going to have something different.'

Paddy thought for a moment and said, 'OK, lads. That's fine. Turn around, and run the other way for a change.'

Today, players are supposed to fit in with a certain body profile, have the right body-fat percentage and be able to pass the bleep test and do a certain number of shuttle runs within a certain time. As a result, we often produce athletes but not players who can kick the ball properly. No player bought into the mantra of 'Fitness, Fitness, Fitness' more than Larry Tompkins, but he complemented his obsession to be fit with the fine skills of the game.

Tompkins first came to prominence in 1979, when he was selected to play for the Kildare senior team, having also lined out for the minor and under-21 football team that year. After emigrating to New York, he returned to Ireland in the mid '80s and opted to declare for Cork following a dispute with the Lilywhites over the purchase of an airline ticket. On that Cork team, he linked up with another former Kildare player, Shea Fahy, who would be chosen as footballer of the year in 1990. Having lost All-Ireland finals in 1987 and '88 to Meath, Tompkins starred in Cork's All-Ireland wins of 1989 and '90, captaining the team in 1990. Nine years later, he coached Cork when they lost the All-Ireland final to Meath.

The 1989 All-Ireland was yet another case of 'what might have been' for Mayo. Their former All-Star midfielder T.J. Kilgallon recalls the game vividly.

'After Anthony Finnerty got the goal, we were in the driving seat, because, having lost the previous two years, they [Cork] were starting to doubt themselves – but in the last ten minutes we went into disarray and let them off the hook. They finished strongly and got the final three points. Cork had probably the finest footballer in the country at the time in Larry Tompkins. When Cork were in trouble, he was the guy who stepped up to the plate, and he could always be relied on to get six or seven points in any match. When you have a player like him, especially someone like Tompkins, who was a real driving force, you will be successful.'

Mayo's Kevin McStay also remembers the game clearly.

'We were millimetres from winning the All-Ireland in '89. We hit the post twice, and the ball bounced back into play. They hit the post twice, but, each time, the ball went over the bar. One of their players double-hopped the ball and scored a point, but the ref, Paddy Collins, who was normally an excellent referee, missed it. After scoring the goal, Anthony got another chance, but the late John Kerins got a touch to it. The umpire backed away because he was afraid the ball was going to hit him. He missed John's touch, and, instead of giving us a 45, he flagged it wide. Our free-taker, Michael Fitzmaurice, was on fire that day and hadn't missed a placed ball, including a 45. If we had got a point at that stage it would have been a big help to us.

'Cork were a more experienced team than us, having contested the All-Ireland final the previous two years, but they were very brittle at that stage of the game. As a forward, I could see their nerves in the way the backs were shouting at each other, but we allowed them to settle rather than keep them on the ropes. When you think back to that team, you have to say that the heartbeat of the team was Larry Tompkins. He was their engine, driving through defences and getting points from play and always reliable from frees. To win All-Irelands you need a top-class free-taker, and Tompkins was certainly that. He was exceptionally committed and would put his body on the line to do anything that was necessary for Cork to win. I especially think of their All-Ireland triumph in 1990. Larry picked up a cruciate ligament injury in that game, but he played through the pain barrier and scored four points to lead Cork to back-to-back All-Irelands. I am sure the fact that Tompkins and the Cork lads were up against their bitter rivals Meath drove him on to push Cork over the line.'

Pat Spillane offers a nuanced assessment of Tompkins.

'Talking to Cork fans after they lost badly to Kerry in the 2007 All-Ireland final, the only consolation they had was that, as they saw it, at least Larry Tompkins was no longer in charge of the team. Larry was a great player but getting a Cork fan to say something nice about his time as Cork manager is as difficult as pushing custard up a hill. Larry is a lovely fella and a gentleman. He was probably the first professional Gaelic footballer – not in the sense that he was getting paid but because he trained morning, noon and night, seven days a week. He devoted his entire life to it. The problem was that even though he captained Cork to an All-Ireland in 1990, people in Cork still, to this day, think of him as a "blow-in", which means he was grudgingly accepted. The failing that Larry had as a manager was that he tried to train the team to be like him, to be as dedicated, determined and fanatical about fitness as he was. He had them running up hills. He brought them on beaches for early-morning runs. Eugene McGee was the first to do this with UCD. Ger Loughnane did it with the Clare hurlers. Since that ploy did not work for Larry, no other team have used it since.'

100

THE MILLENNIUM MAN
BRIAN WHELAHAN

History never stops, but Croke Park sometimes hits the pause button for a moment to bask in the glories of yesteryear. Tradition is an essential ingredient of the game's sporting dish. Who will ever forget Offaly's Séamus Darby's sensational late goal that deprived Kerry of their fifth All-Ireland final triumph in 1982 or D.J. Carey's five-star performance in the 2000 All-Ireland final? For many, though, an abiding memory of Croke Park will always be Brian Whelahan – after conjuring up a performance of exceptional class against the aristocrats of hurling, Kilkenny – with his arm raised aloft in triumph, drinking in the moment after turning defeat into victory in the 1998 All-Ireland final.

Brian Whelahan's quality was first readily apparent to a national audience in Offaly's victory over Clare in the 1989 All-Ireland minor final. With his brothers Simon and Barry as his teammates, he turned Birr into one of the powers of club hurling, winning four All-Ireland titles. To cement the family connection, the team was coached by their father, Pad Joe.

Brian won his first senior medal against Limerick in 1994. Offaly went into the game full of confidence. In fact, so self-assured were they that the side's greatest character, the effervescent Johnny Pilkington, was making victory speeches before the game – all the more remarkable because he was not even the captain! The team were managed by Limerick's Éamonn Cregan, who got very animated during the game, as Joe Dooley has never forgotten.

'I can't remember anything Éamonn said to us before the final. But I recall very vividly his team-talk at half-time. I can assure you it was unprintable! He was very wound up. None of us dared to speak – except briefly among ourselves.'

The end of the game was one of the most dramatic finals ever witnessed when Offaly scored 2–6 in the final five minutes to snatch victory. The following year, the shoe was on the other foot when Offaly lost memorably to Clare. However, Clare manager Ger Loughnane witnessed a little vignette that showcased Whelahan's magic.

'In the '95 All-Ireland, a ball came across the field to the Sparrow [Ger O'Loughlin], and he seemed certain to score. Then the sheer brilliance of Brian Whelahan was illustrated: as the Sparrow flicked the ball, Whelahan hooked him from what seemed a mile away. Whelahan's wrists are like lightning. They're unbelievable. The ball went wide. Although we won, I have to take my hat off to Whelahan. He was one of the greats of the modern game and was pivotal to Offaly's success in the 1990s.'

The year 1998 was dominated by Ger Loughnane and the many controversies that dogged his Clare team: the clashes with officialdom, the rows with referees and the unprecedented media attention. While all the talk was about Clare, the ultimate prize would go to Offaly. After Offaly lost the 1998 Leinster final to Kilkenny, Babs Keating controversially described the Offaly players as 'sheep in a heap'. Babs met with the county board and decided to stay, but the next morning he resigned, allegedly because he was 'shocked' by a newspaper interview with Offaly's star midfielder, Johnny Pilkington, in which Pilkington had questioned Babs's record with the county, stated that Babs had abandoned Offaly's tradition of ground hurling and questioned the tactics against Kilkenny.

In Offaly's hour of crisis, they went in search of a secret weapon. His name was Bond, Michael Bond – or, as the players christened him, 'Double-Uh-Oh'. A few months later Bond would make the most sensational positional switch of Brian Whelahan's career – and effectively win the All-Ireland for Offaly. Before that, there was the small matter of three battles with Clare.

In the All-Ireland semi-final, Clare led Offaly by four points with ten minutes to go, but it required a late free from Jamesie O'Connor to tie the match at 1–13 each after Offaly scored 1–2 without reply. Much of Clare's performance in the replay was a monument to patience, nerve, courage and technical brilliance, the mature masterwork of a great team. As usual, Clare concentrated on setting a dominating, draining pace. This was essential for a team who had to mine goals like nuggets. Houdini could not have escaped from the pit the Offaly team were in, and Mr Micawber would have been hard pressed to find any reason for optimism. Clare's calculated challenge was intensifying towards its thrilling crescendo, but, suddenly . . .

BRIAN WHELAHAN

Nobody knows. That's the mystery, the fun and the drama of hurling. A bizarre incident ensued. Jimmy Cooney intervened and blew full-time two minutes prematurely. A large section of the Offaly supporters staged a sit-in on the field while Johnny Pilkington had a fag and said, 'Wouldn't you think they'd go off for an auld drink?' A new hurling soap opera was about to unfold. To nobody's surprise, the Clare camp were told that there would be a replay in Thurles on the following Saturday. Hence Johnny Pilkington's comment, 'The statement was that you hadn't had Offaly beaten until *The Sunday Game* was over.' Ger Loughnane's verdict on the game was very economical: 'On the day, Offaly were the better team and deserved to win.'

The climax of Whelahan's career came in the 1998 All-Ireland final. Suffering from flu, he was clearly struggling in the half-back line, so Michael Bond boldly moved him to full-forward, where Whelahan's class came to the fore and he scored six points. Then, with just minutes left, he scored a goal that sealed the title in a 2–16 to 1–13 victory over Kilkenny.

Hubert Rigney, the Offaly captain, in his victory speech after the final, said, 'We might have come in the back door, but we're going out the front door.' In one of the great GAA ironies, Offaly had come through the back door despite having voted against it, and Offaly, true to form, voted against the back door the following year.

Although he was voted hurler of the year in both 1994 and '98, Whelahan was sensationally omitted from the 1994 All-Star team. Such was the ensuing level of controversy about this decision that the system of All-Star selection was changed for the following year. Whelahan's place in the pantheon of hurling greats was for ever secured in 2000 when he was the only player from the modern era to be selected on hurling's Team of the Millennium, replacing Tipperary's Jimmy Finn from the Team of the Century. That team in full was:

1   TONY REDDAN (TIPPERARY)
2   JOHN DOYLE (TIPPERARY)
3   NICK O'DONNELL (WEXFORD)
4   BOBBY RACKARD (WEXFORD)
5   PADDY PHELAN (KILKENNY)
6   JOHN KEANE (WATERFORD)
7   BRIAN WHELAHAN (OFFALY)
8   JACK LYNCH (CORK)
9   LORY MEAGHER (KILKENNY)

100 GAA GREATS

10 CHRISTY RING (CORK)

11 MICK MACKEY (LIMERICK)

12 JIMMY LANGTON (KILKENNY)

13 EDDIE KEHER (KILKENNY)

14 RAY CUMMINS (CORK)

15 JIMMY DOYLE (TIPPERARY)